Building Web Reputation Systems

F. Randall Farmer and Bryce Glass

O'REILLY®

Beijing · Cambridge · Farnham · Köln · Sebastopol · Taipei · Tokyo

Building Web Reputation Systems

by F. Randall Farmer and Bryce Glass

Published by O'Reilly Media, Inc., 1005 Gravenstein Highway North, Sebastopol, CA 95472.

O'Reilly books may be purchased for educational, business, or sales promotional use. Online editions are also available for most titles (*http://my.safaribooksonline.com*). For more information, contact our corporate/institutional sales department: 800-998-9938 or *corporate@oreilly.com*.

Editor: Mary E. Treseler
Production Editor: Loranah Dimant
Copyeditor: Genevieve d'Entremont
Proofreader: Loranah Dimant

Indexer: Ellen Troutman Zaig
Cover Designer: Karen Montgomery
Interior Designer: David Futato
Illustrator: Robert Romano

Printing History:
    March 2010:   First Edition.

RepKover.

This book uses RepKover™, a durable and flexible lay-flat binding.

ISBN: 978-0-596-15979-5

[M]

1267556382

Table of Contents

Part II. Extended Elements and Applied Examples

Part III.   Building Web Reputation Systems

Preface

What Is This Book About?

Today's Web is the product of over a *billion* hands and minds. Around the clock and around the globe, people are pumping out contributions small and large: full-length features on Vimeo, video shorts on YouTube, comments on Blogger, discussions on Yahoo! Groups, and tagged-and-titled Del.icio.us bookmarks. User-generated content and robust crowd participation have become the hallmarks of Web 2.0.

But the booming popularity of social media has brought with it a whole new set of challenges for those who create websites and online communities, as well as for the users who consume those sites:

- Problems of *scale* (how to manage—and present—an overwhelming inflow of user contributions)
- Problems of *quality* (how to tell the good stuff from the bad)
- Problems of *engagement* (how to reward contributors in a way that keeps them coming back)
- Problems of *moderation* (how to "stamp out" the worst stuff quickly and efficiently)

Reputation systems can provide an effective solution to all of these problems.

Reputation and Karma: Two Simple Definitions

Reputation
    Information used to make a value judgment about an object or person
Karma
    The reputation(s) for a user

What is reputation in an online community? In its broadest sense, reputation is *information used to make a value judgment about an object or a person.* There are potentially many components to reputation. For example, *karma* is a reputation score for a user in a community, and it may be an aggregation of answers to the following:

- How long has this person been a member of the community?
- What types of activities has she engaged in?
- How well has she performed at them?
- What do other people think about this person?

Having access to a person's reputation might help you make better-informed judgments. Judgments like:

- Can I trust this person?
- Should I transact with him?
- Is it worth my time to listen to him?

The same principles of reputation can also be applied to that person's individual contributions—the video, photo, or textual content that he's authored. Content reputation can answer questions such as:

- What's the best video in this category?
- What are the most interesting photos submitted today?
- Should I bother reading this blog entry?
- Which comments in a thread are truly worth my time?

For the site operator, reputation is at its most powerful when karma (people reputation) is used in concert with content reputation to increase your understanding of your online community and the relative value of its participants and contents. For the community itself, reputation is *relevance.* To the site, reputation represents *value* and *return on investment.*

So what does a *reputation system* do? It powers the whole process: it monitors the community, makes note of the actions that community members take, assesses the community's response to those actions, and keeps a running tally of the history of it all. (Optionally, the system may then *show the results of these calculations back* to users, enabling them to make judgments about the people and things they encounter.)

Reputation systems are the underlying mechanisms behind some of the best-known consumer websites, including Amazon, eBay, Digg, Slashdot, Facebook, and especially media and gaming sites like iTunes and Xbox Live.

But, of course, developing a successful reputation system is not easy. Our experience is that reputation is one part each of engineering, social science, psychology, and economics. Social media architects and designers must pay careful attention to multiple factors: the context in which the community is situated, the incentives they'd like to provide contributors (which often demand a nuanced understanding of the actions they want to encourage and discourage), and the effects that decisions made early in the design process may have on the community spirit downstream.

Building Web Reputation Systems provides a complete, soup-to-nuts process for designing and developing your own community's reputation program. In a guided fashion, you will start with the hard questions:

- How can reputation enhance my business? The community?
- What are the right types of behaviors to encourage?
- What are the right objects (people, things?) to accrue reputation?
- What types of actions should count toward a reputation?

and then you'll learn how to build *reputation models* to accurately reflect all of these inputs. To do so, you'll need a *reputation grammar*, which we've developed and applied to many successful reputation systems used across the Web.

We also provide well-diagrammed reputation patterns for common web needs ("Digg-style" voting systems, ratings and reviews, simple karma) and some extended reputation system reviews and a case study based on actual reputation deployments at industry-leading social sites, including Yahoo!, Flickr, and eBay.

Why Write a Book About Reputation?

We wrote this book because we saw how critical reputation has become to the survival and growth of the Web. Though there are many academic research papers on specific generational algorithms and social effects of reputation systems, we couldn't find a single book that put it all in context—describing it as a separate domain of knowledge, complete with a grammar, emerging best-use patterns, and recurring antipatterns. Until now.

Our extensive experience creating and deploying several reputation systems across a wide range of social media at Yahoo! provided much of our base of knowledge for this book. We add a comprehensive review of other existing applications to venture forth into unexplained territory and offer a working definition of web reputation systems: a survivor's guide for those who would follow. We hope this book will improve the quality of conversation about reputation systems, and help improve the quality of products that are using them.

Who Should Read This Book

This book and the supporting blog and wiki (*http://buildingreputation.com*) are targeted at several audiences:

Primary audience
> Anyone who is *building, operating, or participating* in a website or online application that leverages user-generated content: social networking, ratings, votes, reviews, comments, posts, uploads, games, etc. You'll need to understand reputation systems in order to maximize your user experience and search engine performance, and streamline your operational expenses.

A must-have reference for
> System architects, product managers, community support staff, or user interface designers tasked with designing a reputation system for an online community. (Or any variant thereof: a social collaboration tool, voting mechanism, or a ratings-and-reviews experience.)

Also useful to
> Game designers who deal with reward and incentive systems for social games or any technologist in a role that requires some familiarity with reputation systems who'd like to become conversant in their design and operations.

Successful social media design is hard. Many companies and organizations understand that. Rewarding points for user participation may generate activity and build audience, but site owners should be wary of possible negative impact on content quality. They need this book to help them choose the right reputation model for their site and help them evaluate the health of their deployed social collaboration system.

This book assumes that you have a rudimentary understanding of application logic, can read basic flowcharts, create content for the Web, and have direct experience interacting with users on socially active websites. No programming or web engineering experience is required, though you'll be aided through some of the more technical aspects of this book by some passing familiarity with programmatic thinking.

Organization of This Book

This book is broken into three main parts: Reputation Defined and Illustrated, Extended Elements and Applied Examples, and Building Web Reputation Systems. It was written to be consumed sequentially, but if you are already experienced in developing websites heavy with user-generated content, you may be able to move more quickly through Part I.

Part I: Reputation Defined and Illustrated

Chapter 1 briefly introduces basic concepts and terminology of reputation and sets reputation systems in their proper historical context. With this context in mind, Chapter 2 goes on to define a complete grammar for thinking about reputation and provides a graphical language to clearly describe reputation systems for analysis and development.

Part II: Extended Elements and Applied Examples

In Chapter 3, the primitive reputation grammar elements described in Part I are combined into higher-level *building blocks* that can be used as-is for simple reputation systems or combined to create more complex ones. In Chapter 4, we show how the grammar and blocks we've described can be used to elucidate many of the reputation systems currently deployed across the Web, including Digg, eBay, and Flickr. In this part, practitioners' tips become a regular feature of most chapters; the lessons we've learned are not to be missed—even by the casual reader.

Part III: Building Web Reputation Systems

The last section, comprising more than half the book, goes beyond cookie-cutter reputation needs to offer detailed advice on designing, building, deploying, and operating a custom reputation system. The project begins *not* by drawing a model or screen mockups, but by answering the three big questions posed in Chapter 5 that define and limit your reputation choices. With those answers, Chapter 6 helps to identify your application's objects, methods, and inputs that power your reputation. With all of this in mind, you can start drawing the reputation model.

Chapter 7 helps you decide how to display reputation, and Chapter 8 describes other common uses for reputation, such as providing search relevance. At this point, the reputation model is designed, and the screen mocks are ready. Next up is implementation, testing, and deployment, for which strategies and tips are covered in Chapter 9. We wrap it all up with a case study in Chapter 10. This chapter ties the entire book together, revisiting each of the steps outlined in detail with a single concrete example. It is a successful reputation model that provides inspiration, many insights, and several notes of caution.

Appendix A is intended for technical readers, such as system architects and platform engineers. It describes the *reputation framework*—an execution environment for multiple reputation models. The Yahoo! Reputation Platform is described in detail as an example of a framework that can scale to tens of thousands of transactions per second but had to make some functional trade-offs that are quite illustrative.

Appendix B contains references for related materials for further reading, most of which are available on the Web.

Role-Based Reading (for Those in a Hurry)

Here are a few alternate chapter reading list recommendations, based on your professional role:

[Product | UX | game] designers and application product managers
> We wrote this book primarily for you; Chapters 1 through 10 are all important. If you must skim, be sure to read all of the practitioners tips, warnings, notes, and sidebars to make sure you aren't missing something important. User experience folks should pay extra attention to the pros and cons in Chapters 7 and 8.

System architects, software engineers, platform engineers
> Assuming you're reading this book as part of a plan to deploy a reputation system, read Chapters 1 and 2 completely—the definitions are important to later sections. Skim Chapter 3, but read all the practitioners tips, and pay close attention to the last half of Chapter 4. In Chapter 5, familiarize yourself with the Content Control Patterns and the limiting effects they have on reputation systems. Chapters 6, 9, and 10 are all worth your full attention. Also look at Appendix A and consider whether you need a reputation framework.

Community support staff, [program | project] managers, operations staff
> If you're involved in a support role with reputation systems, read Chapter 1 and review the definitions in Chapter 2. In Chapter 3, be sure to read the practitioners tips, and likewise the advice about why reputation sometimes fails at the end of Chapter 4. Chapters 7 and 8 provide patterns for how reputation faces the users and the company and explain when (and when not) to use them. You're probably in a role that is detailed in Chapter 9; if so, read it. Chapter 10 may be the most important chapter in the book for you—nothing like a practical example to get oriented.

Conventions Used in This Book

The following typographical conventions are used in this book:

Italic
> Indicates new terms, URLs, email addresses, filenames, and file extensions.

`Constant width`
> Used for program listings, as well as within paragraphs to refer to program elements such as variable or function names, databases, data types, environment variables, statements, and keywords.

`Constant width bold`
> Shows commands or other text that should be typed literally by the user.

`Constant width italic`
> Shows text that should be replaced with user-supplied values or by values determined by context.

This icon signifies a tip, suggestion, or general note.

 This icon indicates a warning or caution.

Safari® Books Online

Safari Books Online is an on-demand digital library that lets you easily search over 7,500 technology and creative reference books and videos to find the answers you need quickly.

With a subscription, you can read any page and watch any video from our library online. Read books on your cell phone and mobile devices. Access new titles before they are available for print, and get exclusive access to manuscripts in development and post feedback for the authors. Copy and paste code samples, organize your favorites, download chapters, bookmark key sections, create notes, print out pages, and benefit from tons of other time-saving features.

O'Reilly Media has uploaded this book to the Safari Books Online service. To have full digital access to this book and others on similar topics from O'Reilly and other publishers, sign up for free at *http://my.safaribooksonline.com*.

How to Contact Us

Please address comments and questions concerning this book to the publisher:

O'Reilly Media, Inc.
1005 Gravenstein Highway North
Sebastopol, CA 95472
800-998-9938 (in the United States or Canada)
707-829-0515 (international or local)
707-829-0104 (fax)

We have a web page for this book, where we list errata, examples, and any additional information. You can access this page at:

http://www.oreilly.com/catalog/9780596159795

The authors also have a site for this book at:

http://buildingreputation.com

To comment or ask technical questions about this book, send email to:

> *bookquestions@oreilly.com*

For more information about our books, conferences, Resource Centers, and the O'Reilly Network, see our website at:

> *http://www.oreilly.com*

Acknowledgments

As with any book that reports so much personal experience with a topic, there are more people to thank than we even know or recall—to any we've missed, know that we are grateful for the lessons you helped us learn, even if we're forgetful of your names.

We are first-time authors, so our editorial and publishing supporting cast come foremost to mind:

Mary Treseler, our editor at O'Reilly and our mentor—you helped us learn the ropes and were always supportive when we stumbled.

Havi Hoffman, head of Yahoo! Press—you believed in this project from the beginning, and despite all logistical and legal challenges, you made it happen, along with the unbounded support of your fellow Yahoos: Douglas Crockford, Christian Crumlish, and Neal Sample. Without all of you, there'd be no book at all.

Cate DeHeer, at DutchGirl.com (*http://dutchgirl.com*), our main copy editor—you unified our voices and made us both sound great without losing our personality.

Sanders Kleinfeld, Marlowe Shaeffer, Adam Witwer, and the rest of the support staff at O'Reilly—you made it all go as smoothly as possible.

The Yahoo! Reputation Platform team, in its various incarnations: Alex Chen, Matthias Eichstaedt, Yvonne French, Jason Harmon, Chip Morningstar, Dmitri Smirnov, Farhad Tanzad, Mammad Zadeh—you all helped define, implement, operate, and refine one of the world's finest platforms that provided us with most of the grammar and technical lessons used in this book.

The Yahoo! reputation-enabled product managers: Micah Alpern, Frederique Dame, Miles Libby, Cheralyn Watson, Ori Zaltzman, and so many others—when others scoffed, you were visionary and saw reputation as an unique opportunity to improve your product. So many of the socially oriented stories we've used here are a direct result of your pioneering work.

Our author-mentors: Douglas Crockford, Christian Crumlish, Amy Jo Kim, and Erin Malone—you all helped us understand just what it takes (and what it doesn't) to be an author.

To the readers/commentors on our blog, wiki, and manuscript—by letting us know what you thought as we went along, you significantly improved the first edition of this book. For those of you who comment after this is published—thank you so much for helping us keep this information up-to-date and accurate. Web publishing FTW!

From Randy

First and foremost, I'd like to thank my partner on this project, Bryce Glass, who presented the idea of us writing a book about reputation together just at the time I was feeling the desire to write something but too timid to do it on my own. I knew immediately that this was a great idea, and that he would be the perfect coauthor: I had some the product and engineering experience, and he really understood the UX design issues, as well as being world-class at creating wonderfully simple images to communicate complex concepts. Truly our combined talents produced a book that is greater than the sum of its parts.

Without the explicit encouragement from my wonderful wife, Pamela, this book would never have been started. I began working on it while being nominally unemployed, and at the worst of the 2008 economic downturn. Though I had enough contract work to just barely meet expenses, I could have just continued my search for full-time employment and simply deferred the opportunity to write down my experiences in favor of a steady paycheck. While I was dithering, unsure about taking on the mantle of authorship, she said, "You should go for it!" Her faith in and support for me is an inspiration.

To my parents, Frank and Kathy Farmer, for your constant encouragement to dig ever-deeper into whatever topic I was interested in, I am forever grateful. I hope that sharing my knowledge will help others along a similar path.

Reeve, Cassi, Amanda, and Alice Farmer—you are my pride and joy, and the reason I keep striving to improve the world you will inherit.

I'd also like to acknowledge folks who personally influenced me in significant ways that eventually led me here:

- Thomas Hartsig, Sr., formerly head of the Macomb Intermediate School District Computer Based Instruction group. Tom had the foresight to hire untested high-school programmers to create educational software in the late 1970s. At the MISD I learned that anyone can build a good reputation through hard work and inspiration.

- Steve Arnold, former head of Lucasfilm Games/LucasArts, and everyone there who I worked with during the early 1980s. Nothing convinces you that anything is possible like working for George Lucas.

- Phil Salin, free-market economist, who encouraged me to create reputation systems for his lifelong project The American Information Exchange in the pre-Web 1990s. If he'd only survived and we'd timed it a bit better, we could have been eBay.

- Mark Hull, who hired me into Yahoo! first to create the business plan to build and leverage a reputation platform, then to co-design the Yahoo! 360° social network and help found the Community Platforms group, where the reputation platform would eventually be built.

- Scott Moore and Han Qu, who helped me clarify the Content Control Patterns—thanks, guys!

From Bryce

I, too, would like to thank my coauthor, Randy Farmer. His enthusiasm for, and absolute grasp of, social media and online communities was a large part of what drew me to Yahoo!'s Community Platforms team. Randy—you don't just work at this stuff, you love it, and your energy is contagious.

The real, untold hero of this book—for me—has been my wife, LeeAnn. While I stole precious evenings and weekends away to work on the book, you cared for our son, Edison, and carried our new son, Evan. You have my endless gratitude and—of course—my undying love.

Thank you to my sons' wonderful grandparents for the many weekends of babysitting that freed Daddy up for...yes, more writing.

I'd also like to thank several past and present Yahoos: Christian Crumlish—you've been a great champion of our book, and a great friend as well; Erin Malone—thank you for your friendship and mentoring, and assigning me to work with the Reputation Platform team; Matt Leacock, who supported that platform before me, and is an all-around amazing UX designer and longtime friend; and finally my last manager at Yahoo!, Amanda Linden, who threw her unabashed support and approval behind the book and my involvement in it.

And finally, I'd like to thank my new team at Manta Media, Inc., particularly my manager, Marty Vian, and fellow designer David Roe. You have been supportive in the extreme in helping me get it to the finish line.

PART I

Reputation Defined and Illustrated

Reputation Systems Are Everywhere

Reputation systems impact your life every day, even when you don't realize it. You need reputation to get through life efficiently, because reputation helps you make sound judgments in the absence of any better information. Reputation is even more important on the Web, which has trillions of pages to sort through—each one competing for your attention. Without reputation systems for things like search rankings, ratings and reviews, and spam filters, the Web would have become unusable years ago.

This book will clarify the concepts and terminology of reputation systems and define their mechanisms. With these tools, you can analyze existing models, or even design, deploy, and operate your own online reputation systems.

But, before all that, let us start at the beginning....

An Opinionated Conversation

Imagine the following conversation—maybe you've had one like it yourself. Robert is out to dinner with a client, Bill, and proudly shares some personal news.

He says, "My daughter Wendy is going to Harvard in the fall."

"Really! I'm curious—how did you pick Harvard?" asks Bill.

"Why, it has the best reputation. *Especially* for law, and Wendy wants to be a lawyer."

"Did she consider Yale? My boss is a Yale man—swears by the law school."

"Heh. Yes, depending on who you ask, their programs are quite competitive. In the end, we really liked Harvard's proximity. We won't be more than an hour away."

"Won't it be expensive?"

"It's certainly not cheap...but it *is* prestigious. We'll make trade-offs elsewhere if we have to—it's worth it for my little girl!"

unremarkable story in the details (OK, maybe most us haven't been accepted to ~~ird~~), but this simple exchange demonstrates the power of reputation in our ~~day~~ lives. Reputation is pervasive and inescapable. It's a critical tool that enables us ~~to~~ make decisions, both large (like *Harvard versus Yale*) and small (*what restaurant would impress my client for dinner tonight?*). Robert and Bill's conversation also yields other insights into the nature of reputation.

People Have Reputations, but So Do Things

We often think of reputation in terms of *people* (perhaps because we're each so conscious of our own reputation), but of course a reputation can also be acquired by many types of *things*. In this story, Harvard, a college, obviously has a reputation, but so may a host of other things: the restaurant in which Bill and Robert are sharing a conversation, the dishes that they've ordered, and perhaps the wine that accompanies their meal.

It's probably no coincidence that Bill and Robert have made the specific set of choices that brought them to this moment: reputation has almost certainly played a part in each choice. This book describes a formal, codified system for assessing and evaluating the reputations of both people and things.

Reputation Takes Place Within a Context

Bill praises Harvard for its generally excellent reputation, but that is *not* what's led his family to choose the school: it was Harvard's reputation as a law school in particular. Reputation is earned within a context. Sometimes its value extends outside that context (for example, Harvard is well regarded for academic standards in general). And reputations earned in one context certainly influence reputations in other contexts.

Things can have reputations in multiple contexts simultaneously. In our example, domains of academic excellence are important contexts. But *geography* can define a context as well, and it can sway a final decision. Furthermore, all of an item's reputations need not agree across contexts. In fact, it's highly unlikely that they will. It's entirely possible to have an excellent reputation in one context, an abysmal one in another, and no reputation at all in a third. No one excels at everything, after all.

For example, a dining establishment may have a five-star chef and the best seafood in town, but woefully inadequate parking. Such a situation can lead to seemingly oxymoronic statements such as Yogi Berra's famous line: "No one goes there anymore— it's too crowded."

We Use Reputation to Make Better Decisions

A large part of this book is dedicated to defining reputation in a formal, systema
fashion. But for now, put simply (and somewhat incompletely), reputation is *information used to make a value judgment about a person or a thing*. It's worth examining this assertion in a little more detail.

> Reputation is information used to make a value judgment about an object or a person.

Where does this information come from? It depends—some of it may be information that you, the evaluator, already possess (perhaps through direct experience, longstanding familiarity, or the like). But a significant component of reputation has to do with assimilating information that is *externally produced*, meaning that it does not originate with the person who is evaluating it. We tend to rely more heavily on reputation in circumstances where we don't have firsthand knowledge of the object being evaluated, and the experiences of others can be an invaluable aid in our decision. This is even more true as we move our critical personal and professional decisions online.

What kinds of value judgments are we talking about? All kinds. Value judgments can be decisive, continuous, and expressive. Sometimes a judgment is as simple as declaring that something is noteworthy (*thumbs up* or a *favorite*). Other times you want to know the relative rank or a numeric scale value of something in order to decide how much of your precious resources—attention, time, or money—to dedicate to it. Still other judgments, such as movie reviews or personal testimonials, are less about calculation and more about freeform analysis and opinion. Finally, some judgments, such as "all my friends liked it," make sense only in a small social context.

What about the people and things that we're evaluating? We'll refer to them as *reputable entities* (that is, people or things capable of accruing reputation) throughout this book. Some entities are better candidates for accruing reputation than others, and we'll give guidance on the best strategies for identifying them.

Finally, what kind of information do we mean? Well, almost anything. In a broad sense, if information can be used to judge someone or something, then it informs—in some part—the reputation of that person or thing. In approaching reputation in a formal, systematized way, it's beneficial to think of information in small, discrete units; throughout this book, we'll show that the *reputation statement* is the building block of any reputation system.

The Reputation Statement

Explicit: Talk the Talk

So what are Robert and Bill doing? They're exchanging a series of statements about an entity, Harvard. Some of these statements are obvious: "Harvard is expensive," says Bill. Others are less direct: "Their programs are quite competitive" implies that Robert has in fact compared Harvard to Yale and chosen Harvard. Robert might have said more directly, "For law, Harvard is better than Yale." These direct and indirect assertions feed into the shared model of Harvard's reputation that Robert and Bill are jointly constructing. We will call an asserted claim like this an *explicit reputation statement*.

Implicit: Walk the Walk

Other reputation statements in this story are even less obvious. Consider for a moment Wendy, Robert's daughter—her big news started the whole conversation. While her decision was itself influenced by Harvard's many reputations—as being a fine school, as offering a great law program, as an excellent choice in the Boston area—her *actions* themselves are a form of reputation statement, too. Wendy applied to Harvard in the first place. And, when accepted, she *chose to attend* over her other options. This is a very powerful claim type that we call an *implicit reputation statement*: action taken in relation to an entity. The field of economics calls the idea "revealed preference"; a person's actions speak louder than her words.

The Minimum Reputation Statement

Any of the following types of information might be considered viable reputation statements:

- Assertions made about something by a third party. (Bill, for instance, posits that Harvard "will be expensive.")
- Factual statistics about something.
- Prizes or awards that someone or something has earned in the past.
- Actions that a person might take toward something (for example, Wendy's application to Harvard).

All of these reputation statements—and many more—can be generalized in this way:

a source   makes   a claim   about   a target

As it turns out, this model may be a little *too generalized*; some critical elements are left out. For example, as we've already pointed out, these statements are always made in a context. But we'll explore other enhancements in Chapter 2. For now, the general concepts to get familiar with are *source*, *target*, and *claim*. Here's an example of a reputation statement broken down into its constituent parts. This one happens to be an *explicit* reputation statement by Bill:

Here's another example, an action, which makes an *implicit* reputation statement about the quality of Harvard:

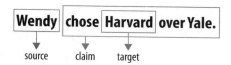

You may be wrestling a bit with the terminology here, particularly the term *claim*. ("Why, Wendy's not claiming anything," you might be thinking. "That's simply what she *did*.") It may help to think of it like this: *we* are going to make the claim—by virtue of watching Wendy's actions—that she believes Harvard is a better choice for her than Yale. We are drawing an implicit assumption of quality from her actions. There is another possible reputation statement hiding in here, one with a claim of did-*not*-choose and a target of Yale.

These are obviously two fairly simple examples. And, as we said earlier, our simplified illustration of a reputation statement is omitting some critical elements. Later, we'll revise that illustration and add a little rigor.

Reputation Systems Bring Structure to Chaos

By what process do these random and disparate reputation statements cohere and become a *reputation*? In "real life," it's sometimes hard to say: boundaries and contexts overlap, and impressions get muddied. Often, real-world reputations are no more advanced than irregular, misshapen lumps of collected statements, coalescing to form a haphazard whole. Ask someone, for example, "What do you think about Indiana?" Or "George W. Bush?" You're liable to get 10 different answers from eight different people. It's up to *you* to keep those claims straight and form a cohesive thought from them.

Systems for monitoring reputation help to formalize and delineate this process. A (sometimes, but not always) welcome side effect is that reputation systems also end up *defining* positive reputations, and suggesting exactly how to tell them from negative

.See the sidebar "Negative and Positive Reputation" on page 17.) Next, we'll
.ss some real-world reputation systems that govern all of our lives.

.n, the remainder of this book proposes a system that accomplishes that very thing
the social web. For the multitude of applications, communities, sites, and social
games that might benefit from a reputation-enriched approach, we'll take you—the
site designer, developer, or architect—through the following process:

- Defining the *targets* (or the best *reputable entities*) in your system
- Identifying likely *sources* of opinion
- Codifying the various *claims* that those sources may make

Reputation Systems Deeply Affect Our Lives

We all use reputation every day to make better decisions about anything, from the
mundane to choices critical for survival. But the flip side is just as important and
pervasive—a multitude of reputation systems currently evaluate you, your performance, and your creations. This effect is also true for the groups that you are a member
of: work, professional, social, or congregational. They all have aggregated reputations
that you are a part of, and their reputation reflects on you as well. These reputations
are often difficult to perceive and sometimes even harder to change.

Local Reputation: It Takes a Village

Many of your personal and group reputations are limited in scope: your latest performance evaluation at work is between you, your boss, and the human resources department; the family living on the corner is known for never cutting their grass; the
hardware store on Main Street gives a 10% discount to regular customers. These are
local reputations that represent much of the fabric that allows neighbors, coworkers,
and other small groups to make quick, efficient decisions about where to go, whom to
see, and what to do.

Local reputation can be highly valuable to those outside of the original context. If the
context can be clearly understood and valued by a larger audience, then "surfacing" a
local reputation more broadly can create significant real-world value for an entity. For
example, assuming a fairly standard definition of a *good sushi restaurant*, displaying a
restaurant's local reputation to visitors can increase the restaurant's business and local
tax revenue. This is exactly what the *Zagat's* guide does—it uses local reputation statements to produce a widely available and profitable reputation system.

Note that—even in this example—a reputation system has to create a plethora of categories (or *contexts*) in order to overcome challenges of aggregating local reputation on
the basis of personal taste. In Manhattan, *Zagat's* lists three types of *American* cuisine
alone: *new*, *regional*, and *traditional*. We will discuss reputation contexts and scope
further in Chapter 6.

On the other hand, a corporate performance review would *not* benefit from broader publication. On the contrary, it is inappropriate, even illegal in some places, to share that type of local reputation in other contexts.

Generally, local reputation has the narrowest context, is the easiest to interpret, and is the most malleable. Sources are so few that it is often possible—or even required—to change or rebuild collective local perception. A retailer displaying a banner that reads "Under New Management" is probably attempting to reset his business's reputation with local customers. Likewise, when you change jobs and get a new boss, you usually have to (or *get to*, depending on how you look at it) start over and rebuild your *good worker* reputation.

Global Reputation: Collective Intelligence

When strangers who do not have access to your local reputation contexts need to make decisions about you, your stuff, or your communities, they often turn to reputations aggregated in much broader contexts. These *global reputations* are maintained by external formal entities—often for-profit corporations that typically are constrained by government regulation.

Global reputations differ from local ones in one significant way; the sources of the reputation statements do not know the personal circumstances of the target. That is, strangers generate reputation claims for other strangers.

You may think, "Why would I listen to strangers' opinions about things I don't yet know how to value?" The answer is simply that a collective opinion is better than ignorance, especially if you are judging the value of the target reputable entity against something precious—such as your time, your health, or your money.

Here are some global reputations you may be familiar with:

- The *FICO credit score* represents your ability to make payments on credit accounts, among many other things.
- Television advertising revenues are closely tied to *Nielsen ratings*. They measure which demographic groups watch which programming.
- For the first 10 years after the Web came into widespread use, *page views* were the primary metric for the success of a site.
- Before plunking down their $10 or more per seat, over 60% of U.S. moviegoers report consulting *online movie reviews and ratings* created by strangers.
- Statistics such as the *Dow Jones Industrial Average*, the *trade deficit*, the *prime interest rate*, the *consumer confidence index*, the *unemployment rate*, and the *spot price of crude oil* are all used as proxies for indicating America's economic health.

Again, these examples are aggregated from both explicit (what people say) and implicit (what people do) claims. Global reputations exist on such a large scale that they are very powerful tools in otherwise information-poor contexts. In all the previous examples, reputation affects the movement of *billions* of dollars every day.

Even seemingly trivial scores such as online movie ratings have so much influence that movie studios have hired professional review writers to pose as regular moviegoers, posting positive ratings early in an attempt to inflate opening weekend attendance figures. This is known in the industry as *buzz marketing*, and it's but one small example of the pervasive and powerful role that formal reputation systems have assumed in our lives.

FICO: A Study in Global Reputation and Its Challenges

Credit scores affect every modern person's life at one time or another. A credit score is the global reputation that has the single greatest impact on the economic transactions in your life. Several credit scoring systems and agencies exist in the United States, but the prevalent reputation tool in the world of creditworthiness is the *FICO credit score* devised by the company Fair Isaac. We'll touch on how the FICO score is determined, how it is used and misused, and how difficult it is to change.

The lessons we learn from the FICO score apply nearly verbatim to reputation systems on the Web.

The FICO score is based on the following factors (all numbers are approximate; see Figure 1-1):

- Start with 850 points—the theoretical maximum score. Everything is downhill from here.
- The largest share, up to 175 points, is deducted for late payments.
- The next most important share, up to 150 points, penalizes you for outstanding balances close to or over available credit limits (capacity).
- Up to 75 points are deducted if your credit history is short. (This effect is reduced if your scores for other factors are high.)
- Another 50 points may be deducted if you have too many new accounts.
- Up to 50 points are reserved for other factors.

Like all reputation scores, the FICO score is aggregated from many separate reputation statements. In this case, the reputation statements are assertions such as *"Randy was 15 days late with his Discover payment last month,"* all made by various individual creditors. So, for the score to be correct, the system must be able to identify the target (Randy) consistently and be updated in a timely and accurate way.

When new sources (creditors) appear, they must comply with the claim structure and be approved by the scoring agency; a bogus source or bad data can seriously taint the resulting scores. Given these constraints and a carefully tuned formulation, the

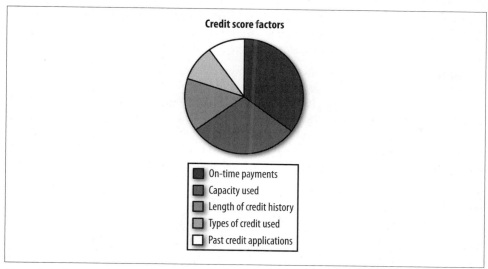

Figure 1-1. *Your credit score is a formalized reputation model made up of numerous inputs.*

FICO score may well be a reasonable representation of something we can call *creditworthiness*.

For most of its history of more than 50 years, the FICO score was shrouded in mystery and nearly inaccessible to consumers, except when they were opening major credit lines (such as when purchasing a home). At the time, this obscurity was considered a *benefit*. A benefit, that is, to lenders and the scoring agencies—that, in operating a high-fee-per-transaction business, were happy to be talking only with one another. But this lack of transparency meant that an error on your FICO score could go undetected for months—or even years—with potentially deleterious effects on your cash flow: increased interest rates, decreased credit limits, and higher lending fees.

However, as it has in most other businesses, the Internet has brought about a reform of sorts in credit scoring. Nowadays you can quickly get a complete credit report or take advantage of a host of features related to it: flags to alert you when others are looking at your credit data, or alarms whenever your score dips or an anomalous reputation statement appears in your file.

> [In the United States] an employer is generally permitted to [perform a credit check], primarily because there is no federal discrimination law that specifically prohibits employment discrimination on the basis of a bad credit report.
>
> —EmployeeIssues.com

As access to credit reports has increased, the credit bureaus have kept pace with the trend and have steadily marketed the reports for a growing number of purposes. More and more transaction-based businesses have started using them (primarily the FICO score) for less and less relevant evaluations. In addition to their original purpose—establishing the terms of a credit account—credit reports are now used by landlords for the less common but *somewhat relevant* purpose of risk mitigation when renting a house or apartment and by some businesses to run background checks on prospective employees—a legal but unreasonably invasive requirement.

Global reputation scores are so powerful and easily accessible that the temptation to apply them outside of their original context is almost irresistible. The rise and spread of the FICO score illustrates what can happen when a reputation that is powerful and ubiquitous in one specific context is used in other, barely related contexts: it transforms the reputation beyond recognition. In this ironic case, your ability to get a job (to make money that will allow you to pay your credit card bills) can be seriously hampered by the fact that your potential boss can determine that you are over your credit limit.

Web FICO?

Several startup companies have attempted to codify a global user reputation to be employed across websites, and some try to leverage a user's preexisting eBay seller's Feedback score as a primary value in their rating. They are trying to create some sort of "real person" or "good citizen" reputation system for use *across all contexts*. As with the FICO score, it is a bad idea to co-opt a reputation system for another purpose, and it dilutes the actual meaning of the score in its original context. The eBay Feedback score reflects only the transaction-worthiness of a specific account, and it does so only for particular products bought or sold on eBay. The user behind that identity may in fact steal candy from babies, cheat at online poker, and fail to pay his credit card bills. Even eBay displays multiple types of reputation ratings within its singular limited context. There is no web FICO because there is no kind of reputation statement that can be legitimately applied to all contexts.

Reputation on the Web

Over the centuries, as human societies became increasingly mobile, people started bumping into one another. Increasingly, we began to interact with complete strangers and our locally acquired knowledge became inadequate for evaluating the trustworthiness of new trading partners and goods. The emergence of various formal and informal reputation systems was necessary and inevitable. These same problems of trust and evaluation are with us today, on the Web. Only...more so. The Web has no centralized history of reputable transactions and no universal identity model. So we can't simply mimic real-world reputation techniques, where once you find someone (or some group) that you trust in one context, you can transfer that trust to another. On the Web, no one knows who you are, or what you've done in the past. There is no multi-context "reputation at large" for users of the Web, at least for the vast majority of users.

Consider what people today are doing online. Popular social media sites are the product of millions of hands and minds. Around the clock and around the globe, the world is pumping out contributions small and large: full-length features on Vimeo, video shorts on YouTube, entries on Blogger, discussions on Yahoo! Groups, and tagged-and-titled Del.icio.us bookmarks. User-generated content and robust crowd participation have become the hallmarks of Web 2.0.

But the booming popularity of social media has created a whole new set of challenges for those who create websites and online communities (not to mention the challenges faced by the users of those sites and communities). Here are just a few of them.

Attention Doesn't Scale

Attention Economics: An approach to the management
of information that treats human attention
as a scarce commodity…

—Wikipedia

If there ever was any question that we live in an attention economy, YouTube has put a definitive end to it. According to YouTube's own data, "every minute, 10 hours of video is uploaded to YouTube." That's over *14,000 hours* of video each and every day. If you started watching *just today's* YouTube contributions nonstop, end to end, you'd be watching for the *next 40 years*. That's a lot of sneezing pandas!

Clearly, no one has the time to personally sift through the massive amount of material uploaded to YouTube. This situation is a problem for all concerned.

- If I'm a *visitor* to YouTube, it's a problem of time management. How can I make sure that I'm finding the best and most relevant stuff in the time I have available?

- If I'm a *video publisher* on YouTube, I have the opposite problem: how can I make sure that my video gets noticed? I think it's good content, but it risks being lost in a sea of competitors.

- And, of course, *YouTube itself* must manage an overwhelming inflow of user contributions, with the attendant costs (storage, bandwidth, and the like). It's in YouTube's best interest to quickly identify abusive content to be removed, and popular content to promote to their users. This decision-making process also has significant cost implications—the most viewed videos can be cached for the best performance, while rarely viewed items can be moved to slower, cheaper storage.

There's a Whole Lotta Crap Out There

Sturgeon's Law: Ninety percent of everything is crud.

—Theodore Sturgeon, author, March 1958

Even in contexts where attention is abundant and the sheer *volume* of user-generated content is not an issue, there is the simple fact that much of what's contributed just may not be that good. Filtering and sorting the best and most relevant content is what web search engines such as Google are all about. Sorting the *wheat from the chaff* is a multibillion-dollar industry.

The *great* content typically is identified by reputation systems, local site editors, or a combination of the two, and it is often featured, promoted, highlighted, or rewarded (see Figure 1-2).

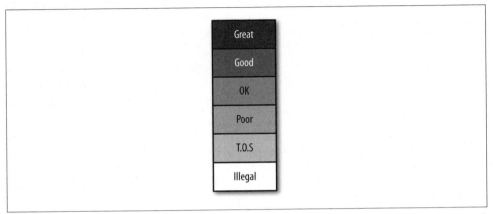

Figure 1-2. Content at the higher end of the scale should be rewarded, trumpeted, and showcased; stuff on the lower registers will be ignored, hidden, or reported to the authorities.

The primary goal of a social media site should be to make user-generated content of *good* quality constitute the bulk of what users interact with regularly. To reach that goal, user incentive reputation systems are often combined with content quality evaluation schemes.

Like an off-color joke delivered in mixed company, seemingly inappropriate content may become high-quality content when it's presented in another context. The quality of such content may be OK, but moving or improving the content will move it up the quality scale. On an ideal social media site, community members would regularly only encounter content that is OK or better.

Unfortunately, when a site has the minimum possible social media features—such as blog comments turned on without oversight or moderation—the result is usually a very high ratio of *poor* content. As user-generated content grows, content moderation of some sort is always required: typically, either employees scan every submission or the site's operators deploy a reputation system to identify bad content. Simply removing the bad content usually isn't good enough—most sites depend on search engine traffic, advertising revenue, or both. To get search traffic, external sites must link to the content, and that means the quality of the content has to be high enough to earn those links.

Then there are submissions that violate the terms of service (TOS) of a social website. Such content needs to be removed in a timely manner to avoid dragging down the average quality of content, degrading the overall value of the site.

Finally, if *illegal* content is posted on a site, not only must it be removed, but the site's operators may be required to report the content to local government officials. Such content obviously must be detected and dealt with as quickly and efficiently as possible.

For sites large and small, the worst content can be quickly identified and removed by a combination of reputation systems and content moderators. But that's not all reputations can do. They also provide a way to identify, highlight, and reward the contributors of the highest quality content, motivating them to produce their very best stuff.

People Are Good. Basically.

Of course, content on your site does not just appear, fully formed, like Athena from the forehead of Zeus. No, we call it *user-generated* content for a reason. And any good reputation system must consider this critical element—the people who power it— before almost anything else.

Visitors to your site will come for a variety of reasons, and each will arrive prearmed with her own motivations, goals, and prejudices. On a truly successful social media site, it may be impossible to generalize about those factors. But it does help to consider the following guidelines, regardless of your particular community and context.

Know thy user

Again, individual motivations can be tricky—in a community of millions like the Web, you'll have as many motivating factors as users (if not more; people are a conflicted lot). But be prepared, at least, to anticipate your contributors' motivations and desires. Will people come to your site and post great content because...

- They crave attention?
- It's intrinsically rewarding to them in some way?
- They expect some monetary reward?
- They're acting altruistically?

In reality, members of your community will act (and act out) for all of these reasons and more. And the better you can understand why they do what they do, the better you can fine-tune your reputation system to reflect the real desires of the people that it represents. We'll talk more about your community members and their individual motivations in Chapter 5, but we'll *generalize* about them a bit here.

Honor creators, synthesizers, and consumers

Not everyone in your community will be a top contributor. This is perfectly natural, expected, and—yes—even desired. Bradley Horowitz (vice president of product management at Google) makes a distinction among *creators*, *synthesizers*, and *consumers* (see Figure 1-3) and speculates on the relative percentages of each that you'll find in a given community:

tors
  1% of the user population might start a group (or a thread within a group).

  thesizers
  10% of the user population might participate actively and actually submit content, whether starting a thread or responding to one.

Consumers
  100% of the user population benefits from the activities of these two groups.

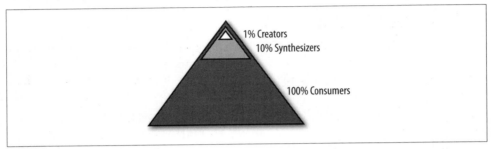

Figure 1-3. In any community, you'll likely find a similar distribution of folks who actively administer the site, those who contribute, and those who engage with it in a more passive fashion.

Again, understanding the roles that members of a community naturally fall into will help you formulate a reputation system that enhances this community dynamic (rather than fights against it). A thoughtful reputation system can help you reward users at *all* levels of participation and encourage them to move continually toward higher levels of participation, without ever discouraging those who are comfortable simply being site consumers.

Throw the bums out

And then there are the bad guys. Not every actor in your community has noble intentions. Attention is a big motivator for some community participants. Unfortunately, for some participants—known as *trolls*—that crassest of motivations is the only one that really matters. Trolls are after your attention, plain and simple, and unfortunately will stoop to any behavioral ploy to get it. But, luckily, they can be deterred (often with only a modicum of effort, when that effort is directed in the right way).

A (by far) more persistent and methodical group of problem users will have a financial motive: if your application is successful, spammers will want to reach your audience and will create robots that abuse your content creation tools to do it. But when given too much prominence, almost any motivation can lead to bad behavior that transgresses the values of the larger community.

The Reputation Virtuous Circle

Negative and Positive Reputation

Positive reputations
> Represent the relative value of an entity or user. Sometimes known as *relevance*, *popularity*, or even *quality*, positive reputation is used to feature the best content and its creators.

Negative reputations
> Identify undesirable content and users for further action. This includes illegal content, TOS violations, and especially spam.

Negative reputation systems are important for saving costs and keeping virtual neighborhoods garbage-free, but their chief value is generally seen as *cost reduction*. For example, a virtual army of robots keeps watch over controversial Wikipedia pages and automatically reverts obvious abuse, such as "blanking"—removing all article content nearly instantaneously—a task that would cost millions of dollars a year if paid human moderators had to perform it. Like a town's police force, negative reputation systems are often *necessary*, but they don't actually make things more attractive to visitors.

Where reputation systems really add value to a site's bottom line is by focusing on identifying the very best user-generated content and offering incentives to users for creating it. Surfacing the best content creates a *virtuous circle* (Figure 1-4): consumers of content visit a site and link to it because it has the best content, and the creators of that content share their best stuff on that site because all the consumers go there.

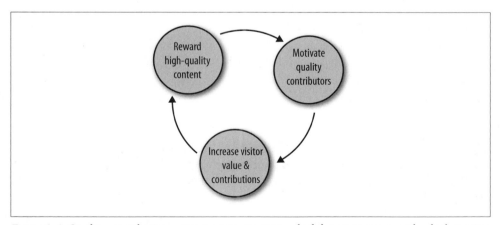

Figure 1-4. Quality contributions attract more attention, which begets more reward, which inspires more quality contributions....

Who's Using Reputation Systems?

Reputation systems are the underlying mechanisms behind some of the best-known consumer websites. For example:

- Amazon's product reviews are probably the most well-known example of object reputation, complete with a built-in meta-moderation model: "Was this review helpful?" Its Top Reviewers program tracks reputable reviews and trusted reviewers to provide context for potential product buyers when evaluating the reviewer's potential biases.

- eBay's feedback score is based on the number of transactions that a seller or buyer has completed. It is aggregated from hundreds or thousands of individual purchase transaction ratings.

- Built on a deep per-post user rating and classification system, Slashdot's karma is an often-referenced program used to surface good content and silence trolls and spammers.

- Xbox Live's (very successful) Achievements reward users for beating minor goals within games and cumulatively add to community members' gamerscores.

Table 1-1 illustrates that *all* of the top 25 websites listed on Alexa.com use at least one reputation system as a critical part of their business, many use several, and quite a few would fail without them. (Note that multiple Google and Yahoo! sites are collapsed in this table.)

Table 1-1. Use of reputation systems on top websites

Website	Vote to promote	Content rating and ranking	Content reviews and comments	Incentive karma (points)	Quality karma	Competitive karma	Abuse scoring
yahoo.*	††[a]	†††	†††	†	†	††	†††
google.*	††	†††	†	-	†	-	†††
youtube.com	†††[b]	††	†††	-	†	†	††
live.com	††	†††	††	†††	†	-	†††
facebook.com	†[c]	†††	††	††	†	†	†††
msn.com	†	†††	†††	-	†	††	††
wikipedia.org	†	-	††	-	†	-	†††
blogger.com	†	†	†††	-	†	-	†††
baidu.com	†	†††	†	†	†††	-	††
rapid-share.com	-[d]	-	-	†††	-	-	††
microsoft.com	-	-	†	-	-	-	†††
hi5.com	†	†	†	†	†	†	††

Website	Vote to promote	Content rating and ranking	Content reviews and comments	Incentive karma (points)	Quality karma	Competitive karma	Abuse scoring
sina.com.cn	†	†	†	†	†	†	†
ebay.com	†	†	-	†	†††	-	†††
mail.ru	†	†	†	-	-	-	†††
fc2.com	-	†	-	-	-	-	††
vkontakte.ru	†	†††	††	††	†	†	†††

[a] Multiple types
[b] Extensively
[c] Yes
[d] Unknown

Challenges in Building Reputation Systems

User-generated sites and online games of all shapes and sizes face common challenges. Even fairly intimate community sites struggle with the same issues as large sites. Regardless of the media types on a site or the audience for which a site is intended, once a reputation system hits a certain threshold of community engagement and contribution, the following problems are likely to affect it:

Problems of scale
    How to manage and present an overwhelming inflow of user contributions

Problems of quality
    How to tell the good stuff from the bad

Problems of engagement
    How to reward contributors in a way that keeps them coming back

Problems of moderation
    How to stamp out the worst stuff quickly and efficiently

Fortunately, a well-considered strategy for employing reputation systems on your site can help you make headway on *all* of these problems. A reputation system compensates for *an individual's* scarcest resource—his attention—by substituting a *community's* greatest asset: collective energy.

Sites with applications that skillfully manage reputations (both of the site's contributors and of their contributions) will prosper. Sites on which the reputation of users and content is ignored or addressed in only the crudest or most reactive way do so at their own peril. Those sites will see the quality of their content sag and participation levels falter, and will themselves earn a reputation as places to avoid.

This book will help you understand, in detail, how reputation systems work and give you the tools you need to apply that knowledge to your site, game, or application. It will help you see how to create your own virtuous circle, producing real value to you and your community. It will also help you design and develop systems to reduce the costs of moderating abuse, especially by putting much of the power back into the hands of your most ardent users.

Related Subjects

We have limited our examination of reputation systems to context-aggregated reputations, and therefore we will only lightly touch on reputation-related subjects. Each of these subjects is covered in detail in other reference works or academic papers (see Appendix B for references to these works):

Search relevance
> Algorithms such as *search rank* and *page rank* are massively complex and require teams of people with doctorates to understand, build, and operate them. If you need a good search engine, license one or use a web service.

Recommender systems
> These are information filters for identifying information items of interest on the basis of similarities of attributes or personal tastes.

Social network filters
> Though this book will help you understand the mechanics of most *social network filters*, it does not cover in depth the engineering challenges required to generate unique reputation scores for every viewing user.

We will not be addressing personal or corporate identity reputation management services, such as search engine optimization (SEO), WebPR, or trademark-monitoring. These are techniques to track and manipulate the very online reputation systems described in this book.

Conceptualizing Reputation Systems

We've demonstrated that reputation is everywhere and that it brings structure to chaos by allowing us to proxy trust when making day-to-day decisions. Therefore reputation is critical for capturing value on the Web, where everything and everybody is reduced to a set of digital identifiers and database records. We demonstrated that all reputation exists in a context. There is no overall web trust reputation—nor should there be. The abuses of the FICO credit score serve well as examples of the dangers therein.

Now that we've named this domain and limited its scope, we next seek to understand the nature of the currently existing examples—successes and failures—to help create both derivative and original reputation systems for new and existing applications. In order to talk consistently about these systems, we started to define a formal grammar, starting with *The Reputation Statement* as its core element. The remainder of this book builds on this premise, starting with Chapter 2, which provides the formal definition of our graphical reputation system grammar. This foundation is used throughout the remainder of the book, and is recommended for all readers.

A (Graphical) Grammar for Reputation

The phrase *reputation system* describes a wide array of practices, technologies, and user-interface elements. In this chapter, we'll build a visual "grammar" to describe the attributes, processes, and presentation of reputation systems. We'll use this grammar throughout subsequent chapters to describe existing reputation systems and define new ones. Furthermore, *you* should be able to use this grammar as well—both to understand and diagram common reputation systems, and to design systems of your own.

> *Meta-modeling*: A formalized specification of domain-specific notations...following a strict rule set.
>
> —*http://en.wikipedia.org/wiki/Metamodeling*

Much reputation-related terminology is inconsistent, confusing, and even contradictory, depending on what site you visit or which expert opinion you read. Over the last 30 years, we've evaluated and developed scores of online and offline reputation systems and identified many concepts and attributes common to them all; enough similarity that we propose a common lexicon and a "graphical grammar"—the common concepts, attributes, and methods involved—to build a foundation for a shared understanding of reputation systems.

Why propose a *graphical* grammar? Reputation is an abstract concept, and deploying it usually requires the participation of many people. In practice, we've consistently seen that having a two-dimensional drawing of the reputation model facilitates the design and implementation phases of the project. Capturing the relationships between the inputs, messages, processes, and outputs in a compact, simple, and accessible format is indispensable. Think of it like a screen mock, but for a critical, normally invisible part of the application.

In describing this grammar, we'll borrow a metaphor from basic chemistry: atoms (reputation statements) and their constituent particles (sources, claims, and targets) are bound with forces (messages and processes) to make up molecules (reputation models), which constitute the core useful substances in the universe. Sometimes different molecules are mixed in solutions (reputation systems) to catalyze the creation of stronger, lighter, or otherwise more useful compounds.

The graphical grammar of reputation systems is continually evolving as the result of changing markets and technologies. Visit this book's companion wiki at *http://buildingreputation.com* for up-to-date information and to participate in this grammar's evolution.

The Reputation Statement and Its Components

As we proceed with our grammar, you'll notice that reputation systems compute many different reputation values that turn out to possess a single common element: the reputation statement. In practice, most input to a reputation model is either already in the form of reputation statements or is quickly transformed into them for easy processing.

Just as matter is made up of atoms, reputation is made up of reputation statements.

Like atoms, reputation statements always have the same basic components, but they vary in specific details. Some are about people, and some are about products. Some are numeric, some are votes, some are comments. Many are created directly by users, but a surprising number is created by software.

Any single atom always has certain particles (protons, neutrons, and electrons). The configurations and numbers of those particles determine the specific properties of an element when it occurs en masse in nature. For example, an element may be stable or volatile, gaseous or solid, and radioactive or inert, but every object with mass is made up of atoms.

The reputation statement is like an atom in that it too has constituent particles: a *source*, a *claim*, and a *target* (see Figure 2-1). The exact characteristics (type and value) of each particle determine what type of element it is and its use in your application.

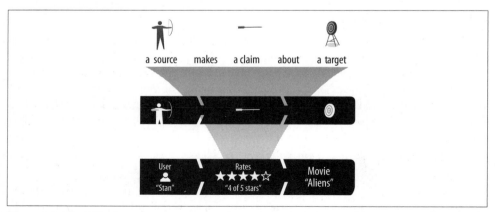

Figure 2-1. Much like in archery, anyone can fire a claim at anything. It doesn't necessarily mean the claim is accurate. Throughout this book, claims will be represented by this stylized arrow shape.

Reputation Sources: Who or What Is Making a Claim?

Every reputation statement is made by someone or something. A claim whose author is unknown is impossible to evaluate: the statement "Some people say product X is great" is meaningless. Who are "some people"? Are they like me? Do they work for the company that makes product X? Without knowing something about who or what made a claim, you can make little use of it.

We start building our grammar from the ground up, and so we need a few primitive objects:

Entity

> An *entity* is any object that can be the source or target of reputation claims. It must always have a unique identifier and is often a database key from an external database. Everything is *for* or *about* entities.

Source

> A *source* is an entity that has made a reputation claim. Though sources are often users, there are several other common sources: input from other reputation models, customer care agents, log crawlers, antispam filters, page scrapers, third-party feeds, recommendation engines, and other reputation roll-ups (see the description of roll-ups in the section "Messages and Processes" on page 26).

User [as Source]

> *Users* are probably the most well-known source of reputation statements. A user represents a single person's interaction with a reputation system. Users are always formal entities, and they may have reputations for which they are the *source* or of which they are the *target*.

Aggregate Source

> Reputation systems are all about collecting and combining or aggregating multiple reputation statements. The reputation statements that hold these collected claims are known as *roll-ups* and always use a special identifier: the aggregate source.

> This sounds like a special exception, but it isn't. This is the very nature of reputation systems, even in life: claims that a movie is number one at the box office don't include a detailed list of everyone who bought a ticket, nor should they. That claim always comes with the name of an aggregation source, such as "according to *Billboard Magazine*."

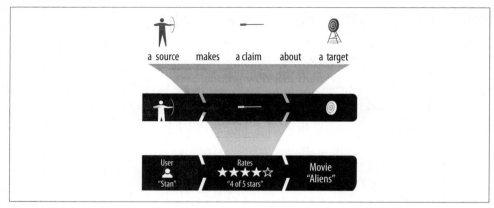

Figure 2-2. A number of common claim types, targeted at a variety of reputable entities.

Reputation Claims: What Is the Target's Value to the Source? On What Scale?

The *claim* is the value that the source assigned to the target in the reputation statement. Each claim is of a particular claim *type* and has a claim value. Figure 2-1 shows a claim with a 5-star rating claim type, and this particular reputation statement has a claim value of 4 (stars).

Claim type

What type of evaluation is this claim? Is it quantitative (numeric) or qualitative (structured)? How should it be interpreted? What processes will be used to normalize, evaluate, store, and display this score? Figure 2-2 shows reputation statements with several different common claim types.

Quantitative or numeric claims

Numeric or quantitative scores are what most people think of as reputation, even if they are displayed in a stylized format such as letter grades, thumbs, stars, or percentage bars. Since computers handle numbers easily, most of the complexity of reputation systems has to do with managing these score classes. Examples of common numerical score classes are accumulators, votes, segmented enumerations (that is, stars), and roll-ups such as averages and rankings.

Qualitative claims

Any reputation information that can't be readily parsed by software is called qualitative, but such information plays a critical role in helping people determine the value of the target. On a typical ratings-and-reviews site, the text comment and the demographics of the review's author set important context for understanding the accompanying 5-star rating. Qualitative scores commonly appear as blocks of text, videos, URLs, photos, and author attributes.

Raw score

> The score is stored in raw form—as the source created it. Keeping the original value is desirable because normalization of the score may cause some loss of precision.

Normalized score

> Numeric scores should be converted to a normalized scale, such as 0.0 to 1.0, to make them easier to compare to each other. Normalized scores are also easier to transform into a claim type other than the one associated with input.
>
> A normalized score is often easier to read than trying to guess what 3 stars means, since we're trained to understand the 0–100 scale early in life and the transformation of a normalized number to 0–100 is trivial to do in one's head. For example, if the community indicated that it was 0.9841 (normalized) in support of your product, you instantly know this is a very good thing.

Reputation Targets: What (or Who) Is the Focus of a Claim?

A reputation statement is always focused on some unique identifiable entity—the *target* of the claim. Reputations are assigned to targets, for example, a new eatery. Later, the application queries the reputation database supplying the same eatery's entity identifier to retrieve its reputation for display: "Yahoo! users rated Chipotle Restaurant 4 out of 5 stars for service." The target is left unspecified (or only partially specified) in database requests based on claims or sources: "What is the best Mexican restaurant near here?" or "What are the ratings that Lara gave for restaurants?"

Target, aka reputable entity

> Any entity that is the target of reputation claims. Examples of reputable entities are users, movies, products, blog posts, videos, tags, guilds, companies, and IP addresses. Even other reputation statements can be reputable entities if users make reputation claims about them—movie reviews, for example.

User as target, aka karma

> When a *user* is the reputable entity target of a claim, we call that *karma*. Karma has many uses. Most uses are simple and limited to corporate networks, but some of the more well-known uses, such as points incentive models and eBay feedback scores, are complex and public (see the section "Karma" on page 176 for a detailed discussion).

Reputation statement as target

> Reputation statements *themselves* are commonly the targets of other reputation statements that refer to them explicitly. See "Complex Behavior: Containers and Reputation Statements As Targets" on page 30 for a full discussion.

Molecules: Constructing Reputation Models Using Messages and Processes

Just as molecules are often made up of many different atoms in various combinations to produce materials with unique and valuable qualities, what makes reputation models so powerful is that they aggregate reputation statements from many sources and often statements of different types. Instead of concerning ourselves with valence and Van der Waals forces, in reputation models we bind the atomic units—the reputation statements—together with *messages* and *processes*.

In the simple reputation model presented in Figure 2-3, messages are represented by arrows and flow in the direction indicated. The boxes are the processes and contain descriptions of the processes that interpret the activating message to update a reputation statement and/or send one or more messages onto other processes. As in chemistry, the entire process is simultaneous; messages may come in at any time, and multiple messages may take different paths through a complex reputation model at the same time.

People often become confused about the limited scope of reputation, and where to draw the lines between multiple reputations, so we need a couple of definitions:

Reputation model
> A reputation model describes all of the reputation statements, events, and processes for a particular context. Usually a model focuses on a single type of reputable entity.
>
> Yahoo! Local, Travel, Movies, TV, etc. are all examples of ratings-and-reviews reputation models. eBay's Seller Feedback model, in which users' ratings of transactions are reflected in sellers' profiles, is a karma reputation model. The example in Figure 2-3 is one of the simplest possible models and was inspired by the *Digg it* vote-to-promote reputation model (see Chapter 6) made popular by Digg.com.

Reputation Context
> A reputation context is the relevant category for a specific reputation. By definition, the reputation's reuse is limited to related contexts. A high ranking for a user of Yahoo! Chess doesn't really tell you whether you should buy something from that user on eBay, but it might tell you something about how committed the user is to board gaming tournaments. See the sections "Reputation Takes Place Within a Context" on page 4 and "FICO: A Study in Global Reputation and Its Challenges" on page 10 for a deeper consideration of the limiting effects of context.

Messages and Processes

Again, look at the simplest reputation model diagram shown in Figure 2-3. The input reputation statement appears on the left and is delivered as a message to the reputation

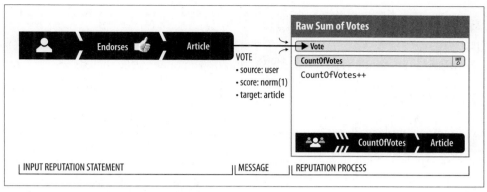

Figure 2-3. Users endorse articles, and the sum of their votes is displayed by that article.

process box. Messages and processes make up the working mechanics of the reputation model:

Reputation message

Reputation messages, represented by the flow lines in reputation model diagrams, are information supplied to a reputation process for some sort of computational action. In this example, the input is a reputation statement delivered as a message to the Raw Sum of Votes process. These messages may come from other processes, explicit user action, or external autonomous software. Don't confuse the party sending the messages with the reputation source; they are usually unrelated. For example, even when the source of a reputation input is a user, the message usually comes from an application—allowing the reputation system to take different actions based on the sender's identity.

Input event (reputation message)

In this book, we call initial messages—those that start the execution flow of a reputation model—*input events*; we show them at the start of a model diagram. Input events are said to be *transient* when the reputation message does not need to be undone or referenced in the future. Transient input events are not stored.

If, on the other hand, an event may need to be displayed or reversed in the future (e.g., if a user abuses the reputation model), it is said to be *reversible* and must be stored either in an external file such as a log or as a reputation statement. Most rating-and-review models have reversible inputs. But for very large-scale systems, such as IP address reputations that identify mail spammers, it's too costly to store a separate input event for every email received. For those reputation models, the transient input method is appropriate.

Reputation process

The large boxes represent one or more *reputation processes*. Using the message parameters, these processes normalize, transform, store, decide how to route new messages, or, most often, calculate a value. Although this book describes several common process types, the logic in these processes is usually customized to the application's requirements for more engineering-level detail about a specific implementation example, see Appendix A.

Stored Reputation Value

A stored reputation value is simply a reputation statement that may be read as part of a reputation process that calculates a new claim value for itself or another reputation statement.

Many reputation processes use message input to transform a reputation statement. In our example in Figure 2-3, when a user clicks "I Digg this URL," the application sends the input event to a reputation process that is a simple counter: CountOfVotes. This counter is a *stored reputation value* that is read for its current value, then incremented by one, and then is stored again. This brings the reputation database up to date and the application may use the target identifier (in Digg's case, a URL) to get the claim value.

Roll-ups

A *roll-up* is a specific kind of stored reputation value—any *aggregated* reputation score that incorporates multiple inputs over time or from multiple processes. *Simple average* and *simple accumulator* are examples of roll-ups.

Reputation Model Explained: Vote to Promote

Figure 2-3 is the first of many reputation model diagrams in this book. We follow each diagram with a detailed explanation.

This model is the *simple accumulator*: It counts votes for a target object. It can count clickthroughs or thumbs-ups, or it can mark an item as a favorite.

Even though most models allow multiple input messages, for clarity we're presenting a simplified model that has only one, in the form of a single reputation statement:

- As users take actions, they cause *votes* to be recorded and start the reputation model by sending them as a messages (represented by the arrows) to the Raw Sum of Votes process.

Likewise, whereas models typically have many processes, this example has only one:

- Raw Sum of Votes: When *vote* messages arrive, the CountOfVotes counter is incremented and stored in a reputation statement of the claim type Counter, set to the value of CountOfVotes and with the same target as the originating vote. The source of this statement is said to be *aggregate* because it is a roll-up—the product of many inputs from many different sources.

See Chapter 3 for a detailed list of common reputation process patterns, and see Chapters 6 and 7 for a discussion of the effects of various score classes on a user interface.

Building on the Simplest Model

Figure 2-4 shows a fuller representation of a Digg.com-like vote-to-promote reputation model. This example adds a new element to determining community interest in an article: adding a reputation for the level of user activity, measured by comments left on the target entity. These two are weighted and combined to produce a rating.

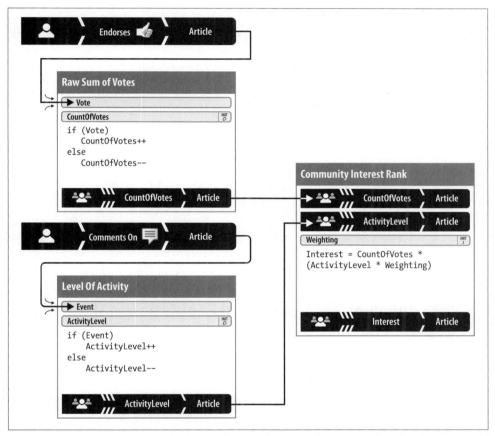

Figure 2-4. Now articles are ranked not only according to endorsements, but also the amount of discussion they generate.

The input messages take the form of two reputation statements:

- When a user *endorses* an article, the thumbs-up vote is represented as a 1.0 and sent as a message to the Raw Sum of Votes process. If a previous thumbs-up vote is *withdrawn*, a score of 0.0 is sent instead.

- When a user *comments on* an article, it is counted as activity and represented as a 1.0 and sent as a message to the *Level of Activity* process. If the comment is later deleted by the user, a score of 0.0 is sent to undo the earlier vote.

This model involves the following reputation processes:

Raw Sum of Votes
> This process either increments (if the input is 1.0) or decrements a roll-up reputation statement containing a simple accumulator called `CountOfVotes`. The process stores the new value and sends it in a message to another process, Community Interest Rank.

Level of Activity
> This process either increments (if the input is 1.0) or decrements a roll-up reputation statement containing a simple accumulator called `ActivityLevel`. It stores the new value back into the statement and sends it in a message to another process, Community Interest Rank.

Community Interest Rank
> This process always recalculates a roll-up reputation statement containing a weighted sum called *interest*, which is the value that the application uses to rank the target article in search results and in other page displays. The calculation uses a local constant—`Weighting`—to combine the values of `CountOfVotes` and `Activity Level` scores disproportionately; in this example, an *endorsement* is worth 10 times the interest score of a single comment. The resulting `Interest` score is stored in a typical roll-up reputation statement: aggregate source, numeric score, and target shared by all of the inputs.

Complex Behavior: Containers and Reputation Statements As Targets

Just as there exist some interesting-looking molecules in nature, and much like hydrogen bonds are especially strong, certain types of reputation statements called *containers* join multiple closely related statements into one super-statement. Most websites with user-generated ratings and comments for products or services provide examples of this kind of reputation statement: they clump together different star ratings with a text comment into an object formally called a *review*. See Figure 2-5 for a typical example, restaurant reviews.

Containers are useful devices for determining the order of reputation statements. Although it's technically true that each individual component of a container *could* be represented and addressed as a statement of its own, that arrangement would be semantically sloppy and lead to unnecessary complexity in your model. The container model maps well to real life. For example, you probably wouldn't think of the series of statements about Dessert Hut made by user Zary22 as a rapid-fire stream of individual

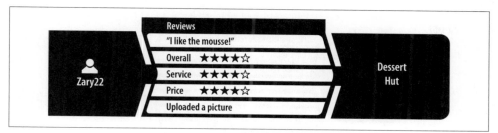

Figure 2-5. A reputation container: some claims make more sense when considered together than when standing alone.

opinions; you'd more likely consider them related and influenced by one another. Taken as a whole, the statements express Zary22's experience at Dessert Hut.

 A *container* is a compound reputation statement with multiple claims for the same source and target.

Once a reputation statement exists in your system, consider how you might make it a reputable entity itself, as in Figure 2-6. This indirection provides for subtle yet powerful feedback. For example, people regularly form their own opinions *about* the opinions of others based on some external criteria or context. ("Jack *hated The Dark Knight*, but he and I never see eye to eye anyway.")

Another feature of review-based reputation systems is that they often incorporate a form of built-in user feedback about reviews written by other users. We'll call this feature the Was This Helpful? pattern. (See Figure 2-7.) When a user indicates whether a review was helpful, the target is a review (container) written earlier by a different user.

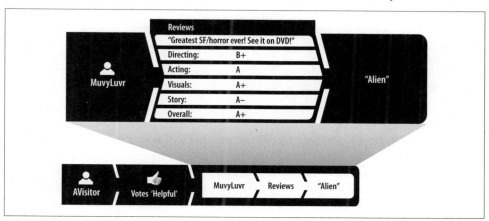

Figure 2-6. A reputation statement can itself be the target of a helpful vote. Here, MuvyLuvr has written a review that others can then rate.

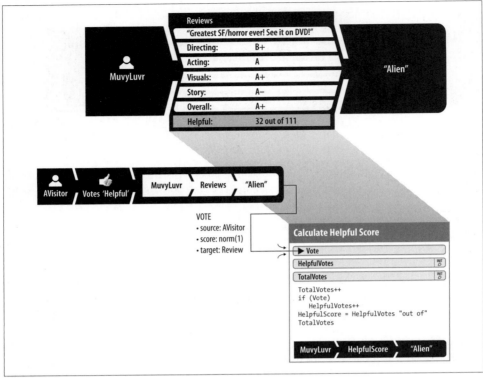

Figure 2-7. Helpful votes for a review are rolled up into an aggregate HelpfulScore. It's often more efficient to just store this score back to the review container for easy retrieval.

The input message takes the form of a single reputation statement:

- A user *votes* on the quality of another reputation statement, in this case a review: a thumbs-up vote is represented by a 1.0 value, and a thumbs-down vote by a 0.0 value.

This model includes only one reputation process:

- Calculate Helpful Score: When the message arrives, load the `TotalVotes` stored reputation value, increment, and store it. If the *vote* is not zero, the process increments `HelpfulVotes`. Finally, set the `HelpfulScore` to a text representation of the score suitable for display: "`HelpfulVotes` out of `TotalVotes`." This representation is usually stored in the very same review container that the voter was judging (i.e., had targeted) as helpful. This configuration simplifies indexing and retrieval, e.g., "Retrieve a list of the most helpful movie reviews by MuvyLuvr" and "Sort the list of movie reviews of *Aliens* by helpful score." Though the original review writer isn't the author of his helpful votes, his review is responsible for them and should contain them.

You'll see variations on this simple pattern of reputation-statements-as-targets repeated throughout this book. It makes it possible to build fairly advanced meta-moderation capabilities into a reputation system. Not only can you ask a community "What's good?"; you can also ask "...and whom do you believe?"

Solutions: Mixing Models to Make Systems

In one more invocation of our chemistry metaphor, consider that physical materials are rarely made of a single type of molecule. Chemists combine molecules into solutions, compounds, and mixtures to get the exact properties they want. But not all substances mix well—oil and water, for example. The same is true in combining multiple reputation model contexts in a single reputation system. It's important to combine only those models with compatible reputation contexts.

Reputation system

> A *reputation system* is a set of one or more interacting reputation models. An example is SlashDot.com, which combines two reputation models: an entity reputation model of users' evaluations of individual message board postings and a karma reputation model for determining the number of moderation opportunities granted to users to evaluate posts. It is a "the best users have the most control" reputation system. See Figure 2-8.

Reputation framework

> The *reputation framework* is the execution environment for one or more reputation systems. It handles message routing, storing, and retrieving statements, and maintaining and executing the model processes. Appendix A describes an implementation of a reputation framework.

Figure 2-8 shows a simple abuse reporting system that integrates two different reputation models in a single *weighted voting* model that takes weights for the IP addresses of the abuse reporters from an external karma system. This example also illustrates an explicit output, common in many implementations. In this example, the output is an event sent to the application environment suggesting that the target comment be dealt with. In this case, the content would need to be reviewed and either hidden or destroyed. Many services also consider punitive action against the content creator's account, such as suspension of access.

For the *reporter trustworthiness* context, the inputs and mechanism of this external reputation model are opaque—we don't know how the model works—because it is on a foreign service, namely TrustedSource.org by McAfee, Inc. Its service provides us one input, and it is different from previous examples:

1. When a reputation system is prompted to request a new trust score for a particular IP address—perhaps by a periodic timer or on demand by external means—it retrieves the `TrustedSourceReputation` as input using the web service API, represented here as a URL. The result is one of the following categories: `Trusted`,

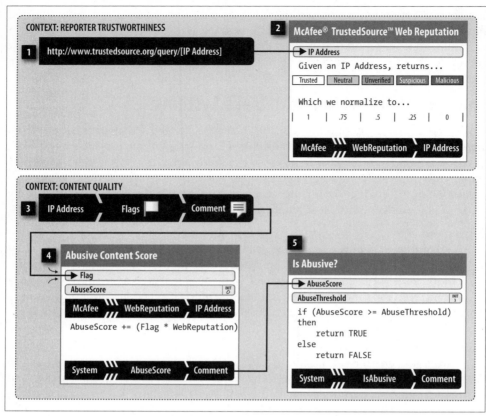

Figure 2-8. Two or more separate models can work in symphony to create a larger, more robust reputation system.

`Neutral`, `Unverified`, `Suspicious`, or `Malicious`, which the system passes to the McAfee TrustedSource Web Reputation process.

This message arrives at a reputation process that transforms the external IP reputation, in a published API format, into the reputation system's normalized range:

2. McAfee TrustedSource Web Reputation: Using a transformation table, the system normalizes the `TrustedSourceReputation` into `WebReputation` with a range from 0.0 (no trust) to 1.0 (maximum trust). The system stores the normalized score in a reputation statement with a source of TrustedSource.org, claim type *simple karma*, with the claim value equal to the normalized `WebReputation`, and a target of the IP address being evaluated.

The main context of this reputation is *content quality*, which is designed to collect *flags* from users whenever they think that the comment in question violates the site's terms of service. When enough users whose web providers have a high enough reputation flag the content, the reputation system sends out a special event. This reputation model is a *weighted voting* model.

This model has one input:

3. A user, connected using a specific IP address, *flags* a target comment as violating the site's terms of service. The value of the flag is always 1.0 and is sent to the Abusive Content Score process.

This model involves two processes—one to accumulate the total abuse score, and another to decide when to alert the outer application:

4. The Abusive Content Score process uses one external variable: `WebReputation`. This variable is stored in a reputation statement with the same target IP address as was provided with the flag input message. The `AbuseScore` starts at 0 and is *increased* by the value of `Flag` multiplied by `WebReputation`. The system stores the score in a reputation statement with an aggregate source, numeric score type, and the comment identifier as the target, then passes the statement in a message to the Is Abusive? process.

5. Is Abusive? then tests the `AbuseScore` against an internal constant, called `AbuseThreshold`, in order to determine whether to highlight the target comment for special attention by the application. In a simple (request-reply) framework implementation, this reputation system returns the result of the Is Abusive? process as `TRUE` or `FALSE` to indicate whether the comment is considered to be abusive. For high-performance asynchronous (fire-and-forget) reputation platforms such as the one described in Appendix A, an alert is triggered only when the result is `TRUE`.

From Reputation Grammar to...

This chapter defined the graphical reputation grammar, from bottom (reputation statements made of sources, claims, and targets) to top (models, systems, and frameworks). All members of any team defining a reputation-enhanced application should find this reference material helpful in understanding their reputation systems.

But at this point, readers with different team functional roles might want to look at different parts of the book next:

Product managers, application designers
Chapter 3 expands the grammar with a comprehensive review of common source, claim, target, and process types that serve as the basis of most reputation models. Think of these as the building blocks that you would start with when thinking about designing your customized reputation model.

Reputation framework engineers, software architects

If you're interested in technical details and want to know more about implementing reputation systems and dealing with issues such as reliability, reversibility, and scale, look at Appendix A for a detailed discussion of reputation frameworks before proceeding.

Reputation enthusiasts

If you're considering skipping the detailed extension of the grammar provided in Chapter 3, be sure not to miss the section "Practitioner's Tips: Reputation Is Tricky" on page 57 for some detailed insights before skipping ahead to Chapter 4, which provides a detailed look at common deployed reputation systems.

PART II

Extended Elements and Applied Examples

Building Blocks and Reputation Tips

By now you should feel fairly conversant in the *lingua franca* of reputation systems (the graphical grammar presented in Chapter 2), and you've had some exposure to their constituent bits and pieces. We've gone over reputation statements, messages, and processes, and you've become familiar with some rudimentary but serviceable models.

In this chapter, we "level up" and explore reputation claims in greater detail. We describe a taxonomy of claim types, exploring reputation roll-ups: actual computations on incoming messages that affect a particular output. Functionally, different types of roll-ups yield very different types of reputations, so we offer guidance on when to use which roll-ups. We end the chapter with practical advice in a section of "practitioner's tricks."

Extending the Grammar: Building Blocks

Though understanding the elements of the reputation grammar is essential, building reputation models from the atoms up every time is time consuming and tedious. There's a lot of benefit to developing tools and shorthand for common patterns and using those to configure reputation statements and templates for well-understood reputation models.

The Data: Claim Types

Remember, a fundamental component of a reputation statement is the *claim*—the assertion of quality that a *source* makes about a *target*. In "The Reputation Statement" on page 6, we discussed how claims can be either explicit (a direct statement of quality, intended by the statement's source to act as such) or implicit (representing a source-user's concrete actions associated with a target entity). These fundamentally different approaches are important because the *combination* of implicit and explicit claims can yield some very nuanced and robust reputation models. In other words, we should pay attention to what people say, but we should give equal weight to what they *do* to determine which entities hold the community's interest.

Claims also can be of different *types*. One helpful distinction is between qualitative claims (claims that describe one or more qualities that may or may not be easily *measured*) and quantitative claims, which are claims that can be measured (and, in fact, are largely generated, communicated, and read back as *numbers* of some kind).

Reputation statements have claim values, which you can generally think of as "what you get back when you ask for a reputation's current state." So, for instance, we can always query the system for Movies.Review.Overall.Average and get back a normalized score within the range of 0–1.

Note that the format of a claim does not always map exactly to the format in which you may wish to display (or, for that matter, gather) that claim. It's more likely that you'd want to translate the Movies.Review.Overall.Average to show your users three colored stars (out of five) instead of a normalized score or percentage.

Qualitative claim types

Qualitative claims attempt to describe some quality of a reputable object. This quality may be as general as the object's overall "quality" ("This is an excellent restaurant!") or as specific as some particular dimension or aspect of the entity ("The cinematography was stunning!"). Generally, qualitative claim types are *fuzzier* than hard quantitative claims, so qualitative claims quite often end up being useful implicit claims.

This is not to say, however, that qualitative claims can't have a quantitative value when considered en masse: almost any claim type can at least be counted and displayed in the form of some simple cumulative score (or "aggregator"—we discuss the various reputation roll-ups later in "Processes: Computing Reputation" on page 46). So while we can't necessarily assign an evaluative score to a user-contributed text comment, for instance (at least not without the rest of the community involved), it's quite common on the Web to see a *count* of the number of comments left about an entity, as a crude indicator of that item's popularity or the level of interest it draws.

The following sections describe some common types of qualitative claims.

Text comments. User-contributed text comments are perhaps the most common, defining feature of the user-generated content on the Web. Though a debate rages about the value of such comments (which in any case differs from site to site and from community to community), no one denies that the ability to leave text comments about an item of content—whether it's a blog entry, an article, or a YouTube video—is a wildly popular form of expression on the Web.

Text comment fields typically are provided as a freeform means of expression: a little white box that users can fill in any way they choose. However, better social sites will attempt to direct comments by providing guidelines or suggestions about what may be considered on- or off-topic.

Users' comments are usually freeform (unstructured) textual data. They typically are character-constrained in some way, but the constraints vary depending on the context: the character allowance for a message board posting is generally much greater than Twitter's famous 140-character limit.

In comment fields, you can choose whether to accommodate rich-text entry and display, and you can apply certain content filters to comments up front (for instance, you can choose to prohibit profanity or disallow fully formed URLs).

Comments are often just one component of a larger compound reputation statement. Movie reviews, for instance, typically are a combination of 5-star qualitative claims (and perhaps different ones for particular aspects of the film) and one or more freeform comment-type claims.

Comments are powerful reputation claims when interpreted by humans, but they may not be easy for automated systems to evaluate. The best way to evaluate text comments varies depending on the context. If a comment is just one component of a user review, the comment can contribute to a "completeness" score for that review: reviews with comments are deemed more complete than those without (and, in fact, the comment field may be required for the review to be accepted at all).

If the comments in your system are directed at another contributor's content (for example, user comments about a photo album or message board replies to a thread), consider evaluating comments as a measure of interest or activity around that reputable entity.

Here are examples of claims in the form of text comments:

- Flickr's Interestingness algorithm likely accounts for the rate of commenting activity targeted at evaluating the quality of photos.
- On Yahoo! Local, it's possible to give an establishment a full review (with star ratings, freeform comments, and bar ratings for subfacets of a user's experience with the establishment). Or a user can simply leave a rating of 1 to 5 stars. (This option encourages quick engagement with the site.) It's easy to see that there's greater business value (and utility to the community) in full reviews with well-written text comments, provided Yahoo! Local tracks the value of the reviews internally.

In our research at Yahoo!, we often probed notions of authenticity to look at how readers interpret the veracity of a claim or evaluate the authority or competence of a claimant.

We wanted to know: when people read reviews online (or blog entries, or tweets), what are the specific cues that make them more likely to accept what they're reading as accurate? Is there something about the presentation of material that makes it more trustworthy? Or is it the way the content author is presented? (Does an "expert" badge convince anyone?)

Time and again, we found that it's the content itself—the review, entry, or comment being evaluated—that makes up readers' minds. If an argument is well stated, if it seems reasonable, and if readers can agree with some aspect of it, then they are more likely to trust the content—no matter what meta-embellishment or framing it's given.

Conversely, research shows that users don't see poorly written reviews with typos or shoddy logic as coming from legitimate or trustworthy sources. People really do pay attention to content.

Media uploads. Reputation value can be derived from other types of qualitative claim types besides just freeform textual data. Any time a user uploads media—either in response to another piece of content (see Figure 3-1) or as a subcomponent of the primary contribution itself—that activity is worth noting as a claim type.

We distinguish textual claims from other media for two reasons:

- While text comments typically are entered in context (users type them right into the browser as they interact with your site), media uploads usually require a slightly deeper level of commitment and planning on the user's part. For example, a user might need to use an external device of some kind and edit the media in some way before uploading it.

- Therefore, you may want to weight these types of contributions differently from text comments (or not, depending on the context) reflecting increased contribution value.

A media upload consists of qualitative claim types that are not textual in nature:

- Video
- Images
- Audio
- Links
- Collections of any of the above

When a media object is uploaded in response to another content submission, consider it as input indicating the level of activity related to the item or the level of interest in it.

Figure 3-1. "Video Responses" to a YouTube video may boost its interest reputation.

When the upload is an integral part of a content submission, factor its presence, absence, or level of completion into the quality rating for that entity.

Here are examples of claims in the form of media uploads:

- Since YouTube video responses require extra effort by the contributors and lead to viewers spending more time on the site, they should have a larger influence on the popularity rank than simple text comments.

- A restaurant review site may attribute greater value to a review that features uploaded pictures of the reviewer's meal: it makes for a compelling display and gives a more well-rounded view of that reviewer's dining experience.

Relevant external objects. A third type of qualitative claim is the presence or absence of inputs that are external to a reputation system. Reputation-based search relevance algorithms (which, again, lie outside the scope of this book) such as Google PageRank rely heavily on this type of claim.

A common format for such a claim is a link to an externally reachable and verifiable item of supporting data. This approach includes embedding Web 2.0 media widgets into other claim types, such as text comments.

When an external reference is provided in response to another content submission, consider it as input indicating the level of activity related to the item or the level of interest in it.

When the external reference is an integral part of a content submission, factor its presence or absence into the quality rating or level of completion for that entity.

Here are examples of claims based on external objects:

- Some shopping review sites encourage cross-linking to other products or offsite resources as an indicator of review completeness. Cross-linking demonstrates that the review author has done her homework and fully considered all options.

- On blogs, the trackback feature originally had some value as an externally verifiable indicator of a post's quality or interest level. (Sadly, however, trackbacks have been a highly gamed spam mechanism for years.)

Quantitative claim types

Quantitative claims are the nuts and bolts of modern reputation systems, and they're probably what you think of first when you consider ways to assess or express an opinion about the quality of an item. Quantitative claims can be measured (by their very nature, they *are* measurements). For that reason, computationally and conceptually, they are easier to incorporate into a reputation system.

Normalized value. Normalized value is the most common type of claim in reputation systems. A normalized value is always expressed as a floating-point number in a range from 0.0 to 1.0. Within the range of 0.0 to 1.0, closer to 0 is worse and closer to 1 is better. Normalization is a best practice for handling claim values because it provides ease of interpretation, integration, debugging, and general flexibility. A reputation system rarely, if ever, displays a normalized value to users. Instead, normalized values are denormalized into a display format that is appropriate for the context of your application (they may be converted back to stars, for example).

One strength of normalized values is their general flexibility. They are the easiest of all quantitative types on which to perform math operations, they are the only quantitative claim type that is finitely bounded, and they allow reputation inputs gathered in a number of different formats to be normalized with ease (and then denormalized back to a display-specific form suitable for the context in which you want to display).

Another strength of normalized values is the general utility of the format: normalizing data is the only way to perform cross-object and cross-reputation comparisons with any certainty. (Do you want your application to display "5-star restaurants" alongside "4-star hotels"? If so, you'd better normalize those scores somewhere.)

Normalized values are also highly readable: because the bounds of a normalized score are already known, they are very easy (for you, the system architect, or others with access to the data) to read at a glance. With normalized scores, you do not need to understand the context of a score to be able to understand its value as a claim. Very little interpretation is needed.

Rank value. A rank value is a unique positive integer. A set of rank values is limited to the number of targets in a bounded set of targets. For example, given a data set of "100 Movies from the Summer of 2009," it is possible to have a ranked list in which each movie has exactly one value.

Here are some examples of uses for rank values:

- Present claims for large collections of reputable entities: for example, quickly construct a list of the top 10, 20, or 100 objects in a set. One common pattern is displaying leaderboards.

- Compare like items one-to-one, which is common on electronic product sales sites such as Shopping.com.

- Build a ranked list of objects in a collection, as with Amazon's sales rank.

Scalar value. When you think of scalar rating systems, we'd be surprised if—in your mind—you're not seeing stars. Rating systems of 3, 4, and 5 stars abound on the Web and have achieved a level of semipermanence in reputation systems. Perhaps that's because of the ease with which users can engage with star ratings; choosing a number of stars is a nice way to express an opinion beyond simple like or dislike.

More generally, a scalar value is a type of reputation claim in which a user gives an entity a "grade" somewhere along a bounded spectrum. The spectrum may be finely delineated and allow for many gradations of opinion (10-star ratings are not unheard of), or it may be binary (for example, thumbs-up, thumbs-down):

- Star ratings (3-, 4-, and 5-star scales are common)
- Letter grade (A, B, C, D, F)
- Novelty-type themes ("4 out of 5 cupcakes")

Yahoo! Movies features letter grades for reviews. The overall grades are calculated using a combination of professional reviewers' scores (which are transformed from a whole host of different claim types, from the *New York Times* letter-grade style to the classic Siskel and Ebert thumbs-up, thumbs-down format) and Yahoo! user reviews, which are gathered on a 5-star system.

Processes: Computing Reputation

Every reputation model is made up of inputs, messages, processes, and outputs. Processes perform various tasks. In addition to creating roll-ups, in which interim results are calculated, updated, and stored, processes include *transformers*, which change data from one format to another; and *routers*, which handle input, output, and the decision making needed to direct traffic among processes. In reputation model diagrams, individual processes are represented as discrete boxes, but in practice the implementation of a process in an operational system combines multiple roles. For example, a single process may take input; do a complex calculation; send the result as a message to another process; and perhaps return the value to the calling application, which would terminate that branch of the reputation model.

Processes are activated only when they receive an input message.

Roll-ups: Counters, accumulators, averages, mixers, and ratios

A roll-up process is the heart of any reputation system—it's where the primary calculation and storage of reputation statements are performed. Several generic kinds of roll-ups serve as abstract templates for the actual customized versions in operational reputation systems. Each type—counter, accumulator, average, mixer, and ratio—represents the most common simple computational unit in a model. In actual implementations, additional computation is almost always integrated with these simple patterns.

All processes receive one or more inputs, which consist of a reputation source, a target, a contextual claim name, and a claim value. In the upcoming diagrams, unless otherwise stated, the input claim value is a normalized score. All processes that generate a new claim value, such as roll-ups and transformers, are assumed to be able to forward the new claim value to another process, even if that capability is not indicated on the diagram. By default in roll-ups, the resulting computed claim value is stored in a reputation statement by the aggregate source. A common pattern for naming the aggregate claim is to concatenate the claim context name (Movies_Acting) with a roll-up context name (Average). For example, the roll-up of many Movies_Acting_Ratings is the Movies_Acting_Average.

Simple Counter. A Simple Counter roll-up (Figure 3-2) adds one to a stored numeric claim representing all the times that the process received any input.

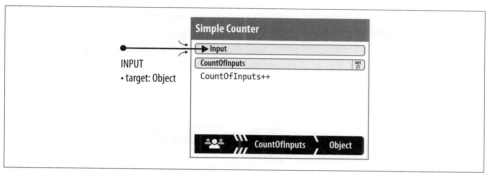

Figure 3-2. A Simple Counter process does just what you'd expect—as inputs come in, it counts them and stores the result.

A Simple Counter roll-up ignores any supplied claim value. Once it receives the input message, it reads (or creates) and adds one to the `CountOfInputs`, which is stored as the claim value for this process.

Here are pros and cons of using a Simple Counter roll-up:

Pros	Cons
Counters are simple to maintain and can easily be optimized for high performance.	A Simple Counter affords no way to recover from abuse. If abuse occurs, see "Reversible Counter" on page 47.
	Counters increase continuously over time, which tends to deflate the value of individual contributions. See "Bias, Freshness, and Decay" on page 60.
	Counters are the most subject of any process to "First-mover effects" on page 63, especially when they are used in public reputation scores and leaderboards.

Reversible Counter. Like a Simple Counter roll-up, a Reversible Counter roll-up ignores any supplied claim value. Once it receives the input message, it either adds or subtracts one to a stored numeric claim, depending on whether there is already a stored claim for this source and target.

Reversible Counters, as shown in Figure 3-3, are useful when there is a high probability of abuse (perhaps because of commercial incentive benefits, such as contests; see "Commercial incentives" on page 115) or when you anticipate the need to rescind inputs by users or the application for other reasons.

Here are pros and cons of using a Reversible Counter roll-up:

Pros	Cons
Counters are easy to understand.	A Reversible Counter scales with the database transaction rate, which makes it at least twice as expensive as a "Simple Counter" on page 47.
Individual contributions can be performed automatically, allowing for correction of abusive input and for bugs.	Reversible Counters require the equivalent of keeping a logfile for every event.
Reversible Counters allow for individual inspection of source activity across targets.	Counters increase continuously over time, which tends to deflate the value of individual contributions. See "Bias, Freshness, and Decay" on page 60.
	Counters are the most subject of any process to "First-mover effects" on page 63, especially when they are used in public reputation scores and leaderboards.

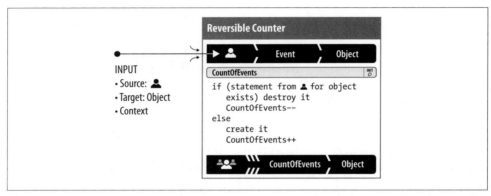

Figure 3-3. A Reversible Counter also counts incoming inputs, but it also remembers them, so that they (and their effects) may be undone later; trust us, this can be very useful.

Simple Accumulator. A Simple Accumulator roll-up, shown in Figure 3-4, adds a single numeric input value to a running sum that is stored in a reputation statement.

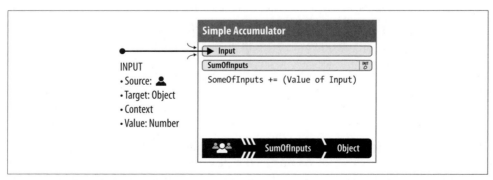

Figure 3-4. A Simple Accumulator process adds arbitrary amounts and stores the sum.

Here are pros and cons of using a Simple Accumulator roll-up:

Pros	Cons
A Simple Accumulator is as simple as it gets; the sums of related targets can be compared mathematically for ranking.	Older inputs can have disproportionately high value.
	A Simple Accumulator affords no way to recover from abuse. If abuse occurs, see "Reversible Accumulator" on page 49.
Storage overhead for simple claim types is low; the system need not store each user's inputs.	If both positive and negative values are allowed, comparison of the sums may become meaningless.

Reversible Accumulator. A reversible accumulator roll-up, shown in Figure 3-5, either (1) stores and adds a new input value to a running sum, or (2) undoes the effects of a previous addition. Consider using a Reversible Accumulator if you would otherwise use a Simple Accumulator, but you want the option either to review how individual sources are contributing to the Sum or to be able to undo the effects of buggy software or abusive use. However, if you expect a very large amount of traffic, you may want to stick with a Simple Accumulator, storing a reputation statement for every contribution can be prohibitively database intensive if traffic is high.

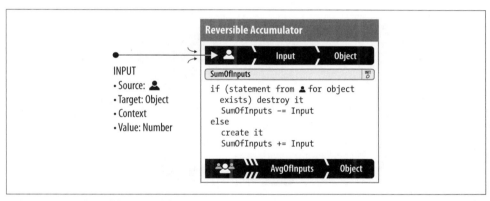

Figure 3-5. A Reversible Accumulator process improves on the Simple model—it remembers inputs so they may be undone.

Here are pros and cons of using a Reversible Accumulator roll-up:

Pros	Cons
Individual contributions can be performed automatically, allowing for correction of abusive input and for bugs.	A Reversible Accumulator scales with the database transaction rate, which makes it at least twice as expensive as a Simple Accumulator.
	Older inputs can have disproportionately high value.
Reversible Accumulators allow for individual inspection of source activity across targets.	If both positive and negative values are allowed, comparison of the sums may become meaningless.

Simple Average. A Simple Average roll-up, shown in Figure 3-6, calculates and stores a running average, including new input.

The Simple Average roll-up is probably the most common reputation score basis. It calculates the mathematical mean of a series of the history of inputs. Its components are a `SumOfInputs`, `CountOfInputs`, and the process claim value, `AvgOfInputs`.

Here are pros and cons of using a Simple Average roll-up:

Pros	Cons
Simple averages are easy for users to understand.	Older inputs can have disproportionately high value compared to the average. See "First-mover effects" on page 63.
	A Simple Average affords no way to recover from abuse. If abuse occurs, see "Reversible Average" on page 50.
	Most systems that compare ratings using Simple Averages suffer from ratings bias effects (see "Ratings bias effects" on page 61) and have uneven rating distributions.
	When Simple Averages are used to compare ratings, in cases when the average has very few components, they don't accurately reflect group sentiment. See "Liquidity: You Won't Get Enough Input" on page 58.

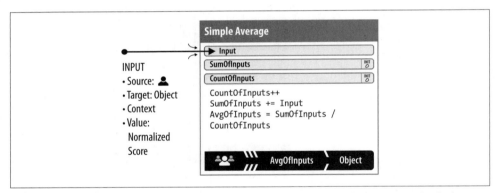

Figure 3-6. A Simple Average process keeps a running total and count for incremental calculations.

Reversible Average. A Reversible Average, shown in Figure 3-7, is a reversible version of Simple Average—it keeps a reputation statement for each input and optionally uses it to reverse the effects of the input.

If a previous input exists for this context, the Reversible Average operation reverses it: the previously stored claim value is removed from the `AverageOfInputs`, the `CountOfInputs` is decremented, and the source's reputation statement is destroyed. If there is no previous input for this context, compute a Simple Average (see the section "Simple Average" on page 50) and store the input claim value in a reputation statement made by this source for the target with this context.

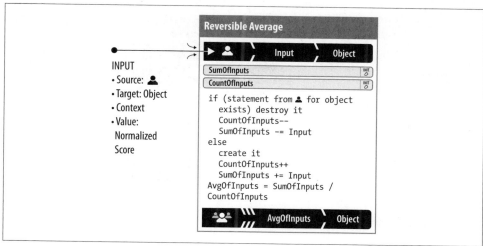

Figure 3-7. A Reversible Average process remembers inputs so they may be undone.

Here are pros and cons of using a Reversible Average roll-up:

Pros	Cons
Reversible Averages are easy for users to understand.	A Reversible Average scales with the database transaction rate, which makes it at least twice as expensive as a Simple Average (see "Simple Average" on page 50).
Individual contributions can be performed automatically, allowing for correction of abusive input and for bugs.	Older inputs can have disproportionately high value compared to the average. See "First-mover effects" on page 63.
Reversible Averages allow for individual inspection of source activity across targets.	Most systems that compare ratings using Simple Averages suffer from ratings bias effects (see "Ratings bias effects" on page 61) and have uneven rating distributions.
	When Reversible Averages are used to compare ratings, in cases when the average has very few components, they don't accurately reflect group sentiment. See "Liquidity: You Won't Get Enough Input" on page 58.

Mixer. A Mixer roll-up, Figure 3-8, combines two or more inputs or read values into a single score according to a weighting or mixing formula. It's preferable, but not required, to normalize the input and output values. Mixers perform most of the custom calculations in complex reputation models.

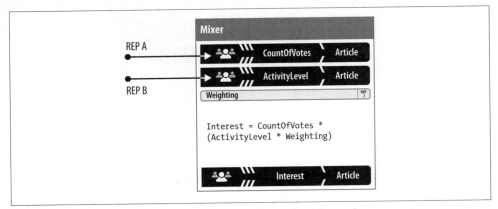

Figure 3-8. A Mixer combines multiple inputs together and weights each.

Simple Ratio. A Simple Ratio roll-up, Figure 3-9, counts the number of inputs (the total), separately counts the number of times the input has a value of exactly 1.0 (for example, hits), and stores the result as a text claim with the value of "(hits) out of (total)."

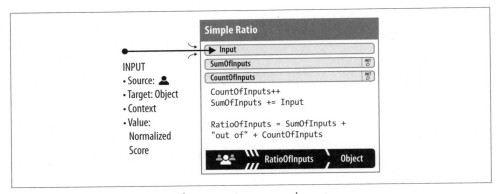

Figure 3-9. A Simple Ratio process keeps running sums and counts.

Reversible Ratio. If the source already has a stored input value for a target, a Reversible Ratio roll-up, Figure 3-10, reverses the effect of the previous hit. Otherwise, this roll-up counts the total number of inputs (the total) and separately counts the number of times the input has a value of exactly 1.0 (hits). It stores the result as a text claim value of "(hits) out of (total)" and also stores the source's input value as a reputation statement for possible reversal and retrieval.

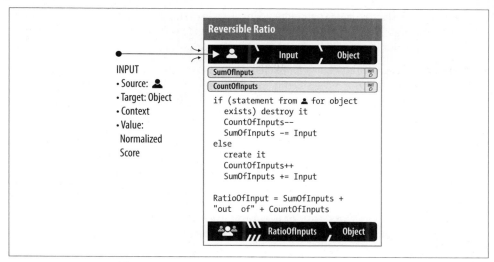

INPUT
- Source: 👤
- Target: Object
- Context
- Value:
  Normalized
  Score

Reversible Ratio

▶ 👤   Input   Object

SumOfInputs   ⬚INIT

CountOfInputs   ⬚INIT

```
if (statement from 👤 for object
    exists) destroy it
    CountOfInputs--
    SumOfInputs -= Input
else
    create it
    CountOfInputs++
    SumOfInputs += Input

RatioOfInput = SumOfInputs +
"out  of" + CountOfInputs
```

👥   RatioOfInputs   Object

Figure 3-10. A Reversible Ratio process remembers inputs so they may be undone.

Transformers: Data normalization

Data transformation is essential in complex reputation systems, in which information enters a model in many different forms. For example, consider an IP address reputation model for a mail system: perhaps it accepts this-email-is-spam votes from users, alongside incoming traffic rates to the mail server, as well as a historical karma score for the user submitting the vote. Each of these values must be transformed into a common numerical range before being combined.

Furthermore, it may be useful to represent the result in a discrete `Spammer/DoNotKnowIf Spammer/NotSpammer` category. In this example, transformation processes, shown in Figure 3-11, do both the normalization and denormalization.

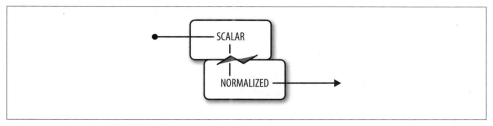

Figure 3-11. Transformers normalize and denormalize data; they are not usually independent processes.

Simple normalization (and weighted transform). Simple normalization is the process of converting from a usually scalar score to the normalized range of 1.0. It is often custom built, and typically accomplished with functions and tables.

Scalar denormalization. Scalar denormalization is the process of converting usually normalized values inputs into a regular scale, such as bronze, silver, gold, number of stars, or rounded percentage. Often custom built, and typically accomplished with functions and tables.

External data transform. An external data transform is a process that accesses a foreign database and converts its data into a locally interpretable score, usually normalized. The example of the McAfee transformation shown in Figure 2-8 illustrates a table-based transformation from external data to a reputation statement with a normalized score. What makes an external data transformer unique is that, because retrieving the original value often is a network operation or is computationally expensive, it may be executed implicitly on demand, periodically, or even only when it receives an explicit request from some external process.

Routers: Messages, Decisions, and Termination

Besides calculating the values in a reputation model, there is important meaning in the way a reputation system is wired internally and back to the application: connecting the inputs to the transformers to the roll-ups to the processes that decide who gets notified of whatever side effects are indicated by the calculation. These are accomplished with a class of building blocks called *routers*. Messaging delivery patterns, decision points, and terminators determine the flow throughout the model as it executes.

Common decision process patterns

We've described the process types as pure primitives, but we don't mean to imply that your reputation processes can't or shouldn't be combinations of the various types. It's completely normal to have a simple accumulator that applies mixer semantics.

There are several common decision process patterns that change the flow of messages into, through, and out of a reputation model: evaluators, terminators, and message routers of various types and combinations.

Simple Terminator. The Simple Terminator process is one that does not send any message to another reputation process, ending the execution of this branch of the model. Optionally a terminator may return its claim value to the application. This is accomplished via a function return, sending a reply, or by signaling to the application environment.

Simple Evaluator. A Simple Evaluator process provides the basic "If...then..." statement of reputation models, usually comparing two inputs and sending a message onto another process(es). Remember that the inputs may arrive asynchronously and separately, so the evaluator may need to have its own state.

Terminating Evaluator. A Terminating Evaluator ends the execution path started by the initial input, usually by returning or sending a signal to the application when some special condition or threshold has been met.

Message Splitter. A Message Splitter, shown in Figure 3-12, replicates a message and forwards it to more than one model event process. This operation starts multiple simultaneous execution paths for one reputation model, depending on the specific characteristics of the reputation framework implementation. See Appendix A for details.

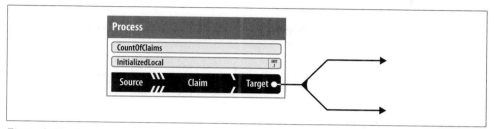

Figure 3-12. A message coming from a process may split and feed into two or more downstream processes.

Conjoint Message Delivery. Conjoint Message Delivery, shown in Figure 3-13, describes the pattern of messages from multiple different input sources being delivered to one process which treats them as if they all have the exact same meaning. For example, in a very large-scale system, multiple servers may send reputation input messages to a shared reputation system environment reporting on user actions. It doesn't matter which server sent the message; the reputation model treats them all the same way. This is drawn as two message lines joining into one input on the left side of the process box.

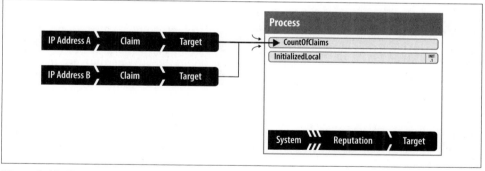

Figure 3-13. Conjoint message paths are represented by merging lines; these two different kinds of inputs will be evaluated in exactly the same way.

Input

Reputation models are effectively dormant when inactive; the model we present in this book doesn't require any persistent processes. Based on that assumption, a reputation model is activated by a specific input arriving as a message to the model. Input gets the ball rolling. Based on the requirements of custom reputation processes, there can be many different forms of input, but a few basic input patterns provide the common basic structure.

Typical inputs. Normally, every message to a reputation process must contain several items: the source, the target, and an input value. Often, the contextual claim name and other values, such as a timestamp and a reputation process ID, also are required for the reputation system to initialize, calculate, and store the required state.

Reputation statements as input. Our diagramming convention shows reputation statements as inputs. That's not always strictly accurate—it's just shorthand for the common method in which the application creates a reputation statement and passes a message containing the statement's context, source, claim, and target to the model. Don't confuse this notational convention with the case when a reputation statement is the target of an input message, which is always represented as a embedded miniature version of the target reputation statement. See "Reputation Targets: What (or Who) Is the Focus of a Claim?" on page 25.

Periodic inputs. Sometimes reputation models are activated on the basis of an input that's not reputation based, such as a timer that will perform an external data transform. At present, this grammar provides no explicit mechanism for reputation models to spontaneously wake up and begin executing, and this has an effect on mechanisms such as those detailed in "Freshness and decay" on page 63. So far, in our experience, spontaneous reputation model activation is not necessary and keeping this constraint out has simplified high-performance implementations. However, there is no particular universal requirement for this limitation.

Output

Many reputation models terminate without explicitly returning a value to the application at all. Instead, they store the output asynchronously in reputation statements. The application then retrieves the results as reputation statements as they are needed—always getting the best possible result, even if it was generated as the result of some other user on some other server in another country.

Return values. Simple reputation environments, in which all the model is implemented serially and executed in-line with the actual input actions, are usually implemented using on request-reply semantics: the reputation model runs for exactly one input at a time and runs until it terminates by returning a copy of the roll-up value that it calculated. Large-scale, asynchronous reputation frameworks, such as the one described in Appendix A, don't return results in this way. Instead, they terminate silently and sometimes send signals (see the next paragraph).

Signals: Breaking out of the reputation framework. Sometimes a reputation model needs to notify the application environment that something significant has happened and special handling is required. To accomplish this, the process sends a *signal*: a message that breaks out of the reputation framework. The mechanism of signaling is specific to each framework implementation, but in our diagramming grammar, signaling is always represented by an arrow leaving the box.

Logging. A reputation logging process provides a specialized form of output: it records a copy of the current score or message into an external store, typically using an asynchronous write. This action is usually the result of an evaluator deciding that a significant event requires special output. For example, if a user karma score has reached a new threshold, an evaluator may decide that the hosting application should send the user a congratulatory message.

Practitioner's Tips: Reputation Is Tricky

When you begin designing a reputation model and system using our graphical grammar, it may be tempting to take elements of the grammar and just plug them together in the simplest possible combinations to create an Amazon-like rating and review system, or a Digg-like voting model, or even a points-based karma incentive model as on StackOverflow. In practice—"in the wild," where people with myriad personal incentives interact with them both as sources of reputation and as consumers—the implementation of reputation systems is fraught with peril. In this section, we describe several pitfalls to avoid in designing reputation models.

The Power and Costs of Normalization

We make much of normalization in this book. Indeed, in almost all of the reputation models we describe, calculations are performed on numbers from 0.0 to 1.0, even when normalization and denormalization might seem to be extraneous steps. Here are the reasons that normalization of claim values is an important, powerful tool for reputation:

Normalized values are easy to understand
> Normalized claim values are always in a fixed, well-understood range. When applications read your claim values from the reputation database, they know that 0.5 means the middle of the range. Without normalization, claim values are ambiguous. A claim value of 5 could mean 5 out of 5 stars, 5 on a 10-point scale, 5 thumbs up, 5 votes out of 50, or 5 points.

Normalized values are portable (messages and data sharing)
> Probably the most compelling reason to normalize the claim values in your reputation statements and messages is that normalized data is portable across various display contexts (see Chapter 7) and can reuse any of the roll-up process code in your reputation framework that accepts and outputs normalized values. Other applications will not require special understanding of your claim values to interpret them.

Normalized values are easy to transform (denormalize)

The most common representation of the average of scalar inputs is a percentage, and this denormalization is accomplished trivially by multiplying the normalized value by 100. Any normalized score may be transformed into a scalar value by using a table or, if the conversion is linear, by performing a simple multiplication. For example, converting to a 5-star rating system could be as simple as multiplying the rating by 0.20 to get the normalized score. To get the stars back, just multiply by 5.0.

Normalization also allows the values of any claim type, such as thumbs-up (1.0)/ thumbs-down (0.0), to be denormalized as a different claim type, such as a percentage (0%–100%) or turned into a 3-point scale of thumbs-up (0.66–1.0), thumbs-down (0.0–0.33), or thumb-to-side (0.33–0.66). Using a normalized score allows this conversion to take place at display time without committing the converted value to the database. Also, the exact same values can be denormalized by different applications with completely different needs.

As with all things, the power of normalization comes with some costs:

Combining normalized scalar values introduces bias

Using different normalized numbers in large reputation systems can cause unexpected biases when the original claim types were scalar values with slightly different ranges. Averaging normalized maximum 4-star ratings (25% each) with maximum 5-star ratings (20% each) leads to rounding errors that cause the scores to clump up if the average is denormalized back to 5 stars. See Table 3-1.

Table 3-1. An example of ugly side effects when normalizing/denormalizing across different scales

Scale	1 stars normalized	2 stars normalized	3 stars normalized	4 stars normalized	5 stars normalized
4 stars	0–25	26–50	51–75	76–100	N/A
5 stars	0–20	21–40	41–60	61–80	81–100
Mean range/ denormalized	0–22 / ★☆☆☆☆	23–45 / ★★☆☆☆	46–67 / ★★★☆☆	68–90 / ★★★★☆	78–100 / ★★★★★

Liquidity: You Won't Get Enough Input

> *When is 4.0 greater than 5.0?*
> *When enough people say it is!*
>
> —F. Randall Farmer,
> Yahoo! Community Analyst, 2007

Consider the following problem with simple averages: it is mathematically unreasonable to compare two similar targets with averages made from significantly different numbers of inputs. For the first target, suppose that there are only three ratings averaging 4.667 stars, which after rounding displays as ★★★★★, and you compare that average score to a target with a much greater number of inputs, say 500, averaging 4.4523 stars, which after rounding displays as only ★★★★☆. The second target, the one with the lower average, better reflects the true consensus of the inputs, since there just isn't enough information on the first target to be sure of anything. Most simple-average displays with too few inputs shift the burden of evaluating the reputation to users by displaying the number of inputs alongside the simple average, usually in parentheses, like this: ★★★★☆ (142).

But pawning off the interpretation of averages on users doesn't help when you're ranking targets on the basis of averages—a lone ★★★★★ rating on a brand-new item will put the item at the top of any ranked results it appears in. This effect is inappropriate and should be compensated for.

We need a way to adjust the ranking of an entity based on the *quantity* of ratings. Ideally, an application performs these calculations on the fly so that no additional storage is required.

We provide the following solution: a high-performance liquidity compensation algorithm to offset variability in very small sample sizes. It's used on Yahoo! sites to which many new targets are added daily, with the result that, often, very few ratings are applied to each one.

RankMean

```
r = SimpleMean m - AdjustmentFactor a +
      LiquidityWeight l * Adjustment Factor a
```

LiquidityWeight

```
l = min(max((NumRatings n - LiquidityFloor f)
                      / LiquidityCeiling c, 0), 1) * 2
```

or

```
r = m - a + min(max((n - f) / c, 0.00), 1.00) * 2.00 * a
```

This formula produces a curve like that in Figure 3-14. Though a more mathematically continuous curve might seem appropriate, this linear approximation can be done with simple nonrecursive calculations and requires no knowledge of previous individual inputs.

The following are suggested initial values for a, c, and f (assuming normalized inputs):

AdjustmentFactor

```
a = 0.10
```

This constant is the fractional amount to remove from the score before adding back in effects based on input volume. For many applications, such as 5-star ratings, it should be within the range of integer rounding error—in this example, if the AdjustmentFactor is set much higher than 10%, a lot of 4-star entities will be ranked before 5-star ones. If it's set too much lower, it might not have the desired effect.

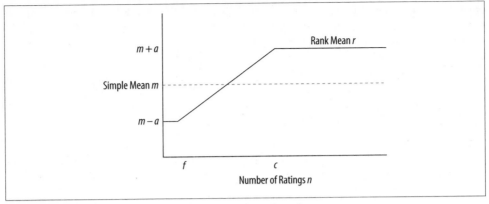

Figure 3-14. The effects of the liquidity compensation algorithm.

LiquidityFloor

> f = 10

> This constant is the threshold for which we consider the number of inputs required to have a positive effect on the rank. In an ideal environment, this number is between 5 and 10, and our experience with large systems indicates that it should never be set lower than 3. Higher numbers help mitigate abuse and get better representation in consensus of opinion.

LiquidityCeiling

> c = 60

> This constant is the threshold beyond which additional inputs will not get a weighting bonus. In short, we trust the average to be representative of the optimum score. This number *must not* be lower than 30, which in statistics is the minimum required for a t-score. Note that the t-score cutoff is 30 for data that is assumed to be unmanipulated (read: random).

We encourage you to consider other values for a, c, and f, especially if you have any data on the characteristics of your sources and their inputs.

Bias, Freshness, and Decay

When you're computing reputation values from user-generated ratings, several common psychological and chronological issues will likely represent themselves in your data. Often, data will be *biased* because of the cultural mores of an audience or simply because of the way the application gathers and shares reputations; for example, an application may favor the display of items that were previously highly rated. Data may also be *stale* because the nature of the target being evaluated is no longer relevant. For example, because of advances in technology, the ratings for the features of a specific model of digital camera, such as the number of pixels in each image, may be irrelevant within a few months. Numerous solutions and workarounds exist for these problems, one of which is to implement a method to *decay* old contributions to your reputations. Read on for details of these problems and what you can do about them.

Ratings bias effects

Figure 3-15 shows the graphs of 5-star ratings from nine different Yahoo! sites with all the volume numbers redacted. We don't need them, since we want to talk only about the shapes of the curves.

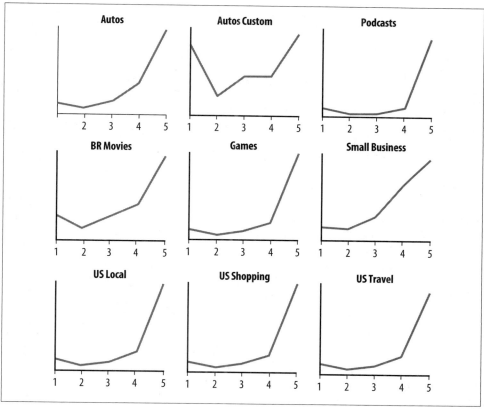

Figure 3-15. Some real ratings distributions on Yahoo! sites. Only one of these distributions suggests a healthy, useful spread of ratings within a community. Can you spot it?

Eight of these graphs have what is known to reputation system aficionados as *J-curves*—where the far right point (5 stars) has the very highest count, 4 stars the next highest, and 1 star a little more than the rest. Generally, a J-curve is considered less than ideal for several reasons. The average aggregate scores, which are all clumped together between 4.5 and 4.7 and therefore all display as 4 or 5 stars, are not so useful in visual sorting of options. Also, a J-curve begs the question: why use a 5-point scale at all?

Wouldn't you get the same effect with a simpler thumbs-up, thumbs-down scale, or maybe even just a super-simple *favorite* pattern?

The outlier among the graphs is for Yahoo! Autos Custom (now shut down), where users rated car profile pages created by other users. That graph has a *W-curve*: lots of 1-, 3-, and 5-star ratings and a healthy share of 4- and 2-star ratings, too. It was a healthy distribution and suggested that a 5-point scale was good for the community.

But why were Yahoo! Autos Custom's ratings so very different from Yahoo! Shopping, Local, Movies, and Travel?

Most likely, the biggest difference was that Autos Custom users were rating *one another's* content. The other sites had users evaluating static, unchanging, or feed-based content in which they didn't have a vested interest.

In fact, if you look at the curves for Shopping and Local, they are practically identical, and have the flattest J-hook, giving the lowest share of 1-star ratings. This similarity was a direct result of the overwhelming use pattern for those sites. Users come to find a great place to eat or the best vacuum to buy. When they search, the results with the *highest ratings appear first*. If a user has experienced that place or thing, he may well also rate it—if it's easy to do so—and most likely will give it 5 stars (see "First-mover effects" on page 63). If the user sees an object that isn't rated but that he likes, he may also rate and/or review it, usually giving it 5 stars so that others can share his discovery—otherwise, why bother? People don't think that it's worth the bother to seek out and create Internet ratings for mediocre places or things. The curves, then, are the direct result of a product design intersecting with users' goals. This pattern—"I'm looking for good things, so I'll help others find good things"—is a prevalent form of ratings bias. An even stronger example happens when users are asked to rate episodes of TV shows. They rate every episode 4.5 stars plus or minus .5 star because *only the fans bother to rate the episodes*, and no fan is ever going to rate an episode below a 3. Look at any popular current TV show on Yahoo! TV or Television Without Pity.

Our closer look at how Yahoo! Autos Custom ratings worked and how users were evaluating the content showed why 1-star ratings were given out so often: users gave feedback to other users to get them to change their behavior. Specifically, you would get one star if you (1) didn't upload a picture of your ride, or (2) uploaded a dealer stock photo of your ride. The site is Autos Custom, after all! Users reserved 5-star ratings for the best of the best. Ratings of 2 through 4 stars were actually used to evaluate the quality and completeness of the car's profile. Unlike all the sites graphed here, the 5-star scale truly represented a broad sentiment, and people worked to improve their scores.

One ratings curve isn't shown here: the U-curve, in which 1 star and 5 stars are disproportionately selected. Some highly controversial objects on Amazon are targets of this rating curve. Yahoo's now-defunct personal music service also saw this kind of curve when new music was introduced to established users: 1 star came to mean "Never play this song again" and 5 meant "More like this one, please." If you're seeing

U-curves, consider that users may be telling you something other than what you want to measure (or that you might need a different rating scale).

First-mover effects

When an application handles quantitative measures based on user input, whether it's ratings or measuring participation by counting the number of contributions to a site, several issues arise—all resulting from bootstrapping of communities—that we group together under the term *first-mover effects*:

Early behavior modeling and early ratings bias
> The first people to contribute to a site have a disproportionate effect on the character and future contributions of others. After all, this is social media, and people usually try to fit into any new environment. For example, if the tone of comments is negative, new contributors will also tend to be negative, which will also lead to bias in any user-generated ratings. See "Ratings bias effects" on page 61.
>
> When an operator introduces user-generated content and associated reputation systems, it is important to take explicit steps to model behavior for the earliest users in order to set the pattern for those who follow.

Discouraging new contributors
> Take special care with systems that contain leaderboards (see "Leaderboard ranking" on page 189) when they're used either for content or for users. Items displayed on leaderboards *tend to stay* on the leaderboards, because the more people who see those items and click, rate, and comment on them, the more who will follow suit, creating a self-sustaining feedback loop.
>
> This loop not only keeps newer items and users from breaking into the leaderboards, it discourages new users from even making the effort to participate by giving the impression that they are too late to influence the result in any significant way.
>
> Though this phenomenon applies to all reputation scores, even for digital cameras, it's particularly acute in the case of simple point-based karma systems, which give active users ever more points for activity so that leaders, over years of feverish activity, amass millions of points, making it mathematically impossible for new users to ever catch up.

Freshness and decay

As the previous section showed, time leaches value from reputation, but there's also the simple problem of ratings becoming stale over time as their target reputable entities change or become unfashionable. Businesses change ownership, technology becomes obsolete, cultural mores shift.

The key insight to dealing with this problem is to remember the expression, "What did you do for me *this* week?" When you're considering how your reputation system will display reputation and use it indirectly to modify the experience of users, remember to account for time value. A common method for compensating for time in reputation values is to apply a decay function: subtract value from the older reputations as time goes on, at a rate that is appropriate to the context. For example, digital camera ratings for resolution should probably lose half their weight every year, whereas restaurant reviews should only lose 10% of their value in the same interval.

Here are some specific algorithms for decaying a reputation score over time:

Linear aggregate decay
> Every score in the corpus is decreased by a fixed percentage per unit time elapsed, whenever it is recalculated. This is high performance, but scarcely updated reputations will have disproportionately high values. To compensate, a timer input can perform the decay process at regular intervals.

Dynamic decay recalculation
> Every time a score is added to the aggregate, recalculate the value of every contributing score. This method provides a smoother curve, but it tends to become computationally expensive $O(n^2)$ over time.

Window-based decay recalculation
> The Yahoo! Spammer IP reputation system has used a time-window-based decay calculation: fixed time or a fixed-size window of previous contributing claim values is kept with the reputation for dynamic recalculation when needed. New values push old values out of the window, and the aggregate reputation is recalculated from those that remain. This method produces a score with the most recent information available, but the information for low-liquidity aggregates may still be old.

Time-limited recalculation
> This is the de facto method that most engineers use to present any information in an application: use all of the ratings in a time range from the database and compute the score just in time. This is the most costly method, because it involves always hitting the database to recalculate an aggregate reputation (say, for a ranked list of hotels), when 99% of the time the resulting value is exactly the same as it was in the previous iteration. This method also may throw away still contextually valid reputation. Performance and reliability are usually best served with the alternate approaches described previously.

Implementer's Notes

The massive-scale Yahoo! Reputation Platform, detailed in Appendix A, implemented the reputation building blocks, such as the accumulator, sum, and even rolling average, in both the reputation model execution engine and in the database layer. This division of labor provided important performance improvements because the read-modify-write logic for stored reputation values are kept as close to the data store as possible. For small systems, it may be reasonable to keep the entire reputation system in memory at once, thus avoiding this complication. But be careful. If your site is as successful as you hope it might someday be, making an all-memory-based design may well come back to bite you, hard.

Making Buildings from Blocks

In this chapter, we extended the grammar by defining various reputation building blocks out of which hundreds of currently deployed reputation systems are built. We also shared tips about a few surprises we've encountered that emerge when these processes interact with real human beings.

In Chapter 4, we combine and customize these blocks to describe full-fledged reputation models and systems that are available on the Web today. We look at a selection of common patterns, including voting, points, and karma. We also review complex reputations, such as those at eBay and Flickr, in considerable detail. Diagramming these currently operational examples demonstrates the expressiveness of the grammar, and the lessons learned from their challenges provide important experiences to consider when designing new models.

CHAPTER 4

Common Reputation Models

Now we're going to start putting our simple reputation building blocks from Chapter 3 to work. Let's look at some actual reputation models to understand how the claims, inputs, and processes described in the last chapter can be combined to model a target entity's reputation.

In this chapter, we name and describe a number of simple and broadly deployed reputation models, such as vote to promote, simple ratings, and points. You probably have some degree of familiarity with these patterns by simple virtue of being an active online participant. You see them all over the place; they're the bread and butter of today's social web. Later in this chapter, we show you how to combine these simple models and expand upon them to make real-world models.

Understanding how these simple models combine to form more complete ones will help you identify them when you see them in the wild. All of this will become important later in the book, as you start to design and architect your own tailored reputation models.

Simple Models

At their very simplest, some of the models we present next are really no more than fancified reputation primitives: counters, accumulators, and the like. Notice, however, that just because these models are simple doesn't mean that they're not useful. Variations on the favorites-and-flags, voting, ratings-and-reviews, and karma models are abundant on the Web, and the operators of many sites find that, at least in the beginning, these simple models suit their needs perfectly.

favorites-and-flags model excels at identifying outliers in a collection of entities. The outliers may be exceptional either for their perceived quality or for their lack of same. The general idea is this: give your community controls for identifying or calling attention to items of exceptional quality (or exceptionally low quality).

These controls may take the form of explicit votes for a reputable entity, or they may be more subtle implicit indicators of quality (such as the ability to bookmark content or send a link to it to a friend). A count of the number of times these controls are accessed forms the initial input into the system; the model uses that count to tabulate the entities' reputations.

In its simplest form, a favorites-and-flags model can be implemented as a simple counter (Figure 4-1). When you start to combine them into more complex models, you'll probably need the additional flexibility of a reversible counter.

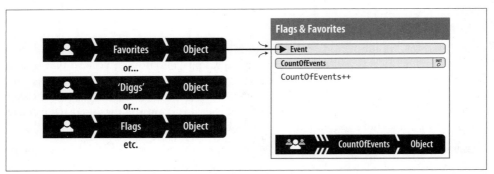

Figure 4-1. Favorites, flags, or send-to-a-friend models can be built with a Simple Counter process— count 'em up and keep score.

The favorites-and-flags model has three variants: vote to promote, favorites, and report abuse.

Vote to promote

The vote-to-promote model, a variant of the favorites-and-flags model, has been popularized by crowd-sourced news sites such as Digg, Reddit, and Yahoo! Buzz. In a vote-to-promote system, a user promotes a particular content item in a community pool of submissions. This promotion takes the form of a vote for that item, and items with more votes rise in the rankings to be displayed with more prominence.

Vote to promote differs from this-or-that voting (see the section "This-or-That Voting" on page 69) primarily in the degree of boundedness around the user's options. Vote to promote enacts an opinion on a reputable object within a large, potentially unbounded set (sites like StumbleUpon, for instance, have the entire Web as its candidate pool of potential objects).

Favorites

Counting the number of times that members of your community bookmark a content item can be a powerful method for tabulating content reputation. This method provides a primary value (see the sidebar "Provide a Primary Value" on page 132) to the user: bookmarking an item gives the user persistent access to it, and the ability to save, store, or retrieve it later. And, of course, it also provides a secondary value to the reputation system.

Report abuse

Unfortunately, there are many motivations in user-generated content applications for users to abuse the system. So it follows that reputation systems play a significant role in monitoring and flagging bad content. This is not that far removed from bookmarking the good stuff. The most basic type of reputation model for abuse moderation involves keeping track of the number of times the community has flagged something as abusive. Craigslist uses this mechanism, and sets a custom threshold for each item listed based on a per-user, per-category, and even per-city basis—though the value and the formulation are always kept secret from the users.

Typically, once a certain threshold is reached, either the application or human agents (staff) will act upon the content accordingly, or some piece of application logic will determine the proper automated outcome: remove the "offending" item, properly categorize it (for instance, add an "adult content" disclaimer to it), or add it to a prioritized queue for human agent intervention.

If your application is at a scale where automated responses to abuse reports are necessary, you'll probably want to consider tracking reputations for abuse reporters themselves. See "Who watches the watchers?" on page 209 for more.

This-or-That Voting

If you give your users options for expressing their opinion about something, you are giving them a vote. A very common use of the voting model (which we've referenced throughout this book) is to allow community members to vote on the usefulness, accuracy, or appeal of something.

To differentiate from more open-ended voting schemes like vote to promote, it may help to think of these types of actions as "this-or-that" voting: choosing from the most attractive option within a bounded set of possibilities (see Figure 4-2).

It's often more convenient to store that reputation statement back as a part of the reputable entity that it applies to, making it easier, for example, to fetch and display a "Was this review helpful?" score (see Figure 2-7 in Chapter 2).

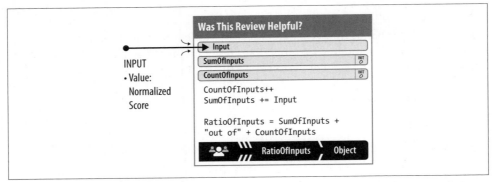

Figure 4-2. Those "Helpful Review" scores that you see are often nothing more than a Simple Ratio.

Ratings

When an application offers users the ability to express an explicit opinion about the quality of something, it typically employs a ratings model (Figure 4-3). There are a number of different scalar-value ratings: stars, bars, "HotOrNot," or a 10-point scale. (We discuss how to choose from among the various types of ratings inputs in the section "Determining Inputs" on page 131.) In the ratings model, ratings are gathered from multiple individual users and rolled up as a community average score for that target.

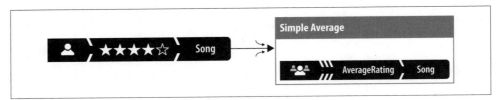

Figure 4-3. Individual ratings contribute to a community average.

Reviews

Some ratings are most effective when they travel together. More complex reputable entities frequently require more nuanced reputation models, and the ratings-and-review model, shown in Figure 4-4, allows users to express a variety of reactions to a target. Although each rated facet could be stored and evaluated as its own specific reputation, semantically that wouldn't make much sense; it's the review in its entirety that is the primary unit of interest.

In the reviews model, a user gives a target a series of ratings and provides one or more freeform text opinions. Each individual facet of a review feeds into a community average.

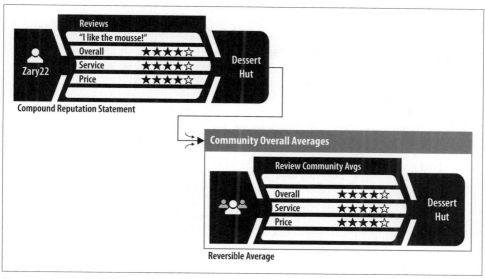

Figure 4-4. A full user review typically is made up of a number of ratings and some freeform text comments. Those ratings with a numerical value can, of course, contribute to aggregate community averages as well.

Points

For some applications, you may want a very specific and granular accounting of user activity on your site. The points model, shown in Figure 4-5, provides just such a capability. With points, your system counts up the hits, actions, and other activities that your users engage in and keeps a running sum of the awards.

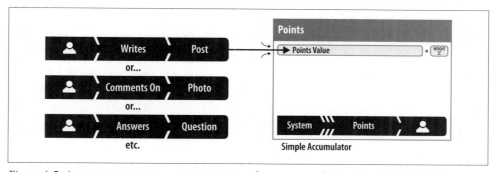

Figure 4-5. As a user engages in various activities, they are recorded, weighted, and tallied.

This is a tricky model to get right. In particular, you face two dangers:

- Tying inputs to point values almost forces a certain amount of transparency into your system. It is hard to reward activities with points without also communicating to your users what those relative point values are. (See "Keep Your Barn Door Closed (but Expect Peeking)" on page 91.)

- You risk unduly influencing certain behaviors over others: it's almost certain that some minority of your users (or, in a success-disaster scenario, the *majority* of your users) will make points-based decisions about which actions they'll take.

 There are significant differences between points awarded for reputation purposes and monetary points that you may dole out to users as currency. The two are frequently confounded, but reputation points should not be spendable.

If your application's users must actually surrender part of their own intrinsic value in order to obtain goods or services, you will be punishing your best users, and you'll quickly lose track of people's real relative worths. Your system won't be able to tell the difference between truly valuable contributors and those who are just good hoarders and never spend the points allotted to them.

It would be far better to *link* the two systems but allow them to remain independent of each other: a currency system for your game or site should be orthogonal to your reputation system. Regardless of how much currency exchanges hands in your community, each user's underlying intrinsic karma should be allowed to grow or decay uninhibited by the demands of commerce.

Karma

A karma model is reputation for users. In the section "Solutions: Mixing Models to Make Systems" on page 33, we explained that a karma model usually is used in support of other reputation models to track or create incentives for user behavior. All the complex examples later in this chapter ("Combining the Simple Models" on page 74) generate and/or use a karma model to help calculate a quality score for other purposes, such as search ranking, content highlighting, or selecting the most reputable provider.

There are two primitive forms of karma models: models that measure the amount of user participation and models that measure the quality of contributions. When these types of karma models are combined, we refer to the combined model as *robust*. Including both types of measures in the model gives the highest scores to the users who are both active and produce the best content.

Participation karma

Counting socially and/or commercially significant events by content creators is probably the most common type of participation karma model. This model is often implemented as a point system (see the earlier section "Points" on page 71), in which each action is worth a fixed number of points and the points accumulate. A participation karma model looks exactly like Figure 4-5, where the input event represents the number of points for the action and the source of the activity becomes the target of the karma.

There is also a negative participation karma model, which counts how many bad things a user does. Some people call this model *strikes*, after the three-strikes rule of American baseball. Again, the model is the same, except that the application interprets a high score inversely.

Quality karma

A quality-karma model, such as eBay's seller feedback model (see "eBay Seller Feedback Karma" on page 78), deals solely with the quality of user contributions. In a quality-karma model, the number of contributions is meaningless unless it is accompanied by an indication of whether each contribution is good or bad for business. The best quality-karma scores are always calculated as a side effect of other users evaluating the contributions of the target.

On eBay, a successful auction bid is the subject of the evaluation, and the results roll up to the seller: if there is no transaction, there should be no evaluation. For a detailed discussion of this requirement, see "Karma is complex, built of indirect inputs" on page 176. Look ahead to Figure 4-6 for a diagram of a combined ratings-and-reviews and quality-karma model.

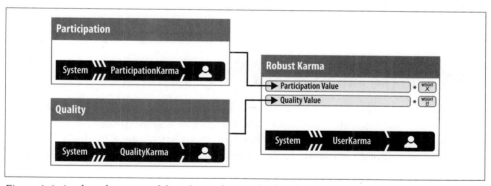

Figure 4-6. A robust-karma model might combine multiple other karma scores—measuring, perhaps, not just a user's output (Participation) but his effectiveness (or Quality) as well.

Robust karma

By itself, a participation-based karma score is inadequate to describe the value of a user's contributions to the community, and we will caution time and again throughout the book that rewarding simple activity is an impoverished way to think about user karma. However, you probably don't want a karma score based solely on quality of contributions, either. Under this circumstance, you may find your system rewarding *cautious* contributors, ones who, out of a desire to keep their quality-ratings high, only contribute to "safe" topics, or—once having attained a certain quality ranking—decide to stop contributing to protect that ranking.

What you really want to do is to combine quality-karma and participation-karma scores into one score—call it robust karma. The robust-karma score represents the *overall* value of a user's contributions: the quality component ensures some thought and care in the preparation of contributions, and the participation side ensures that the contributor is very active, that she's contributed recently, and (probably) that she's surpassed some minimal thresholds for user participation—enough that you can reasonably separate the passionate, dedicated contributors from the fly-by post-then-flee crowd.

The weight you'll give to each component depends on the application. Robust-karma scores often are not displayed to users, but may be used instead for internal ranking or flagging, or as factors influencing search ranking; see "Keep Your Barn Door Closed (but Expect Peeking)" on page 91, later in this chapter, for common reasons for this secrecy. But even when karma scores are displayed, a robust-karma model has the advantage of encouraging users both to contribute the best stuff (as evaluated by their peers) and to do it often.

When negative factors are included in factoring robust-karma scores, it is particularly useful for customer care staff—both to highlight users who have become abusive or users whose contributions decrease the overall value of content on the site, and potentially to provide an increased level of service to proven-excellent users who become involved in a customer service procedure. A robust-karma model helps find the best of the best and the worst of the worst.

Combining the Simple Models

By themselves, the simple models described earlier are not enough to demonstrate a typical deployed large-scale reputation system in action. Just as the ratings-and-reviews model is a combination of the simpler atomic models that we described in Chapter 3, most reputation models combine multiple smaller, simpler models into one complex system.

 We present these models for *understanding*, not for wholesale copying. If we impart one message in this book, we hope it is this: reputation is highly contextual, and what works well in one context will almost inevitably fail in many others. Copying any existing implementation of a model too closely may indeed lead you closer to the surface aspects of the application that you're emulating. Unfortunately, it may also lead you *away* from your own specific business and community objectives.

Part III shows how to design a system specific to your own product and context. You'll see better results for your application if you learn from models presented in this chapter, then set them aside.

User Reviews with Karma

Eventually, a site based on a simple reputation model, such as the ratings-and-reviews model, is bound to become more complex. Probably the most common reason for increasing complexity is the following progression. As an application becomes more successful, it becomes clear that some of the site's users produce higher-quality reviews. These quality contributions begin to significantly increase the value of the site to end users and to the site operator's bottom line. As a result, the site operator looks for ways to recognize these contributors, increase the search ranking value of their reviews, and generally provide incentives for this value-generating behavior. Adding a karma reputation model to the system is a common approach to reaching those goals.

The simplest way to introduce a quality-karma score to a simple ratings-and-reviews reputation system is to introduce a "Was this helpful?" feedback mechanism that visiting readers may use to evaluate each review.

The example in Figure 4-7 is a hypothetical product reputation model, and the reviews focus on 5-star ratings in the categories "overall," "service," and "price." These specifics are for illustration only and are not critical to the design. This model could just as well be used with thumb ratings and any arbitrary categories, such as "sound quality" or "texture."

The combined ratings-and-reviews with karma model has one compound input: the review and the was-this-helpful vote. From these inputs, the community rating averages, the WasThisHelpful ratio, and the reviewer quality-karma rating are generated on the fly. Pay careful attention to the sources and targets of the inputs of this model; they are not the same users, nor are their ratings targeted at the same entities.

The model can be described as follows:

1. The review is a compound reputation statement of claims related by a single source user (the reviewer) about a particular target, such as a business or a product:

   - Each review contains a text-only comment that typically is of limited length and that often must pass simple quality tests, such as minimum size and spell checking, before the application will accept it.

   - The user must provide an overall rating of the target; in this example, in the form of a 5-star rating, although it could be in any scale appropriate to the application.

   - Users who wish to provide additional detail about the target can contribute optional service and/or price scores. A reputation system designer might encourage users to contribute optional scores by increasing their reviewer quality karma if they do so. (This option is not shown in the diagram.)

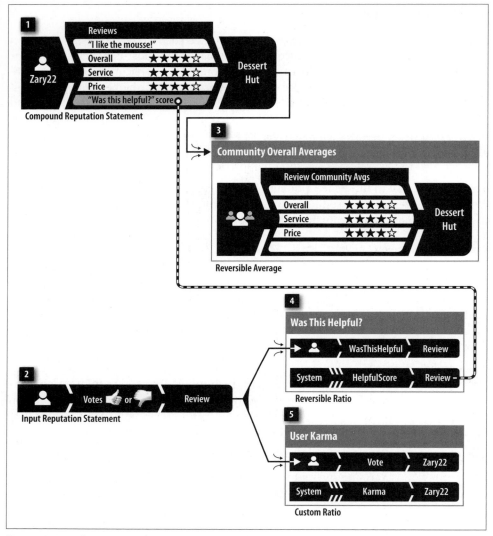

Figure 4-7. In this two-tiered system, users write reviews and other users review those reviews. The outcome is a lot of useful reputation information about the entity in question (here, Dessert Hut) and all the people who review it.

- The last claim included in the compound review reputation statement is the WasThisHelpful ratio, which is initialized to 0 out of 0 and is never actually modified by the reviewer but derived from the was-this-helpful votes of readers.

2. The was-this-helpful vote is not entered by the reviewer but by a user (the reader) who encounters the review later. Readers typically evaluate a review itself by click-

ing one of two icons, "thumb-up" (Yes) or "thumb-down" (No), in response to the prompt "Did you find this review helpful?".

This model has only three processes or outputs and is pretty straightforward. Note, however, the split shown for the was-this-helpful vote, where the message is duplicated and sent both to the Was This Helpful? process and the process that calculates reviewer quality karma. The more complex the reputation model, the more common this kind of split becomes.

Besides indicating that the same input is used in multiple places, a split also offers the opportunity to do parallel and/or distributed processing—the two duplicate messages take separate paths and need not finish at the same time or at all.

3. The Community Overall Averages process calculates the average of all the component ratings in the reviews. The overall, service, and price claims are averaged. Since some of these inputs are optional, keep in mind that each claim type may have a different total count of submitted claim values.

   Because users may need to revise their ratings and the site operator may wish to cancel the effects of ratings by spammers and other abusive behavior, the effects of each review are reversible. This is a simple reversible average process, so it's a good idea to consider the effects of bias and liquidity when calculating and displaying these averages (see the section "Practitioner's Tips: Reputation Is Tricky" on page 57).

4. The Was This Helpful? process is a reversible ratio, keeping track of the total (T) number of votes and the count of positive (P) votes. It stores the output claim in the target review as the `HelpfulScore` ratio claim with the value `P out of T`.

   Policies differ for cases when a reviewer is allowed to make significant changes to a review (for example, changing a formerly glowing comment into a terse "This sucks now!"). Many site operators simply revert all the was-this-helpful votes and reset the ratio. Even if your model doesn't permit edits to a review, for abuse mitigation purposes, this process still needs to be reversible.

5. After a simple point accumulation model, our reviewer quality User Karma process implements probably the simplest karma model possible: track the ratio of total was-this-helpful votes for all the reviews that a user has written to the total number of votes received. We've labeled this a custom ratio because we assume that the application will be programmed to include certain features in the calculation such as requiring a minimum number of votes before considering any display of karma to a user. Likewise, it is typical to create a nonlinear scale when grouping users into karma display formats, such as badges like "top 100 reviewer." See the next section and Chapter 7 for more on display patterns for karma.

   Karma models, especially public karma models, are subject to massive abuse by users interested in personal status or commercial gain. For that reason, this process must be reversible.

Now that we have a community-generated quality-karma claim for each user (at least those who have written a review noteworthy enough to invite helpful votes), you may notice that this model doesn't use that score as an input or weight in calculating other scores. This configuration is a reminder that reputation models all exist within an application context, and therefore the most appropriate use for this score will be determined by your application's needs.

Perhaps you will keep the quality-karma score as a corporate (internal) reputation, helping to determine which users should get escalating customer support. Perhaps the score will be public, displayed next to every one of a user's reviews as a status symbol for all to see. It might even be personal, shared only with each reviewer, so that reviewers can see what the overall community thinks of their contributions. Each of these choices has different ramifications, which we discuss in Chapter 6 in detail.

eBay Seller Feedback Karma

eBay contains the Internet's most well-known and studied user reputation or karma system: seller feedback. Its reputation model, like most others that are several years old, is complex and continuously adapting to new business goals, changing regulations, improved understanding of customer needs, and the never-ending need to combat reputation manipulation through abuse. See Appendix B for a brief survey of relevant research papers about this system and Chapter 9 for further discussion of the continuous evolution of reputation systems in general.

Rather than detail the entire feedback karma model here, we focus on claims that are from the buyer and about the seller. An important note about eBay feedback is that buyer claims exist in a specific context: a market transaction, which is a successful bid at auction for an item listed by a seller. This specificity leads to a generally higher-quality karma score for sellers than they would get if anyone could just walk up and rate a seller without even demonstrating that they'd ever done business with them; see "Implicit: Walk the Walk" on page 6.

 The reputation model in Figure 4-8 was derived from the following eBay pages: *http://pages.ebay.com/help/feedback/scores-reputation.html* and *http://pages.ebay.com/sellerinformation/PowerSeller/requirements.html*, both current as of March 2010.

We have simplified the model for illustration, specifically by omitting the processing for the requirement that only buyer feedback and detailed seller ratings (DSRs) *provided over the previous 12 months* are considered when calculating the positive feedback ratio, DSR community averages, and—by extension—power seller status. Also, eBay reports user feedback counters for the last month and quarter, which we are omitting here for the sake of clarity. Abuse mitigation features, which are not publicly available, are also excluded.

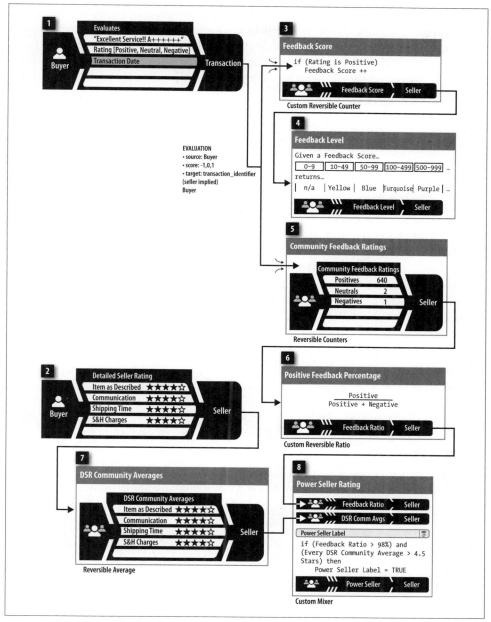

Figure 4-8. This simplified diagram shows how buyers influence a seller's karma scores on eBay. Though the specifics are unique to eBay, the pattern is common to many karma systems.

Figure 4-8 illustrates the seller feedback karma reputation model, which is made of typical model components: two compound buyer input claims—seller feedback and detailed seller ratings—and several roll-ups of the seller's karma, including community feedback ratings (a counter), feedback level (a named level), positive feedback percentage (a ratio), and the power seller rating (a label).

The context for the buyer's claims is a transaction identifier—the buyer may not leave any feedback before successfully placing a winning bid on an item listed by the seller in the auction market. Presumably, the feedback primarily describes the quality and delivery of the goods purchased. A buyer may provide two different sets of complex claims, and the limits on each vary:

1. Typically, when a buyer wins an auction, the delivery phase of the transaction starts and the seller is motivated to deliver the goods of the quality advertised in a timely manner. After either a timer expires or the goods have been delivered, the buyer is encouraged to leave feedback on the seller, a compound claim in the form of a three-level rating—positive, neutral, or negative—and a short text-only comment about the seller and/or transaction. The ratings make up the main component of seller feedback karma.

2. Once each week in which a buyer completes a transaction with a seller, the buyer may leave detailed seller ratings, a compound claim of four separate 5-star ratings in these categories: "item as described," "communications," "shipping time," and "shipping and handling charges." The only use of these ratings, other than aggregation for community averages, is to qualify the seller as a power seller.

eBay displays an extensive set of karma scores for sellers: the amount of time the seller has been a member of eBay, color-coded stars, percentages that indicate positive feedback, more than a dozen statistics that track past transactions, and lists of testimonial comments from past buyers or sellers. This is just a *partial* list of the seller reputations that eBay puts on display.

The full list of displayed reputations almost serves as a menu of reputation types present in the model. Every process box represents a claim displayed as a public reputation to everyone, so to provide a complete picture of eBay seller reputation, we simply detail each output claim separately.

3. The Feedback Score counts every positive rating given by a buyer as part of seller feedback, a compound claim associated with a single transaction. This number is cumulative for the lifetime of the account, and it generally loses its value over time; buyers tend to notice it only if it has a low value.

   It is fairly common for a buyer to change this score, within some time limitations, so this effect must be reversible. Sellers spend a lot of time and effort working to change negative and neutral ratings to positive ratings to gain or to avoid losing a Power Seller Rating.

   When this score changes, it is used to calculate the feedback level.

4. The Feedback Level process generates a graphical representation (in colored stars) of the feedback score. This is usually a simple data transformation and normalization process; here we've represented it as a mapping table, illustrating only a small subset of the mappings.

 This visual system of stars on eBay relies, in part, on the assumption that users will know that a red shooting star is a better rating than a purple star. But we have our doubts about the utility of this representation for buyers. Iconic scores such as these often mean more to their owners, and they might represent only a slight incentive for increasing activity in an environment in which each successful interaction equals cash in your pocket.

5. The Community Feedback Ratings process generates a compound claim containing the historical counts for each of the three possible seller feedback ratings—positive, neutral, and negative—over the last 12 months, so that the totals can be presented in a table showing the results for the last month, 6 months, and year. Older ratings are decayed continuously, though eBay does not disclose how often this data is updated if new ratings don't arrive. One possibility would be to update the data whenever the seller posts a new item for sale.

   The positive and negative ratings are used to calculate the positive feedback percentage.

6. The Positive Feedback Percentage process divides the positive feedback ratings by the sum of the positive and negative feedback ratings over the last 12 months. Note that the neutral ratings are not included in the calculation.

 This is a recent change reflecting eBay's confidence in the success of updates deployed in the summer of 2008 to prevent bad sellers from using retaliatory ratings against buyers who are unhappy with a transaction (known as tit-for-tat negatives). Initially this calculation included neutral ratings because eBay feared that negative feedback would be transformed into neutral ratings. It was not.

   This score is an input into the power seller rating, which is a highly coveted rating to achieve. This means that each and every individual positive and negative rating given on eBay is a critical one—it can mean the difference for a seller between acquiring the coveted power seller status or *not*.

7. The Detailed Seller Ratings (DSR) Community Averages are simple reversible averages for each of the four ratings categories: "item as described," "communications," "shipping time," and "shipping and handling charges." There is a limit on how often a buyer may contribute DSRs.

eBay only recently added these categories as a new reputation model because including them as factors in the overall seller feedback ratings diluted the overall quality of seller and buyer feedback. Sellers could end up in disproportionate trouble just because of a bad shipping company or a delivery that took a long time to reach a remote location. Likewise, buyers were bidding low prices only to end up feeling gouged by shipping and handling charges.

Fine-grained feedback allows one-off small problems to be averaged out across the DSR community averages instead of being translated into red-star negative scores that poison overall trust. Fine-grained feedback for sellers is also actionable by them and motivates them to improve, since these DSR scores make up half of the power seller rating.

8. The Power Seller Rating, appearing next to the seller's ID, is a prestigious label that signals the highest level of trust. It includes several factors external to this model, but two critical components are the positive feedback percentage, which must be at least 98%, and the DSR community averages, which each must be at least 4.5 stars (around 90% positive). Interestingly, the DSR scores are more flexible than the feedback average, which tilts the rating toward overall evaluation of the transaction rather than the related details.

Though the context for the buyer's claims is a single transaction or history of transactions, the context for the aggregate reputations that are generated is *trust in the eBay marketplace itself*. If the buyers can't trust the sellers to deliver against their promises, eBay cannot do business. When considering the roll-ups, we transform the single-transaction claims into trust in the seller, and—by extension—that same trust rolls up into eBay. This chain of trust is so integral and critical to eBay's continued success that it must continuously update the marketplace's interface and reputation systems.

Flickr Interestingness Scores for Content Quality

The popular online photo service Flickr uses reputation to qualify new user submissions and track user behavior that violates Flickr's terms of service. Most notably, Flickr uses a completely custom reputation model called "interestingness" for identifying the highest-quality photographs submitted from the millions uploaded every week. Flickr uses that reputation score to rank photos by user and, in searches, by tag.

Interestingness is also the key to Flickr's "Explore" page (*http://flickr.com/explore*), which displays a daily calendar of the photos with the highest interestingness ratings, and users may use a graphical calendar to look back at the worthy photographs from any previous day. It's like a daily leaderboard for newly uploaded content.

The version of Flickr interestingness that we are presenting here is an abstraction based on several different pieces of evidence: the U.S. patent application (Number 2006/0242139 A1) filed by Flickr, comments that Flickr staff have made on their own message boards, observations by power users in the community, and our own experience in building such reputation systems.

We offer two pieces of advice for anyone building similar systems: there is no substitute for gathering historical data when you are deciding how to clip and weight your calculations, and—even if you get your initial settings correct—you will need to adjust them over time to adapt to the use patterns that will emerge as the direct result of implementing reputation. (See the section "Emergent effects and emergent defects" on page 236.)

Figure 4-9 has two primary outputs: photo **interestingness** and interesting photographer **Karma**, and everything else feeds into those two key claims.

Of special note in this model is the existence of a karma loop (represented in the figure by a dashed-pipe). A user's reputation score influences how much "weight" her opinion carries when evaluating others' work (commenting on it, favoriting it, or adding to groups): photographers with higher interestingness karma on Flickr have a greater voice in determining what constitutes "interesting" on the site.

Each day, Flickr generates and stores a list of the top 500 most interesting photos for the "Explore" page. It also updates the current interestingness score of each and every photo each time one of the input events occurs. Here, we illustrate a real-time model for that update, though it isn't at all clear that Flickr actually does these calculations in real time, and there are several good reasons to consider delaying that action. See "Keep Your Barn Door Closed (but Expect Peeking)" on page 91.

Since there are four main paths through the model, we've grouped all the inputs by the kind of reputation feedback they represent: viewer activities, tagging, flagging, and republishing. Each path provides a different kind of input into the final reputations.

1. *Viewer activities* represent the actions that a viewing user performs on a photo. Each action is considered a significant endorsement of the photo's content because any action requires special effort by the user. We have assumed that all actions carry equal weight, but that is not a requirement of the model:

   - A viewer can attach a note to the photo by adding a rectangle over a region of the photo and typing a short note.

   - When a viewer comments on a photo, that comment is displayed for all other viewers to see. The first comment is usually the most important, because it encourages other viewers to join the conversation. We don't know whether Flickr weighs the first comment more heavily than subsequent ones. (Though that is certainly common practice in some reputation models.)

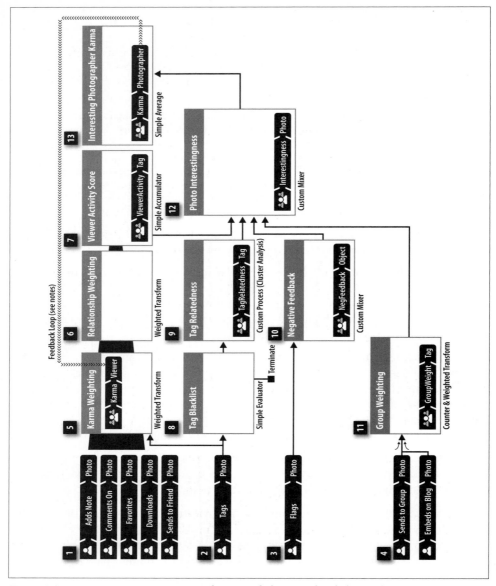

Figure 4-9. Interestingness ratings are used in several places on the Flickr site, but most noticeably on the "Explore" page, a daily calendar of photos selected using this content reputation model.

- By clicking the "Add to Favorites" icon, a viewer not only endorses a photo but shares that endorsement—the photo now appears in the viewer's profile, on her "My Favorites" page.

- If a viewer downloads the photo (depending on a photo's privacy settings, image downloads are available in various sizes), that is also counted as a viewer activity. (Again, we don't know for sure, but it would be smart on Flickr's part to count multiple repeat downloads as *only one action*, lest they risk creating a back door to attention-gaming shenanigans.)

- Finally, the viewer can click "Send to Friend," creating an email with a link to the photo. If the viewer addresses the message to multiple users or even a list, this action could be considered republishing. However, applications generally can't distinguish a list address from an individual person's address, so for reputation purposes, we assume that the addressee is always an individual.

2. *Tagging* is the action of adding short text strings describing the photo for categorization. Flickr tags are similar pregenerated categories, but they exist in a *folksonomy*: whatever tags users apply to a photo, that's what the photo is about. Common tags include 2009, me, Randy, Bryce, Fluffy, and cameraphone, along with the expected descriptive categories of wedding, dog, tree, landscape, purple, tall, and irony—which sometimes means "made of iron"!

Tagging gets special treatment in a reputation model because users must apply extra effort to tag an object, and determining whether one tag is more likely to be accurate than another requires complicated computation. Likewise, certain tags, though popular, should not be considered for reputation purposes at all. Tags have their own quantitative contribution to interestingness, but they also are considered viewer activities, so the input is split into both paths.

3. Sadly, many popular photographs turn out to be pornographic or in violation of Flickr's terms of service.

On many sites—if left untended—porn tends to quickly generate a high-quality reputation score. Remember, "quality" as we're discussing it is, to some degree, a measure of attention. Nothing garners attention like appealing to prurient interests.

The smart reputation designer can, in fact, leverage this unfortunate truth. Build a corporate-user "porn probability" reputation into your system—one that identifies content with a high (or *too-high*) velocity of attention and puts it in a prioritized queue for human agents to review.

Flagging is the process by which users mark content as inappropriate for the service. This is a negative reputation vote: by tagging a photo as abusive, the user is saying "this doesn't belong here." This strong action should decrease the interestingness score *fast*—faster, in fact, than the other inputs can raise it.

4. *Republishing* actions represent a user's decision to increase the audience for a photo by either adding it to a Flickr group or embedding it in a web page. Users can accomplish either by using the blog publishing tools in Flickr's interface or by

copying and pasting an HTML snippet that the application provides. Flickr's patent doesn't specifically say that these two actions are treated similarly, but it seems reasonable to do so.

Generally, four things determine a Flickr photo's interestingness (represented by the four parallel paths in Figure 4-9): the viewer activity score, which represents the effect of viewers taking a specific action on a photo; tag relatedness, which represents a tag's similarity to others associated with other tagged photos; the negative feedback adjustment, which reflects reasons to downgrade or disqualify the tag; and group weighting, which has an early positive effect on reputation with the first few events.

5. The events coming into the Karma Weighting process are assumed to have a normalized value of 0.5, because the process is likely to increase it. The process reads the interesting-photographer karma of the user taking the action (not the person who owns the photo) and increases the viewer activity value by some weighting amount before passing it onto the next process. As a simple example, we'll suggest that the increase in value will be a maximum of 0.25—with no effect for a viewer with no karma and 0.25 for a hypothetical awesome user whose every photo is beloved by one and all. The resulting score will be in the range 0.5 to 0.75. We assume that this interim value is not stored in a reputation statement for performance reasons.

6. Next, the Relationship Weighting process takes the input score (in the range of 0.5 to 0.75) and determines the relationship strength of the viewer to the photographer. The patent indicates that a stronger relationship should grant a higher weight to any viewer activity. Again, for our simple example, we'll add up to 0.25 for a mutual first-degree relationship between the users. Lower values can be added for one-way (follower) relationships or even relationships as members of the same Flickr groups. The result is now in the range of 0.5 to 1.0 and is ready to be added into the historical contributions for this photo.

7. The Viewer Activity Score is a simple accumulator and custom denormalizer that sums up all the normalized event scores that have been weighted. In our example, they arrive in the range of 0.5 to 1.0. It seems likely that this score is the primary basis for interestingness. The patent indicates that each sum is marked with a timestamp to track changes in viewer activity score over time.

   The sum is then denormalized against the available range, from 0.5 to the maximum known viewer activity score, to produce an output from 0.0 to 1.0, which represents the normalized accumulated score stored in the reputation system so that it can be used to recalculate photo interestingness as needed.

8. Unlike most of the reputation messages we've considered so far, the incoming message to the tagging process path does not include any numeric value at all; it contains only the text tag that the viewer is adding to the photo. The tag is first subjected to the Tag Blacklist process, a simple evaluator that checks the tag against

a list of forbidden words. If the flow is terminated for this event, there is no contribution to photo interestingness for this tag.

 Separately, it seems likely that Flickr would want a tag on the list of forbidden words to have a negative, penalizing effect on the karma score for the person who added it.

Otherwise, the tag is considered worthy of further reputation consideration and is sent on to the Tag Relatedness process. Only if the tag was on the list of forbidden words is it likely that any record of this process would be saved for future reference.

9. The nonblacklisted tag then undergoes the Tag Relatedness process, which is a custom computation of reputation based on cluster analysis described in the patent in this way (from Flickr's U.S. Patent Application No. 2006/0242139 A1):

> [0032] As part of the relatedness computation, the statistics engine may employ a statistical clustering analysis known in the art to determine the statistical proximity between metadata (e.g., tags), and to group the metadata and associated media objects according to corresponding cluster. For example, out of 10,000 images tagged with the word "Vancouver," one statistical cluster within a threshold proximity level may include images also tagged with "Canada" and "British Columbia." Another statistical cluster within the threshold proximity may instead be tagged with "Washington" and "space needle" along with "Vancouver." Clustering analysis allows the statistics engine to associate "Vancouver" with both the "Vancouver-Canada" cluster and the "Vancouver-Washington" cluster. The media server may provide for display to the user the two sets of related tags to indicate they belong to different clusters corresponding to different subject matter areas, for example.

This is a good example of a black-box process that may be calculated outside of the formal reputation system. Such processes are often housed on optimized machines or run continuously on data samples in order to give best-effort results in real time.

For our model, we assume that the output will be a normalized score from 0.0 (no confidence) to 1.0 (high confidence) representing how likely the tag is related to the content. The simple average of all the scores for the tags on this photo is stored in the reputation system so that it can be used to recalculate photo interestingness as needed.

10. The Negative Feedback path determines the effects of flagging a photo as abusive content. Flickr documentation is nearly nonexistent on this topic (for good reason; see "Keep Your Barn Door Closed (but Expect Peeking)" on page 91), but it seems reasonable to assume that even a small number of negative feedback events should be enough to nullify most, if not all, of a photo's interestingness score.

For illustration, let's say that it would take only five abuse reports to do the most damage possible to a photo's reputation. Using this math, each abuse report event would be worth 0.2. Negative feedback can be thought of as a Reversible Accumulator with a maximum value of 1.0.

 This model doesn't account for abuse by users ganging up on a photo and flagging it as abusive when it is not. (See "Who watches the watchers?" on page 209). That is a different reputation model, which we illustrate in detail in Chapter 10.

11. The last component of the process is the republishing path. When a photo gets even more exposure by being shared on channels such as blogs and Flickr groups, then Flickr assigns some additional reputation value to it, shown here as the Group Weighting process.

    Flickr official forum posts indicate that for the first five or so actions, this value quickly increases to its maximum value—1.0 in our system. After that, it stabilizes, so this process is also a simple accumulator, adding 0.2 for every event and capping at 1.0.

12. All of the inputs to Photo Interestingness, a simple mixer, are normalized scores from 0.0 to 1.0 and represent either positive (viewer activity score, tag relatedness, group weighting) or negative (negative feedback) effects on the claim.

    The exact formulation for this calculation is not detailed in any documentation, nor is it clear that anyone who doesn't work for Flickr understands all its subtleties. But...for illustration purposes, we propose this drastically simplified formulation: photo interestingness is made up of 20% each of group weighting and tag relatedness plus 60% viewer activity score minus negative feedback.

    A common early modification to a formulation like this is to increase the positive percentages enough so that no minor component is required for a high score. For example, you could increase the 60% viewer activity score to 80% and then cap the result at 1.0 before applying any negative effects.

    A copy of this claim value is stored in the same high-performance database as the rest of the search-related metadata for the target photo.

13. The Interesting Photographer Karma score is recalculated each time the interestingness reputation of one of the photos changes. This liquidity compensated average is sufficient when using this karma to evaluate other user's photos.

The Flickr model is undoubtedly complex and has spurred a lot of discussion and mythology in the photographer community on Flickr.

It's important to reinforce the point that all of this computational work is in support of three very exact contexts: interestingness works specifically to influence photos' search rank on the site, their display order on user profiles, and ultimately whether or not they're featured on the site-wide "Explore" page. It's the third context, Explore, that introduces one more important reputation mechanic: randomization.

Each day's photo interestingness calculations produce a ranked list of photos. If the content of the "Explore" page were 100% determined by those calculations, it could get boring. First-mover effects can predict that you would *probably* always see the same photos by the same photographers at the top of the list (see the section "First-mover effects" on page 63). Flickr lessens this effect by including a random factor in the selection of the photos.

Each day, the top 500 photos appear in randomized order. In theory, the photo with the 500th-ranked photo interestingness score *could* be displayed first and the one with the highest photo interestingness score could be displayed last. The next day, if they're still on the top-500 list, they could both appear somewhere in the middle.

This system has two wonderful effects:

- A more diverse set of high-quality photos and photographers gets featured, encouraging more participation by the users producing the best content.
- It mitigates abuse, because the photo interestingness score is not displayed and the randomness of the display prevents it from being deduced. Randomness makes it nearly impossible to reverse-engineer the specifics of the reputation model—there is simply too much noise in the system to be certain of the effects of smaller contributions to the score.

What's truly wonderful is that this randomness doesn't harm Explore's efficacy in the least; given the scale and activity of the Flickr community, each and every day there are more than enough high-quality photos to fill a 500-photo list. Jumbling up the order for display doesn't detract from the experience of browsing them by one whit.

When and Why Simple Models Fail

As a business owner on today's Web, probably the greatest thing about social media is that the users themselves create the media from which you, the site operator, capture value. This means, however, that the quality of your site is directly related to the quality of the content created by your users.

This can present problems. Sure, the content is cheap, but you usually get what you pay for, and you will probably need to pay more to improve the quality. Additionally, some users have a different set of motivations than you might prefer.

We offer design advice to mitigate potential problems with social collaboration and suggestions for specific nontechnical solutions.

Party Crashers

As illustrated in the real-life models earlier, reputation can be a successful motivation for users to contribute large volumes of content and/or high-quality content to your application. At the very least, reputation can provide critical money-saving value to your customer care department by allowing users to prioritize the bad content for attention and likewise flag power users and content to be featured.

But mechanical reputation systems, of necessity, are always subject to unwanted or unanticipated manipulation; they are only algorithms, after all. They cannot account for the many, sometimes conflicting, motivations for users' behavior on a site. One of the strongest motivations of users who invade reputation systems is commercial. Spam invaded email. Marketing firms invade movie review and social media sites. And drop-shippers are omnipresent on eBay.

eBay drop-shippers put the middleman back into the online market; they are people who resell items that they don't even own. It works roughly like this:

1. A seller develops a good reputation, gaining a seller feedback karma of at least 25 for selling items that she personally owns.

2. The seller buys some drop-shipping software, which helps locate items for sale on eBay and elsewhere cheaply, or joins an online drop-shipping service that has the software and presents the items in a web interface.

3. The seller finds cheap items to sell and lists them on eBay for a higher price than they're available from the drop-shipper but lower than other eBay sellers are selling them for. The seller includes an average or above-average shipping and handling charge.

4. The seller sells an item to a buyer, receives payment, and sends an order for the item, along with a drop-shipping payment, to the drop-shipper, who then delivers the item to the buyer.

This model of doing business was not anticipated by the eBay seller feedback karma model, which only includes buyers and sellers as reputation entities. Drop-shippers are a third party in what was assumed to be a two-party transaction, and they cause the reputation model to break in various ways:

- The drop-shippers sometimes fail to deliver the goods as promised to the buyer. The buyer then gets mad and leaves negative feedback: the dreaded red star. That would be fine, but it is the seller—who never saw or handled the good—that receives the mark of shame, not the actual shipping party.

- This arrangement is a big problem for the seller, who cannot afford the negative feedback if she plans to continue selling on eBay.

- The typical options for rectifying a bungled transaction won't work in a drop-shipper transaction: it is useless for the buyer to return the defective goods to the seller. (They never originated from the seller anyway.) Trying to unwind the shipment (the buyer returns the item to the seller; the seller returns it to the drop-shipper, if that is even possible; the drop-shipper buys or waits for a replacement item and finally ships it) would take too long for the buyer, who expects immediate recompense.

In effect, the seller *can't make the order right* with the customer without refunding the purchase price in a timely manner. This puts them out-of-pocket for the price of the goods along with the hassle of trying to recover the money from the drop-shipper.

But a simple refund alone sometimes isn't enough for the buyer! Depending on the amount of perceived hassle and effort this transaction has cost the buyer, he is still likely to rate the transaction negatively overall. (And rightfully so. Once it's become evident that a seller is working through a drop-shipper, many of their excuses and delays start to ring very hollow.) So a seller may have, at this point, outlayed a lot of her own time and money to rectify a bad transaction only to *still* suffer the penalties of a red star.

What option does the seller have left to maintain her positive reputation? You guessed it—a payoff. Not only will a concerned seller eat the price of the goods—and any shipping involved—but she will also pay an additional *cash bounty* (typically up to $20.00) to get buyers to flip a red star to green.

What is the cost of clearing negative feedback on drop-shipped goods? The cost of the item + $20.00 + lost time negotiating with the buyer. That's the cost that reputation imposes on drop-shipping on eBay.

The lesson here is that a reputation model will be reinterpreted by users as they find new ways to use your site. Site operators need to keep a wary eye on the specific behavior patterns they see emerging and adapt accordingly. Chapter 9 provides more detail and specific recommendations for prospective reputation modelers.

Keep Your Barn Door Closed (but Expect Peeking)

You will—at some point—be faced with a decision about how *open* (or not) to be about the details of your reputation system. Exactly how much of your model's inner workings should you reveal to the community? Users inevitably will want to know:

- What reputations is the system keeping? (Remember, not all reputations will be visible to users; see "Corporate Reputations Are Internal Use Only: Keep Them Hush-hush" on page 172.)
- What are the inputs that feed into those reputations?
- How are they weighted? (That is, what are the *important* inputs?)

This decision is not at all trivial: if you err on the side of extreme secrecy, you risk damaging your community's trust in the system that you've provided. Your users may come to question its fairness or—if the inner workings remain *too* opaque—they may flat-out doubt the system's accuracy.

Most reputation-intensive sites today attempt at least to alleviate some of the community's curiosity about how content reputations and user reputations are earned. It's not like you can keep your system a *complete* secret.

Equally bad, however, is divulging *too much* detail about your reputation system to the community. And more site designers probably make this mistake, especially in the early stages of deploying the system and growing the community. As an example, consider the highly specific breakdown of actions on the Yahoo! Answers site, and the points rewarded for each (see Figure 4-10).

Points and Levels

To encourage participation and reward great answers, Yahoo! Answers has a system of points and levels. The number of points you get depends on the specific action you take. The points table below summarizes the point values for different actions. While you can't use points to buy or redeem anything, they do allow everyone to recognize how active and helpful you've been. (And they give you another excuse to brag to your friends.)

Points Table

Action	Points
Begin participating on Yahoo! Answers	One Time: 100
Ask a question	-5
Choose a best answer for your question	3
No Best Answer was selected by voters on your question	Points Returned: 5
Answer a question	2
Deleting an answer	-2
Log in to Yahoo! Answers	Once daily: 1

Figure 4-10. How to succeed at Yahoo! Answers? The site courteously provides you with a scorecard.

Why might this breakdown be a mistake? For a number of reasons. Assigning overt point values to specific actions goes beyond *enhancing* the user experience and starts to directly influence it. Arguably, it may tip right over into the realm of *dictating* user behavior, which generally is frowned upon.

A detailed breakdown also arms the malcontents in your community with exactly the information they need to deconstruct your model. And they won't even need to guess at things like relative weightings of inputs into the system; the relative value of different inputs is right there on the site, writ large. Try, instead, to use language that is clear and truthful without necessarily being comprehensive and exhaustively complete, like this example from the Yahoo! UK Message Boards:

> The exact formula that determines medal-achievement will not be made public (and is subject to change) but, in general, it may be influenced by the following factors: community response to your messages (how highly others rate your messages); the amount of (quality) contributions that you make to the boards; and how often and accurately you rate *others' messages*.

Staying vague does not mean, of course, that some in your community won't continue to wonder, speculate, and talk among themselves about the specifics of your reputation system. Algorithm gossip has become something of a minor sport on collaborative sites like Digg and YouTube.

For some participants, guessing at the workings of reputations like "highest rated" or "most popular" is probably just that—an entertaining game and nothing more. Others, however, see only the benefit of any insight they might be able to gain into the system's inner workings: greater visibility for themselves and their content, more influence within the community, and the greater currency that follows both. (See "Egocentric incentives" on page 118.)

The following are some helpful strategies for masking the inner workings of your reputation models and algorithms.

Decay and delay

Time is on your side. Or it *can* be, in one of a couple of ways. First, consider the use of time-based decay in your models: recent actions "count for" more than actions in the distant past, and the effects of older actions decay (lessen) over time. Incorporating time-based delays has several benefits:

- Reputation leaders can't rest on their laurels. When reputations decay, they have to be earned back continually. This requirement encourages your community to stay active and engage with your site frequently.

- Decay is an effective counter to the stagnation that naturally results from network effects (see "First-mover effects" on page 63). Older, more established participants will not tend to linger at the top of rankings quite as much.

- Those who *do* probe the system to gain an unfair advantage will not reap long-term benefits from doing so unless they continue to do it within the constraints imposed by the decay. (Coincidentally, this profile of behavior makes it easier to spot—and correct for—users who are gaming the system.)

It's also beneficial to delay the results of newly triggered inputs. If a reasonable window of time exists between the triggering of an input (marking a photo as a favorite, for instance) and the resulting effect on that object's reputation (moving the photo higher in a visible ranking), it confounds a gaming user's ability to do easy what-if comparisons (particularly if the period of delay is itself unpredictable).

When the reputation effects of various actions are instantaneous, you've given the gamers of your system a powerful analytic tool for reverse-engineering your models.

Provide a moving target

We've already cautioned that it's important to keep your system flexible (see "Plan for Change" on page 226). That's not just good advice from a technical standpoint, but from a social and strategic one as well. Put simply: leave yourself enough wiggle room to adjust the impact of different inputs in the system (add new inputs, change their relative weightings, or eliminate ones that were previously considered). That flexibility gives you an effective tool for confounding gaming of the system. If you suspect that a particular input is being exploited, you at least have the option of tweaking the model to compensate for the abuse. You will also want the flexibility of introducing new types of reputations to your site (or retiring ones that are no longer serving a purpose).

It is tricky, however, to enact changes like these without affecting the social contract you've established with the community. Once you've codified a certain set of desired behaviors on your site, some users will (understandably) be upset if the rug gets pulled out from under them. This risk is yet another argument for avoiding disclosure of too many details about the mechanics of the system, or for downplaying the system's importance.

Reputation from Theory to Practice

Parts I and II of this book focused on reputation *theory*:

- Understanding reputation systems through defining the key concepts
- Defining a visual grammar for reputation systems
- Creating a set of key building blocks and using them to describe simple reputation models
- Using it all to illuminate popular complex reputation systems found in the wild

Along the way, we sprinkled in practitioner's tips to share what we've learned from existing reputation systems to help you understand what could, and already has, gone wrong.

Now you're prepared for the second section of the book: applying this theory to a specific application—yours. Chapter 5 starts the project off with three basic questions about your application design. In haste, many projects skip over one or more of these critical considerations, and the results are often very costly.

Building Web
Reputation Systems

Planning Your System's Design

Parts I and II were *theory*—a comprehensive description of the graphical grammar and the tools needed to conceptualize reputation systems. The remaining chapters put all of that theory into *practice*. We describe how to define the requirements for a reputation model; design web interfaces for the gathering of user evaluations; provide patterns for the display and utilization of reputation; and provide advice on implementation, testing, tuning, and understanding community effects on your system.

Every reputation system starts as an idea from copying a competitor's model or doing something innovative. In our experience, that initial design motivation usually ignores the most important questions that should be asked before rushing into such a long-term commitment.

Asking the Right Questions

When you're planning a reputation system—as in most endeavors in life—you'll get much better answers if you spend a little time up front considering the right questions. This is the point where we pause to do just that. We explore some very simple questions: why are we doing this? What do we hope to get out of it? How will we know we've succeeded?

The answers to these questions undoubtedly will not be quite so simple. Community sites on the Web vary wildly in makeup, involving different cultures, customs, business models, and rules for behavior. Designing a successful reputation system means designing a system that's successful for your particular set of circumstances. You'll therefore need a fairly well-tuned understanding of your community and the social outcomes that you hope to achieve.

We'll get you started. Some careful planning and consideration now will save you a world of heartache later.

Here are the questions that we help you answer in this chapter:

- What are your goals for your application?
  - Is generating revenue based on your content a primary focus of your business?
  - Will user activity be a critical measure of success?
  - What about loyalty (keeping the same users coming back month after month)?
- What is your content control pattern?
  - Who is going to create, review, and moderate your site's content and/or community?
  - What services do staff, professional feed content, or external services provide?
  - What roles do the users play?

  The answers to these questions will tell you how comprehensive a reputation system you need. In some cases, the answer will be none at all. Each content control pattern includes recommendations and examples of incentive models to consider for your system.

- Given your goals and the content models, what types of incentives are likely to work well for you?
  - Should you rely on altruistic, commercial, or egocentric incentives, or some combination of those?
  - Will karma play a role in your system? Should it?

  Understanding how the various incentive models have been demonstrated to work in similar environments will narrow down the choices you make as you proceed to Chapter 6.

What Are Your Goals?

Marney Beard was a longtime design and project manager at Sun Microsystems, and she had a wonderful guideline for participating in any team endeavor. Marney would say, "It's all right to *start* selfish. As long as you don't *end* there." (Marney first gave this advice to her kids, but it turns out to be equally useful in the compromise-laden world of product development.)

So, following Marney's excellent advice, we encourage you to—for a moment—take a very self-centered view of your plans for a rich reputation system for your website. Yes, ultimately your system will be a balance among your goals, your community's desires, and the tolerances and motivations of everyone who visits the site. But for now, let's just talk about *you*.

Both people and content reputations can be used to strengthen one or more aspects of your business. There is no shame in that. As long as we're starting selfish, let's get downright crass. How can imbuing your site with an historical sense of people and content reputation help your bottom line?

User engagement

Perhaps you'd like to deepen user engagement—either the amount of time that u
spend in your community or the number and breadth of activities that they partake in.
For a host of reasons, users who are more engaged are more valuable, both to your
community and to your business.

Offering incentives to users may persuade them to try more of your offering than they
would try by virtue of their own natural curiosity alone. Offline marketers have long
been aware of this phenomenon; promotions such as sweepstakes, contests, and give-
aways are all designed to influence customer behavior and deepen engagement.

User engagement can be defined in many different ways. Eric T. Peterson offers up a
pretty good list of basic metrics for engagement. He posits that the most engaged users
are those who do the following (list adapted from *http://blog.webanalyticsdemystified
.com/weblog/2006/12/how-do-you-calculate-engagement-part-i.html*):

- View critical content on your site
- Have returned to your site recently (made multiple visits)
- Return directly to your site (not by following a link) some of the time
- Have long sessions, with some regularity, on your site
- Have subscribed to at least one of your site's available data feeds

This list is definitely skewed toward an advertiser's or a content publisher's view of
engagement on the Web. It's also loaded with subjective measures. (For example, what
constitutes a "long" session? Which content is "critical"?) But that's fine. We want
subjective—at this point, we can tailor our reputation approach to achieve exactly what
we hope to get out of it.

So what would be a good set of metrics to determine community engagement on your
site? Again, the best answer to that question *for you* will be intimately tied to the goals
that you're trying to achieve.

Tara Hunt, as part of a longer discussion on Metrics for Healthy Communities, offers
the following suggestions (list adapted from *http://www.horsepigcow.com/2007/10/03/
metrics-forhealthy-communities/*):

- The rate of attrition in your community, especially with new members.
- The average length of time it takes for a newbie to become a regular contributor.
- Multiple community crossover. If your members are part of many communities,
  how do they interact with your site? Flickr photos? Twittering? Etc.?
- The number of both giving actions and receiving actions—for example, posters
  give (advice, knowledge, etc.), and readers receive. (See Figure 5-1.)
- Community participation in tending and policing the community to keep it a nice
  place (for example, users who report content as spam, who edit a wiki for better
  layout, etc.).

Figure 5-1. No matter how you measure it, Bernadette e. is one active and engaged "Yelper."

This is a good list, but it's still highly subjective. Once you decide *how* you'd like your users to engage with your site and community, you'll need to determine how to measure that engagement.

Speaking of Metrics...

In Chapter 9, we ask you to evaluate your site's performance against the goals that you define in this chapter. Of course, that exercise will be much more effective if you can compare actual data from before and after the rollout of your reputation system.

To be able to make that comparison, you will need to anticipate the metrics that will help you evaluate the system's performance; to make sure *now* that your site or application is configured to provide that data; and to ensure that the data is being appropriately logged and saved for the time when you'll need it for decision making, tweaking, and tuning your system.

After all, there's nothing quite like setting out to do a before-and-after comparison only to realize that you weren't keeping proper data *before*.

Establishing loyalty

Perhaps you're interested in building brand loyalty among your site's visitors, establishing a relationship with them that extends beyond the boundaries of one visit or session. Yahoo! Fantasy Sports employs a fun reputation system, shown in Figure 5-2, enhanced with nicely illustrated trophies for achieving milestones (such as a winning season in a league) for various sports.

This simple feature serves many purposes: the trophies are fun and engaging, they may serve as an incentive for community members to excel at a sport, they help extend each user's identity and give the user way to express her own unique set of interests and biases to the community, and they are *also* an effective way of establishing a continuing

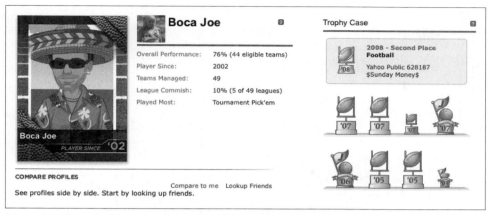

Figure 5-2. "Boca Joe" has played a variety of fantasy sports on Yahoo! since 2002. Do you suppose the reputation he's earned on the site helps brings him back each year?

bond with Fantasy Sports players—one that persists from season to season and sport to sport.

Any time a Yahoo! Fantasy Sports user is considering a switch to a competing service (fantasy sports in general is big business, and there are any number of very capable competitors), the existence of the service's trophies provides tangible evidence of the switching cost for doing so: a reputation reset.

Coaxing out shy advertisers

Maybe you are concerned about your site's ability to attract advertisers. User-generated content is a hot Internet trend that's almost become synonymous with Web 2.0, but it has also been slow to attract advertisers—particularly big, traditional (but deep-pocketed) companies worried about displaying their own brand in the Wild West environment that's sometimes evident on sites like YouTube or Flickr.

Once again, reputation systems offer a way out of this conundrum. By tracking the high-quality contributors and contributions on your site, you can guarantee to advertisers that their brand will be associated only with content that meets or exceeds certain standards of quality.

In fact, you can even craft your system to reward particular *aspects* of contribution. Perhaps, for instance, you'd like to keep a "clean contributor" reputation that takes into account a user's typical profanity level and also weighs abuse reports against him into the mix. Without some form of filtering based on quality and legality, there's simply no way that a prominent and respected advertiser like Johnson's would associate its brand with YouTube's user-contributed, typically anything-goes videos (see Figure 5-3).

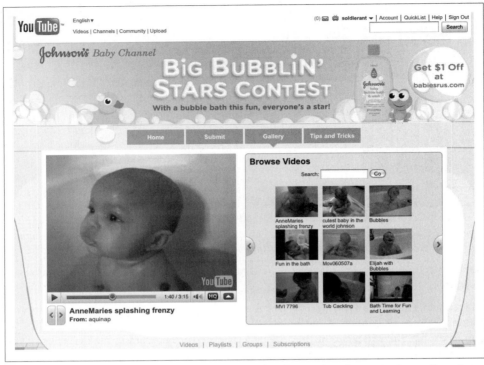

Figure 5-3. The Johnson's Baby Channel on YouTube places a lot of trust in the quality of user submissions.

Of course, another way to allay advertisers' fears is by generally improving the quality (both real and perceived) of content generated by the members of your community.

Improving content quality

Reputation systems really shine at helping you make value judgments about the relative quality of content that users submit to your site. Chapter 8 focuses on the myriad techniques for filtering out bad content and encouraging high-quality contributions. For now, it's only necessary to think of "content" in broad strokes. First, let's examine content control patterns—patterns of content generation and management on a site. The patterns will help you make smarter decisions about your reputation system.

Content Control Patterns

The question of whether you need a reputation system at all and, if so, the particular models that will serve you best, are largely a function of how content is generated and managed on your site. Consider the workflow and life cycle of content that you have planned for your community, and the various actors who will influence that workflow.

First, *who* will handle your community's content? Will users be doing most of the content creation and management? Or staff? ("Staff" can be employees, trusted third-party content providers, or even deputized members of the community, depending on the level of trust and responsibility that you give them.)

In most communities, content control is a function of some combination of users and staff, so we'll examine the types of activities that each might be doing. Consider all the potential activities that make up the content life cycle at a very granular level:

- Who will draft the content?
- Will anyone edit it or otherwise determine its readiness for publishing?
- Who is responsible for actually publishing it to your site?
- Can anyone edit content that's live?
- Can live content be evaluated in some way? Who will do that?
- What effect does evaluation have on content?
  — Can an evaluator promote or demote the prominence of content?
  — Can an evaluator remove content from the site altogether?

You'll ultimately have to answer all of these fine-grained questions, but we can abstract them somewhat at this stage. Right now, the questions you really need to pay attention to are these three:

- Who will create the content on your site? Users or staff?
- Who will evaluate the content?
- Who has responsibility for removing content that is inappropriate?

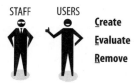

STAFF USERS
Create
Evaluate
Remove

There are eight different content control patterns for these questions—one for each unique combination of answers. For convenience, we've given each pattern a name, but the names are just placeholders for discussion, not suggestions for recategorizing your product marketing.

If you have multiple content control patterns for your site, consider them all and focus on any shared reputation opportunities. For example, you may have a community site with a hierarchy of categories that are created, evaluated, and removed by staff. Perhaps the content *within* that hierarchy is created by users.

In that case, two patterns apply: the staff-tended category tree is an example of the Web 1.0 content control pattern, and as such it can effectively be ignored when selecting your reputation models. Focus instead on the options suggested by the Submit-Publish pattern formed by the users populating the tree.

Web 1.0: Staff creates, evaluates, and removes

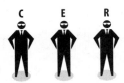

When your staff is in complete control of all of the content on your site—even if it is supplied by third-party services or data feeds—you are using a Web 1.0 content control pattern. There's really not much a reputation system can do for you in this case; no user participation equals no reputation needs. Sure, you could grant users reputation points for visiting pages on your site or clicking indiscriminately, but to what end? Without some sort of visible result to participating, they will soon give up and go away.

Neither is it probably worth the expense to build a content reputation system for use solely by staff, unless you have a staff of hundreds evaluating tens of thousands of content items or more.

Bug report: Staff creates and evaluates, users remove

In this content control pattern, the site encourages users to petition for removal or major revision of corporate content—items in a database created and reviewed by staff. Users don't add any content that other users can interact with. Instead, they provide feedback intended to *eventually* change the content. Examples include bug tracking and customer feedback platforms and sites, such as Bugzilla and GetSatisfaction. Each site allows users to tell the provider about an idea or problem, but it doesn't have any immediate effect on the site or other users.

A simpler form of this pattern is when users simply click a button to report content as inappropriate, in bad taste, old, or duplicate. The software decides when to hide the content item in question. AdSense, for example, allows customers who run sites to mark specific advertisements as inappropriate matches for their site—teaching Google about their preferences as content publishers.

Typically, this pattern doesn't require a reputation system; user participation is a rare event and may not even require a validated login. In cases where a large number of interactions per user are appropriate, a corporate reputation system that rates a user's effectiveness at performing a task can quickly identify submissions from the best contributors.

This pattern resembles the Submit pattern (see "Submit-publish: Users create, staff evaluates and removes" on page 107), though the moderation process in that pattern typically is less socially oriented than the review process in this pattern (since the feedback is intended for the application operators only). These systems often contain strong negative feedback, which is crucial to understanding your business but isn't appropriate for review by the general public.

Reviews: Staff creates and removes, users evaluate

This popular content control pattern—the first generation of online reputation systems—gave users the power to leave ratings and reviews of otherwise static web content, which then was used to produce ranked lists of like items. Early, and still prominent, sites using this pattern include Amazon.com and dozens of movie, local services, and product aggregators. Even blog comments can be considered user evaluation of otherwise tightly controlled content (the posts) on sites like BoingBoing or The Huffington Post.

The simplest form of this pattern is implicit ratings only, such as Yahoo! News, which tracks the most emailed stories for the day and the week. The user simply clicks a button labeled "Email this story," and the site produces a reputation rank for the story.

Historically, users who write reviews usually have been motivated by altruism (see "Incentives for User Participation, Quality, and Moderation" on page 111). Until strong personal communications tools arrived—such as social networking, news feeds, and multidevice messaging (connecting SMS, email, the Web, and so on)—users didn't produce as many ratings and reviews as many sites were looking for. There were often more site content items than user reviews, leaving many content items (such as obscure restaurants or specialized books) without reviews.

Some site operators have tried to use commercial (direct payment) incentives to encourage users to submit more and better reviews. Epinions offered users several forms of payment for posting reviews. Almost all of those applications eventually were shut down, leaving only a revenue-sharing model for reviews that are tracked to actual purchases. In every other case, payment for reviews seemed to have created a strong incentive to game the system (by generating false was-this-helpful votes, for example), which actually lowered the quality of information on a site. Paying for participation almost never results in high-quality contributions.

More recently, sites such as Yelp have created egocentric incentives for encouraging users to post reviews: Yelp lets other users rate reviewers' contributions across dimensions such as "useful," "funny," and "cool," and it tracks and displays more than 20 metrics of reviewer popularity. This configuration encourages more participation by certain mastery-oriented users, but it may result in an overly specialized audience for the site by selecting for people with certain tastes. Yelp's whimsical ratings can be a distraction to older audiences, discouraging some from contributing.

What makes the reviews content control pattern special is that it is *by and for* other users. It's why the was-this-helpful reputation pattern has emerged as a popular participation method in recent years—hardly anyone wants to take several minutes to write a review, but it only takes a second to click a thumb-shaped button. Now a review itself can have a quality score and its author can have the related karma. In effect, the review becomes its own context and is subject to a different content control pattern: "Basic social media: Users create and evaluate, staff removes" on page 109.

Surveys: Staff creates, users evaluate and remove

In the surveys content control pattern, users evaluate and eliminate content as fast as staff can feed it to them. This pattern's scarcity in public web applications usually is related to the expense of supplying content of sufficient minimum quality. Consider this pattern a user-empowered version of the reviews content control pattern, where content is flowing so swiftly that only the fittest survive the user's wrath. Probably the most obvious example of this pattern is the television program *American Idol* and other elimination competitions that depend on user voting to decide what is removed and what remains, until the best of the best is selected and the process begins anew. In this example, the professional judges are the staff that selects the initial acts (content) that the users (the home audience) will see perform (content) from week to week, and the users among the home audience who vote via telephone act as the evaluators and removers.

The keys to using this pattern successfully are as follows:

- Keep the primary content flowing at a controlled rate appropriate for the level of consumption by the users, and keep the minimum quality consistent or improving over time.

- Make sure that the users have the tools they need to make good evaluations and fully understand what happens to content that is removed.

- Consider carefully what level of abuse mitigation reputation systems you may need to counteract any cheating. If your application will significantly increase or decrease the commercial or egocentric value of content, it will provide incentives for people to abuse your system. For example, this web robot helped win Chicken George a spot as a housemate on *Big Brother: All Stars* (from the Vote for the Worst website):

  > Click here to open up an autoscript that will continue to vote for chicken George every few seconds. Get it set up on every computer that you can, it will vote without you having to do anything.

Submit-publish: Users create, staff evaluates and removes

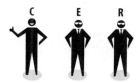

In the submit-publish content control pattern, users create content that will be reviewed for publication and/or promotion by the site. Two common evaluation patterns exist for staff review of content: proactive and reactive. Proactive content review (or moderation) is when the content is not immediately published to the site and is instead placed in a queue for staff to approve or reject. Reactive content review trusts users' content until someone complains and only then does the staff evaluate the content and remove it if needed.

Some websites that display this pattern are television content sites, such as the site for the TV program *Survivor*. That site encourages viewers to send video to the program rather than posting it, and they don't publish it unless the viewer is chosen for the show. Citizen news sites such as Yahoo! You Witness News accept photos and videos and screen them as quickly as possible before publishing them to their sites. Likewise, food magazine sites may accept recipe submissions that they check for safety and copyright issues before republishing.

Since the feedback loop for this content control pattern typically lasts days, or at best hours, and the number of submissions per user is minuscule, the main incentives that tend to drive people fall under the altruism category: "I'm doing this because I think it needs to be done, and someone has to do it." Attribution should be optional but encouraged, and karma is often worth calculating when the traffic levels are so low.

An alternative incentive that has proven effective to get short-term increases in participation for this pattern is commercial: offer a cash prize drawing for the best, funniest, or wackiest submissions. In fact, this pattern is used on many contest sites, such as YouTube's Symphony Orchestra contest (*http://www.youtube.com/symphony*). YouTube had judges sift through user-submitted videos to find exceptional performers to fly to New York City for a live symphony concert performance of a new piece written for the occasion by the renowned Chinese composer Tan Dun, which was then republished on YouTube. As Michael Tilson Thomas, director of music, San Francisco Symphony, said:

> How do you get to Carnegie Hall? Upload! Upload! Upload!

Agents: Users create and remove, staff evaluates

The agents content control pattern rarely appears as a standalone form of content control, but it often appears as a subpattern in a more complex system. The staff acts as a prioritizing filter of the incoming user-generated content, which is passed on to other users for simple consumption or rejection. A simple example is early web indexes, such as the 100% staff-edited Yahoo! Directory, which was the Web's most popular index until web search demonstrated that it could better handle the Web's exponential growth and the types of detailed queries required to find the fine-grained content available.

Agents are often used in hierarchical arrangements to provide scale, because each layer of hierarchy decreases the work on each individual evaluator several times over, which can make it possible for a few dozen people to evaluate a very large amount of user-generated content. We mentioned that the contest portion of *American Idol* was a surveys content control pattern, but talent selection initially goes through a series of agents, each prioritizing and passing them on to a judge, until some of the near-finalists (selected by yet another agent) appear on camera before the celebrity judges. The judges choose the talent (the content) for the season, but they don't choose who appears in the qualification episodes—the producer does.

The agents pattern generally doesn't have many reputation system requirements, depending on how much power you invest in the users to remove content. In the case of the Yahoo! Directory, the company may choose to pay attention to the links that remain unclicked in order to optimize its content. If, on the other hand, your users have a lot of authority over the removal of content, consider the abuse mitigation issues raised in the "Surveys: Staff Creates, Users Evaluate and Remove" pattern (see "Surveys: Staff creates, users evaluate and remove" on page 106).

Basic social media: Users create and evaluate, staff removes

An application that lets users create and evaluate a significant portion of the site's content is what people are calling basic social media these days. On most sites with a basic social media content control pattern, content removal is controlled by staff, for two primary reasons:

Legal exposure

Compliance with local and international laws on content and who may consume it cause most site operators to draw the line on user control here. In Germany, for instance, certain Nazi imagery is banned from websites, even if the content is from an American user, so German sites filter for it. No amount of user voting will overturn that decision. U.S. laws that affect what content may be displayed and to whom include the Children's Online Privacy and Protection Act (COPPA) and the Child Online Protection Act (COPA), which govern children's interaction with identity and advertising, and the Digital Copyright Millennium Act (DCMA), which requires sites with user-generated content to remove items that are alleged to violate copyright on the request of the content's copyright holder.

Minimum editorial quality and revenue exposure

When user-generated content is popular but causes the company grave business distress, it is often removed by staff. A good example of a conflict between user-generated content and business goals surfaces on sites with third-party advertising: Ford Motor Company wouldn't be happy if one of its advertisements appeared next to a post that read, "The Ford Taurus sucks! Buy a Scion instead." Even if there is no way to monitor for sentiment, often a minimum quality of contribution is required for the greater health of the community and business. Compare the comments on just about any YouTube video to those on popular Flickr photos. This suggests that the standard for content quality should be as high as cost allows.

Often, operators of new sites start out with an empty shell, expecting users to create and evaluate en masse, but most such sites never gather a critical mass of content creators, because the operators didn't account for the small fraction of users who are creators (see "Honor creators, synthesizers, and consumers" on page 15). But if you bootstrap yourself past the not-enough-creators problem, through advertising, reputation, partnerships, and/or a lot of hard work, the feedback loop can start working for you (see "The Reputation Virtuous Circle" on page 17). The Web is filled with examples of significant growth with this content control pattern: Digg, YouTube, Slashdot, JPG Magazine, etc.

The challenge comes when you become as successful as you dreamed, and two things happen: people begin to value their status as a contributor to your social media ecosystem, and your staff simply can't keep up with the site abuse that accompanies the increase in the site's popularity. Plan to implement your reputation system for success—to help users find the best stuff their peers are creating and to allow them to point your moderation staff at the bad stuff that needs attention. Consider content reputation and karma in your application design from the beginning, because it's often disruptive to introduce systems of users judging each other's content after community norms are well established.

The Full Monty: Users create, evaluate, and remove

What? You want to give users complete control over the content? Are you sure? Before you decide, read the section "Basic social media: Users create and evaluate, staff removes" on page 109 to find out why most site operators don't give communities control over most content removal.

We call this content control pattern the Full Monty, after the musical about desperate blue-collar guys who've lost their jobs and have nothing to lose, so they let it all hang out at a benefit performance, dancing naked with only hats for covering. It's kinda like that—all risk, but very empowering and a lot of fun.

There are a few obvious examples of appropriate uses of this pattern. Wikis were specifically designed for full user control over content (that is, if you have reason to trust everyone with the keys to the kingdom, get the tools out of the way). The Full Monty pattern works very well inside companies and nonprofit organizations, and even in ad hoc workgroups. In these cases, some other mechanism of social control is at work—for example, an employment contract or the risk of being shamed or banished from the group. Combined with the power for anyone to restore any damage (intentional or otherwise) done by another, these mechanisms provide enough control for the pattern to work.

But what about public contexts in which no social contract exists to define acceptable behavior? Wikipedia, for example, doesn't really use this pattern: it employs an army of robots and professional editors who watch every change and enforce policy in real time. Wikipedia follows a pattern much more like the one described in "Basic social media: Users create and evaluate, staff removes" on page 109.

When no external social contract exists to govern users' actions, you have a wide-open community, and you need to substitute a reputation system in order to place a value on the objects and the users involved in it. Consider Yahoo! Answers (covered in detail in Chapter 10). Yahoo! Answers decided to let users themselves remove content from display on the site because of the staff backlog. Because response time for abusive content complaints averaged 12 hours, most of the potential damage had already been done by the time the offending content was removed. By building a corporate karma system that allowed users to report abusive content, Yahoo! Answers dropped the average amount of time that bad content was displayed to 30 seconds. Sure, customer care staff was still involved with the hardcore problem cases of swastikas, child abuse, and porn spammers, but most abusive content came to be completely policed by users.

Notice that catching bad content is not the same as identifying good content. In a universe where the users are in complete control, the best you can hope to do is encourage the kinds of contributions you want through modeling the behavior you want to see, constantly tweaking your reputation systems, improving your incentive models, and providing clear lines of communication between your company and customers.

Incentives for User Participation, Quality, and Moderation

Why do people do the things they do? If you believe classical economics, it's because of incentives. An incentive creates an expectation in a person's mind (of reward, or delight, or punishment) that leads them to behave in a certain way. If you're going to attempt to motivate your users, you'll need some understanding of incentives and how they influence behavior.

Predictably irrational

When analyzing what role reputation may have in your application, you need to look at what motivates your users and what incentives you may need to provide to facilitate your goals. Out of necessity, this will take us on a short side trip through the intersection of human psychology and market economics.

In Chapter 4 of his book *Predictably Irrational* (HarperCollins), Duke University Professor of behavioral economics Dan Ariely describes a view of two separate incentive exchanges for doing work and the norms that set the rules for them; he calls them social norms and market norms.

Social norms govern doing work for other people because they asked you to—often because doing the favor makes you feel good. Ariely says these exchanges are "wrapped up in our social nature and our need for community. They are usually warm and fuzzy." Market norms, on the other hand, are cold and mediated by wages, prices, and cash: "There's nothing warm and fuzzy about [them]," writes Ariely. Market norms come from the land of "you get what you pay for."

Social and market norms don't mix well. Ariely gives several examples of confusion when these incentive models mix. In one, he describes a hypothetical scene after a family home-cooked holiday dinner, in which he offers to pay his mother $400, and the outrage that would ensue, and the cost of the social damage (which would take a long time to repair). In a second example, less purely hypothetical and more common, Ariely shows what happens when social and market norms are mixed in dating and sex. A guy takes a girl out on a series of expensive dates. Should he expect increased social interaction—maybe at least a passionate kiss? "On the fourth date he casually mentions how much this romance is costing him. Now he's crossed the line (and has upset his date!). He should have known you can't mix social and market norms—especially in this case—without implying that the lady is a tramp."

Ariely goes on to detail an experiment that verifies that social and market exchanges differ significantly, at least when it comes to very small units of work. The work-effort he tested is similar to many of reputation evaluations we're trying to create incentives for. The task in the experiments was trivial: use a mouse to drag a circle into a square on a computer screen as many times as possible in five minutes. Three groups were tested: one group was offered no compensation for participating in the test, one group was offered 50 cents, and the last group was offered $5. Though the subjects who were paid $5 did more work than those who were paid 50 cents, the subjects who did the most work were the ones who were offered no money at all. When the money was substituted with a gift of the same value (a Snickers bar and a box of Godiva chocolates), the work distinction went away—it seems that gifts operate in the domain of social norms, and the candy recipients worked as hard as the subjects who weren't compensated. But when a price sticker was left on the chocolates so that the subjects could see the monetary value of the reward, it was again market norms that applied, and the striking difference in work results reappeared—with volunteers working harder than subjects who received priced candy.

Incentives and reputation

When considering how a content control pattern might help you develop a reputation system, be careful to consider two sets of needs: what incentives would be appropriate for your users in return for the tasks you are asking them to do on your behalf? And what particular goals do you have for your application? Each set of needs may point to a different reputation model—but try to accommodate both.

Ariely talked about two categories of norms—social and market—but for reputation systems, we talk about three main groups of online incentive behaviors:

- *Altruistic* motivation, for the good of others
- *Commercial* motivation, to generate revenue
- *Egocentric* motivation, for self-gratification

Interestingly, these behaviors map somewhat to social norms (altruistic and egocentric) and market norms (commercial and egocentric). Notice that egocentric motivation is listed both a social and a market norm. This is because market-like reputation systems (like points or virtual currencies) are being used to create successful work incentives for egocentric users. In effect, egocentric motivation crosses the two categories in a entirely new virtual social environment—an online reputation-based incentive system—in which these social and market norms can coexist in ways that we might normally find socially repugnant in the real world. In reputation-based incentive systems, bragging can be good.

Altruistic or sharing incentives

Altruistic, or sharing, incentives reflect the giving nature of users who have something to share—a story, a comment, a photo, an evaluation—and who feel compelled to share it on your site. Their incentives are internal. They may feel an obligation to another user or to a friend, or they may feel loyal to (or despise) your brand.

Altruistic or sharing incentives can be characterized into several categories:

- *Tit-for-tat* or *pay-it-forward* incentives: "I do it because someone else did it for me first."
- *Friendship* incentives: "I do it because I care about others who will consume this."
- *Know-it-all* or *crusader* or *opinionated* incentives: "I do it because I know something everyone else needs to know."
- *Other* altruistic incentives: If you know of other incentives driven by altruism or sharing, please contribute them to the website for this book: *http://buildingreputation.com*.

When you're considering reputation models that offer altruistic incentives, remember that these incentives exist in the realm of social norms; they're all about sharing, not accumulating commercial value or karma points. Avoid aggrandizing users driven by altruistic incentives—they don't want their contributions to be counted, recognized, ranked, evaluated, compensated, or rewarded in any significant way. Comparing their work to anyone else's will actually discourage them from participating.

Tit-for-tat and pay-it-forward incentives. A tit-for-tat incentive is at work when a user has received a benefit either from the site or from the other users of the site, and then contributes to the site to return the favor. Early social sites, which contained only staff-provided content and followed a content control patterns such as reviews, provided no incentives to participate. On those sites, users most often indicated that they were motivated to contribute only because another user's review on the site helped them.

A pay-it-forward incentive (from the book by that title by Catherine Ryan Hyde, and the motion picture in 2000) is at work when a user contributes to a site with the goal of improving the state of the world by doing an unrequested deed of kindness toward another—with the hope that the recipient would do the same thing for one or more other people, creating a never-ending and always expanding world of altruism. It can be a model for corporate reputation systems that track altruistic contributions as an indicator of community health.

Friendship incentives. In Fall 2004, when the Yahoo! 360° social network first introduced the vitality stream (later made popular by Facebook and Twitter as the personal news feed), it included activity snippets of various types, such as status and summary items that were generated by Yahoo! Local whenever a user's friends wrote a review of a restaurant or hotel. From the day the vitality stream was launched, Yahoo! Local saw a sustained 45% increase in the number of reviews written daily. A Yahoo! 360° user was over *50 times* more likely to write a review than a typical Yahoo! Local user.

The knowledge that friends would be notified when you wrote a review—in effect notifying them both of where you went and what you thought—became a much stronger altruistic motivator than the tit-for-tat incentive. There's really no reputation system involved in the friendship incentive; it's simply a matter of displaying users' contributions to their friends through news feed events, in item searches, or whenever they happen to encounter a reputable entity that a friend evaluated.

Crusader, opinionated incentives, and know-it-all. Some users are motivated to contribute to a site by a passion of some kind. Some passions are temporary; for example, the *crusaders* are like those who've had a terrible customer experience and might wish to share their frustration with the anonymous masses, perhaps exacting some minor revenge on the business in question. Some passions stem from deeply held religious or political beliefs that they feel compelled to share; these are the *opinionated*. The *know-it-all* users' passions emerge from topical expertise and others who are just killing time. In any case, people seem to have a lot to say that has very mixed commercial value. Just glancing at the comments on a popular YouTube video will show many of these motivations all jumbled together.

This group of altruistic incentives is a mixed bag. It can result in some great contributions as well as a lot of junk (as we mentioned in "There's a Whole Lotta Crap Out There" on page 13). If you have reason to believe that a large portion of your most influential community members will be motivated by controversial ideas, carefully consider the costs of evaluation and removal in the content control pattern that you choose. Having a large community that is out of control can be worse than having no community at all.

On any movie review site, look at the way people respond to one another's reviews for hot-button movies like *Fahrenheit 9/11* (Figure 5-4) or *The Passion of the Christ*. If the site offers "Was this review helpful?" voting, the reviews with the highest total votes are likely to be very polarized. Clearly, in these contexts the word *helpful* means "agreement with the review-writer's viewpoint."

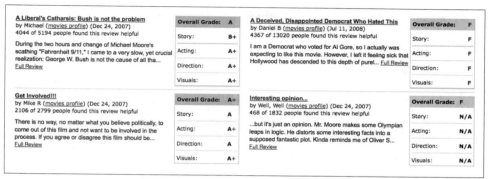

Figure 5-4. In the context of movie reviews, it appears as if the community has interpreted the "Was This Helpful?" question in its own way. They're probably using that input to agree or disagree with a viewpoint, rather than gauging how "useful" it may or may not be.

Commercial incentives

Commercial incentives fall squarely in the range of Ariely's market norms. They reflect people's motivation to do something for money, though the money may not come in the form of direct payment from the user to the content creator. Advertisers have a nearly scientific understanding of the significant commercial value of something they call branding. Likewise, influential bloggers know that their posts build their brand, which often involves the perception of them as subject matter experts. The standing that they establish may lead to opportunities such as speaking engagements, consulting contracts, improved permanent positions at universities or prominent corporations, or even a book deal. A few bloggers may actually receive payment for their online content, but more are capturing commercial value indirectly.

Reputation models that exhibit content control patterns based on commercial incentives must communicate a much stronger user identity. They need strong and distinctive user profiles with links to each user's valuable contributions and content. For example, as part of reinforcing her personal brand, an expert in textile design would want to share links to content that she thinks her fans will find noteworthy.

But don't confuse the need to support strong profiles for contributors with the need for a strong or prominent karma system. When a new brand is being introduced to a market, whether it's a new kind of dish soap or a new blogger on a topic, a karma system that favors established participants can be a disincentive to contribute content. A community decides how to treat newcomers—with open arms or with suspicion. An example of the latter is eBay, where all new sellers must "pay their dues" and bend over backward to get a dozen or so positive evaluations before the market at large will embrace them as trustworthy vendors. Whether you need karma in your commercial incentive model depends on the goals you set for your application. One possible rule of thumb: if users are going to pass money directly to other people they don't know, consider adding karma to help establish trust.

There are two main subcategories of commercial incentives:

Direct revenue incentives
Extracting commercial value (better yet, cash) directly from the user as soon as possible

Branding incentives
Creating indirect value by promotion—revenue will follow later

Direct revenue incentives.   A direct revenue incentive is at work whenever someone forks over money for access to a content contributor's work and the payment ends up, sometimes via an intermediary or two, in the contributor's hands. The mechanism for payment can be a subscription, a short-term contract, a transaction for goods or services, on-content advertising like Google's AdSense, or even a PayPal-based tip jar.

When real money is involved, people take trust seriously, and reputation systems play a critical role in establishing trust. By far the most well-known and studied reputation system for online direct revenue business is eBay's buyer and seller feedback (karma) reputation model. Without a way for strangers to gauge the trustworthiness of the other party in a transaction, no online auction market could exist.

When you're considering reputation systems for an application with a direct revenue incentive, step back and make sure that you might not be better off with either an altruistic or an egocentric incentive. Despite what you may have learned in school, money is *not* always the best motivator, and for consumers it's a pretty big barrier to entry. The ill-fated Google Answers failed because it was based on a user-to-user direct revenue incentive model in which competing sites, such as WikiAnswers, provided similar results for free (financed, ironically, by using Google AdSense to monetize answer pages indexed by, you guessed it, Google).

The Zero Price Effect: Free Is Disproportionately Better Than Cheap

In *Predictably Irrational*, Ariely details a series of experiments to show that people have an irrational urge to choose a free item over an unusually low-priced but higher-quality item. First he offered people a single choice between buying a 1-cent Hershey's Kiss and a 15-cent Lindt truffle, and most people bought the higher-quality truffle. But when he dropped the price of both items by one penny, making the Kiss free, a dramatic majority of a new group of buyers instead selected the Kiss. He calls this the zero price effect. For designing incentive systems, it provokes two thoughts:

- Don't delude yourself that you will overcome the zero price effect by pricing items low enough in a user-to-user direct revenue incentive design.

- Even if you give away user contributions for free, you can still have direct revenue: charge advertisers or sponsors instead of charging consumers.

Incentives through branding: Professional promotion. Various forms of indirect commercial incentives can together be referred to as *branding*, the process of professionally promoting people, goods, or organizations. The advertiser's half of the direct revenue incentive model lives here, too. The goal is to expose the audience to your message and eventually capture value in the form of a sale, a subscriber, or a job.

Typically, the desired effects of branding are preceded by numerous branding activities: writing blog posts, running ads, creating widgets to be embedded on other sites, participating in online discussions, attending conferences, and so on. Reputation systems offer one way to close that loop by capturing direct feedback from consumers. They also help measure the success of branding activities.

Take the simple act of sharing a URL on a social site such as Twitter. Without a reputation system, you have no idea how many people followed your link or how many other people shared it. The URL-shortening service Awe.sm, shown in Figure 5-5, provides both features: it tracks how many people click your link and how many different people shared the URL with others.

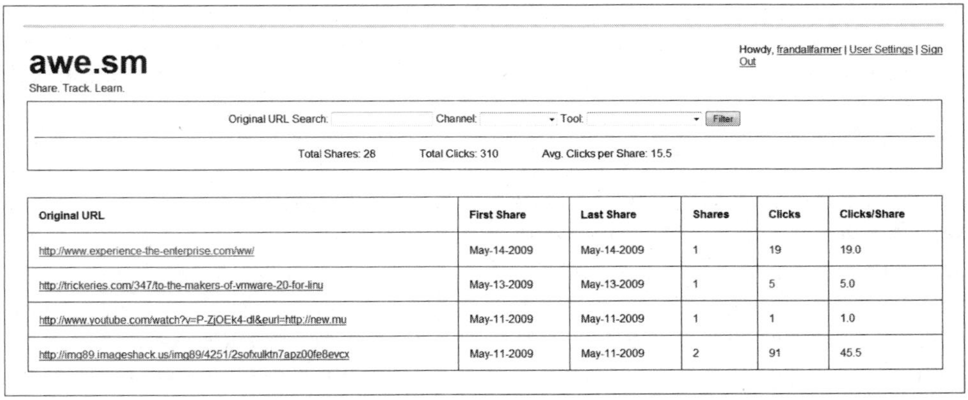

awe.sm
Share. Track. Learn.

Original URL Search: Channel: Tool: [Filter]

Total Shares: 28   Total Clicks: 310   Avg. Clicks per Share: 15.5

Original URL	First Share	Last Share	Shares	Clicks	Clicks/Share
http://www.experience-the-enterprise.com/ww/	May-14-2009	May-14-2009	1	19	19.0
http://trickeries.com/347/to-the-makers-of-vmware-20-for-linu	May-13-2009	May-13-2009	1	5	5.0
http://www.youtube.com/watch?v=P-ZjOEk4-dl&eurl=http://new.mu	May-11-2009	May-11-2009	1	1	1.0
http://img89.imageshack.us/img89/4251/2sofxulktn7apz00fe8evcx	May-11-2009	May-11-2009	2	91	45.5

Figure 5-5. Awe.sm turns URL shortening into a reputation system, measuring how many people click your URL and how many share it with others.

For contributors who are building a brand, public karma systems are a double-edged sword. If a contributor is at the top of his market, his karma can be a big indicator of trustworthiness, but most karma scores can't distinguish inexperience from a newly registered account from complete incompetence—this fact handicaps new entrants.

An application can address this experience-inequity by including time-limited scores in the karma mix. For example, B.F. Skinner was a world-renowned and respected behavioral scientist, but his high reputation has a weakness—it's old. In certain contexts, it's even useless. For example, his great reputation would do me no good if I were looking for a thesis advisor, because he's been dead for almost 20 years.

Egocentric incentives

Egocentric incentives are often exploited in the design online in computer games and many reputation-based websites. The simple desire to accomplish a task taps into deeply hardwired motivations described in behavioral psychology as *classical and operant conditioning* (which involves training subjects to respond to food-related stimulus) and *schedules of reinforcement*. This research indicates that people can be influenced to repeat simple tasks by providing periodic rewards, even a reward as simple as a pleasing sound.

But, an individual animal's behavior in the social vacuum of a research lab is not the same as the ways in which we very social humans reflect our egocentric behaviors to one another. Humans make teams and compete in tournaments. We follow leaderboards comparing ourselves to others and comparing groups that we associate ourselves with. Even if our accomplishments don't help another soul or generate any revenue for us personally, we often want to feel recognized for them. Even if we don't seek accolades from our peers, we want to be able to *demonstrate mastery* of something—to hear the message, "You did it! Good job!"

Therefore, in a reputation system based on egocentric incentives, user profiles are a key requirement. In this kind of system, users need someplace to show off their accomplishments—even if only to themselves. Almost by definition, egocentric incentives involve one or more forms of karma. Even with only a simple system of granting trophies for achievements, users will compare their collections to one another. New norms will appear that look more like market norms than social norms: people will trade favors to advance their karma, people will attempt to cheat to get an advantage, and those who feel they can't compete will opt out altogether.

Egocentric incentives and karma do provide very powerful motivations, but they are almost antithetical to altruistic ones. The egocentric incentives of many systems have been overdesigned, leading to communities consisting almost exclusively of experts. Consider just about any online role playing game that survived more than three years. For example, to retain its highest-level users and the revenue stream they produce, *World of Warcraft* must continually produce new content targeted at those users. If it stops producing new content for its most dedicated users, its business will collapse. This *elder game* focus stunts its own growth by all but abandoning improvements aimed at acquiring new users. When new users do arrive (usually in the wake of a marketing promotion), they end up playing alone because the veteran players are only interested in the new content and don't want to bother going through the long slog of playing through the lowest levels of the game yet again.

We describe three subcategories of egocentric incentives:

Fulfillment incentives
> The desire to complete a task, assigned by oneself, a friend, or the application

Recognition incentives
> The desire for the praise of others

The Quest for Mastery
Personal and private motivation to improve oneself

Fulfillment incentives. The simplest egocentric incentive is the desire to complete a task: to fulfill a goal as work or personal enjoyment. Many reputation model designs that tap the desire of users to complete a complex task can generate knock-on reputations for use by other users or in the system as a whole. For example, free music sites are based on the desire of some users to personalize their own radio stations to gather ratings, which they can then use to recommend music to others. Not only can reputation models that fulfill preexisting user needs gather more reputation claims than altruism and commercial incentives can, but the data typically is of higher quality because it more closely represents users' true desires.

Recognition incentives. Outward-facing egocentric incentives are all related to personal or group recognition. They're driven by admiration, praise, or even envy, and they're focused exclusively on reputation scores. That's all there is to it. Scores often are displayed on one or more public leaderboards, but they can also appear as events in a user's news feed—for example, messages from Zynga's *Mafia Wars* game that tell all your friends you became a Mob Enforcer before they did, or that you gave them the wonderful gift of free energy that will help them get through the game faster.

Recognition is a very strong motivator for many users, but not all. If, for example, you give accumulating points for user actions in a context where altruism or commercial incentives produce the best contributions, your highest-quality contributors will end up leaving the community, while those who churn out lower-value content fill your site with clutter.

Always consider implementing a quality-based reputation system alongside any recognition incentives to provide some balance between quality and quantity. In May 2009, *Wired* writer Nate Ralph wrote "Handed Keys to Kingdom, Gamers Race to Bottom" (*http://www.wired.com/gamelife/2009/05/misson_architect_abuse*) in which he details examples of how Digg, and the games *Little Planet*, and *City of Heroes* were hijacked by people who gamed user recognition reputation systems to the point of seriously decreasing the quality of the applications' key content. Like clockwork, it didn't take long for reputation abuse to hit the iTunes application library as well.

Personal or private incentives: The quest for mastery. Personal or private forms of egocentric incentives can be summarized as motivating a quest for mastery. For example, when people play solitaire or do crossword or sudoku puzzles alone, they do it simply for the stimulation and to see if they can accomplish a specific goal; maybe they want to beat a personal score or time or even just manage to complete the game. The same is true for all single-player computer games, which are much more complex. Even multiple-player games, online and off, such as *World of Warcraft* or *Scrabble*, have strong personal achievement components, such as bonus multipliers or character mastery levels.

Notice especially that players of online single-player computer games—or casual game sites, as they are known in the industry—skew more female and older than most game-player stereotypes you may have encountered. According to the Consumer Electronics Association, 65% of the gamers are women. And women between the ages of 35 and 49 are more likely to visit online gaming websites than even teenage boys. So, if you expect more women than men to use your application, consider staying away from recognition incentives and using mastery-based incentives instead.

Common mastery incentives include achievements (feedback that the user has accomplished one of a set of multiple goals), ranks or levels with caps (acknowledgments of discrete increases in performance—for example, Ensign, Corporal, Lieutenant, and General—but with a clear achievable maximum), and performance scores such as percentage accuracy, where 100% is the desired perfect score.

Resist the temptation to keep extending the top tier of your mastery incentives. Doing so would lead to user fatigue and abuse of the system. Let the user win. It's OK. They've already given you a lot of great contributions and likely will move on to other areas of your site.

Summary: Motivation and Incentive

- *Altruistic* motivation: for the good of others
    - *Tit-for-tat* or *pay-it-forward* incentives: "I do it because someone else did it for me first."
    - *Friendship* incentives: "I do it because I care about others who will consume this."
    - *Know-it-all* or *crusader* or *opinionated* incentives: "I do it because I know something everyone else needs to know."

- *Commercial* motivation: to generate revenue
    - *Direct revenue* incentives: Extracting commercial value (better yet, cash) directly from the user as soon as possible
    - *Branding* incentives: Creating indirect value by promotion—revenue will follow later
- *Egocentric* motivation: for self-gratification
    - *Fulfillment* incentives: The desire to complete a task, assigned by oneself, a friend, or the application
    - *Recognition* incentives: The desire for the praise of others
    - *The Quest for Mastery*: Personal and private motivation to improve oneself

---

Consider Your Community

Introducing a reputation system into your community will almost certainly affect its character and behavior in some way. Some of these effects will be positive (we hope! I mean, that's why you're reading this book, right?). But there are potentially negative side effects to be aware of, too. It is almost impossible to predict exactly what community effects will result from implementing a reputation system because—and we bet you can guess what we're going to say here—it is so bound to the particular context for which you are designing. But the following sections present a number of community factors to consider early in the process.

What are people there to do?

This question may seem simple, but it's one that often goes unasked: what, exactly, is the purpose of this community? What are the actions, activities, and engagements that users expect when they come to your site? Will those actions be aided by the overt presence of content- or people-based reputations? Or will the mechanisms used to generate reputations (event-driven inputs, visible indicators, and the like) actually detract from the primary experience that your users are here to enjoy?

Is this a new community? Or an established one?

Many of the models and techniques that we cover in this book are equally applicable, whether your community is a brand-new, aspiring one or has been around a while and already has acquired a certain dynamic. However, it may be slightly more difficult to introduce a robust reputation system into an existing and thriving community than to have baked-in reputation from the beginning. Here's why:

- An established community already has shared mores and customs. Whether the community's rules have been formalized or not, users do indeed have expectations about how to participate, including an understanding of what types of actions and behaviors are viewed as transgressive. The more established and the more strongly held those community values are, the more important it is for you to match your reputation system's inputs and rewards to those values.

- Some communities may have been around long enough to suffer from problems of scale that would not affect an early stage or brand-new site. The amount of conversation (or noise, depending on how you look at it) might already be overwhelming. And some sites face migration issues:
  - Should you grandfather in old content or just leave it out of the new system?
  - Will you expect people to go back and grade old content retroactively? (In all likelihood, they won't.)

- In particular, it may be difficult to make changes to an existing reputation system. Whether the changes are as trivial and opaque as tweaking some of the parameters that determine a video's popularity ranking or as visible and significant as introducing a new level designation for top performers, you are likely to encounter resistance (or, at the very least, curiosity) from your community. You are, in effect, changing the rules of your community, so expect the typical reaction: some will welcome the changes, others (typically, users who benefited most under the old rules) will denounce them.

We don't mean to imply, however, that designing a reputation system for a new, greenfield community is an easy task. For a new community, rather than identify the community characteristics that you'd like to enhance (or leave unharmed), your task is to imagine the community effects that you're hoping to influence, then make smart decisions to achieve those outcomes.

The competitive spectrum

Is your community a friendly, welcoming place? Helpful? Collaborative? Argumentative or spirited? Downright combative? Communities can put a whole range of behaviors on display, and it can be dangerous to generalize too much about any specific community. But it's important to at least consider the overall character of the community that you plan to influence through your reputation system.

A very telling aspect of community character (though it's not the only one worth considering) is the level of perceived competitiveness in your community (see Figure 5-6). That aspect includes the individual goals of community members and to what degree those goals coexist peacefully or conflict. What are the actions that community members engage in? How might those actions impinge on the experiences of other community members? Do comparisons or contests among people produce the desired behaviors?

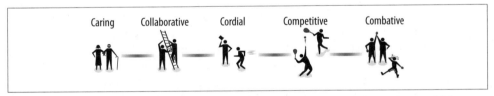

Figure 5-6. The competitive spectrum may help suggest the appropriate reputation model for your community's needs.

In general, the more competitive a group of people in a community is, the more appropriate it is to compare those people (and the artifacts that they generate) to one another.

Read that last bit again, and carefully. A common mistake made by product architects (especially for social web experiences) is assuming a higher level of competitiveness than what really exists. Because reputation systems and their attendant incentive systems are often intended to emulate the principles of engaging game designs, designers often gravitate toward the aggressively competitive—and comparative—end of the spectrum.

Even the intermediate stages along the spectrum can be deceiving. For example, where would you place a community like Match.com or Yahoo! Personals along the spectrum? Perhaps your first instinct was to say, "I would place a dating site firmly in the 'competitive' part of the spectrum." People are competing for attention, right? And dates?

Remember, though, the entire context for reputation in this example. Most importantly, remember the desires of the person who is doing the evaluating on these sites. A visitor to a dating site probably doesn't want competition, and she may not view her activity on the site as competitive at all but as a collaborative endeavor. She's looking for a potential dating partner who meets her own particular criteria and needs—not necessarily "the best person on the site."

"The Competitive Spectrum" is expanded upon in Christian Crumlish and Erin Malone's *Designing Social Interfaces (http://oreilly.com/cata log/9780596154936)* (O'Reilly).

Better Questions

Our goal for this chapter was to get you asking the right questions about reputation for your application. Do you need reputation at all? How might it promote more and better participation? How might it conflict with your goals for community use of your application? We've given you a lot to consider in this chapter, but your answers to these questions will be invaluable as you dive into Chapter 6, where we teach you how to define the what, who, how, and limits of your reputation system.

Objects, Inputs, Scope, and Mechanism

Having answered the three key questions posed in Chapter 5 (see "Asking the Right Questions" on page 97), you should have a pretty good idea of what you want to accomplish with your system. In this chapter, we start showing you *how* to accomplish those goals. We'll start identifying the components of your reputation system and we systematically determine these details:

- Which *objects* (people or things) will play a part in the reputation system? Some objects will themselves be reputable entities and will accrue and lose reputation over time. Other objects may not directly benefit from having a reputation but may play a part in the system nevertheless.

- What *inputs* will feed into your system? Inputs frequently will take the form of *actions* that your users may take, but other inputs are possible, and we'll discuss them in some detail.

- In the case of user-expressed opinions and actions, what are the appropriate *mechanisms* to offer your users? What would be the difference between offering 5-star ratings, thumbs-up voting, or social bookmarking?

In addition, we share a number of practitioner's tips, as always. This time around, we consider the effects of exclusivity on your reputation system (how stingy, or how generous, should you be when doling out reputations?). We also provide some guidance for determining the appropriate scope of your reputations in relation to context.

The Objects in Your System

To accomplish your reputation-related goals, you'll have two main weapons—the objects that your software understands and the software tools, or mechanisms, that you provide to users and embed in processes. To put it simply, if you want to build birdhouses, you need wood and nails (the objects) along with saws and hammers (the tools), and you need someone to do the actual construction (the users).

Architect, Understand Thyself

Where will the relevant objects in your reputation system come from? Why, they're present in your larger application, of course. (Not *all* objects need be contained within the application—see "Relevant external objects" on page 44—but this will be the majority case.) Let's start by thinking clearly about the architecture and makeup of your application.

In places, it may sound as though we're describing a "brownfield" deployment of your reputation system: that is, that we're assuming you already have an application in mind or in production and are merely retrofitting a reputation system onto it. That is not at all the case.

You would consider the same questions and dependencies regardless of whether your host application was already live or was still in the planning stages. It's just much easier for us to talk about reputation as though there were preexisting objects and models to graft it onto. (Planning your application architecture is a whole other book altogether.)

So...what does your application do?

You know your application model, right? You can probably list the five most important objects represented in your system without even breaking a sweat. In fact, a good place to start is by composing an "elevator pitch" for your application; in other words, describe, as succinctly as you can, what your application will do. Here are some examples:

- A social site that lets you share recipes and keep and print shopping lists of ingredients
- A tool that lets you edit music mashups, build playlists of them, and share those lists with your friends
- An intranet application that lets paralegal assistants access and save legal briefs and share them with lawyers in a firm

These are short, sweet, and somewhat vague descriptions of three very different applications, but each one still tells us much of what we need to know to plan our reputation needs. The recipe sharing site likely will benefit from some form of reputation for recipes and will require some way for users to rate them. The shopping lists? Not so much; those are more like utilities for individual users to manage the application data.

If an artifact or object in your system has an audience of one, you probably don't need to *display* a reputation for it. You may, however, opt to keep one or more reputations for those objects' useful inputs—designed to roll up into the reputations of other, more visible objects.

As for the music site, perhaps it's not any one track that's worth assessing but the quality of the playlists. Or maybe what's relevant is users' reputations as deejays (their performance, over time, at building and sustaining an audience). Tracking either one will probably also require keeping mashup tracks as an object in the system, but those tracks may not necessarily be treated as primary reputable entities.

In the intranet application for paralegals, the briefs are the primary atomic unit of interest. Who saved what briefs, how are users adding metadata, and how many people attach themselves to a document? These are all useful bits of information that will help filter and rank briefs to present back to other users.

So the first step toward defining the relevant objects in your reputation system is to start with what's important in the application model, then think forward a little to what types of problems reputation will help your users solve. Then you can start to catalog the elements of your application in a more formal fashion.

Perform an application audit

Although you've thought at a high level about the primary objects in your application model, you've probably overlooked some smaller-order, secondary objects and concepts. These primary and secondary objects relate to one another in interesting ways that we can make use of in our reputation system. An application audit can help you to fully understand the entities and relationships in your application.

Make a complete inventory of every kind of object in your application model that may have anything to do with accomplishing your goals. Some obvious items are user profile records and data objects that are special to your application model: movies, transactions, landmarks, CDs, cameras, or whatever. All of these are clear candidates for tracking as reputable entities.

It is very important to know what objects will be the targets of reputation statements and any new objects you'll need to create for that purpose. Make sure you understand the metadata surrounding each object and how your application will access it. How are the objects organized? Are they searchable by attributes? Which attributes? How are the different objects related to one another?

Some objects in your application model will be visually represented in the interface, so one way to start an audit is with a simple survey of screen designs, at whatever fidelity is available. For in-progress projects, early-stage wireframes are fine—if your application is in production, take some screenshots and print them. Figure 6-1 shows an audit-screengrab for a project already in production, Yahoo! Message Boards.

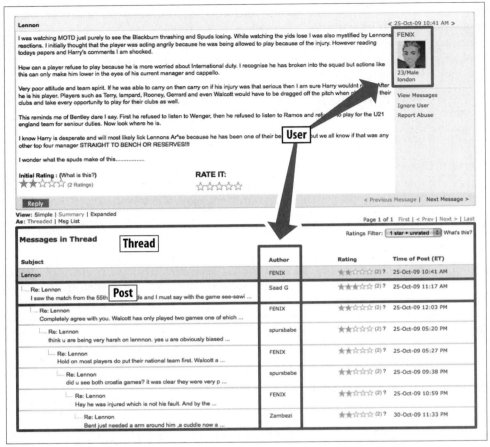

Figure 6-1. Here, users, threads, and posts are all useful entities to model in a message board context.

Also be sure to list items whose creation, editing, or content can be used as input into your reputation model. Some common types of such items are:

- Categorization systems, such as folders, albums, or collections
- Tags
- Comments
- Uploads

Spend some time considering more nuanced sources of information, such as historical activity data, external reputation information, and special processes that provide application-relevant insight.

As an example, consider a profanity filter applied to user-supplied text messages, replacing positive matches with asterisks (****); the real-time results of applying the filter

might provide a way to measure the effects of interface changes on this particular ᵤ
behavior (the use of profanity).

What Makes for a Good Reputable Entity?

An object that makes a good candidate for tracking as a reputable entity in your system probably has one or more of the characteristics outlined in the following sections.

People are interested in it

This probably should go without saying, but—what the heck—let's say it anyway. If your entire application offering is built around a specific type of object, social or otherwise, the object is probably a good candidate for tracking as a reputable entity.

And remember, nothing interests people more than...other people. That phenomenon alone is an argument for at least considering using karma (people reputation) in any application that you might build. Users will always want every possible edge in understanding other actors in a community. What motivates them? What actions have they performed in the past? How might they behave in the future?

When you're considering what objects will be of the most interest to your users, don't overlook other, related objects that also may benefit users. For example, on a photo-sharing site, it seems natural that you'd track a photo's reputation. But what about photo albums? They may not be the very first application object that you think of, but in some situations, it's likely you'll want to direct users' attention to high-quality groupings or collections of photos.

The solution is to track both objects. Each may affect the reputation of the other to some degree, but the inputs and weightings you'll use to generate reputation for each will necessarily differ.

The decision investment is high

Some decisions are easy to make, requiring little investment of time or effort. Likewise, the cost of recovering from such decisions is negligible. For example, suppose I ask myself, "Should I read this blog entry?"

If it's a short entry, and I'm already engaged in the act of reading blogs, and no other distractions are calling me away from that activity, then, yeah, I'll probably go ahead and give it a read. (Of course, the content of the entry itself is a big factor. If neither the entry's title nor a quick skim of the body interests me, I'll likely pass it up.) And, once I've read it, if it turns out not to have been a very good choice? Well, no harm done. I can recover gracefully, move on to the next entry in my feed reader, and proceed on my way.

The level of decision investment is important because it affects the likelihood that a user will make use of available reputation information for an item. In general, the greater the investment in a decision, the more a user will expect (and make use of) robust supporting data (see Figure 6-2).

Figure 6-2. More critical decisions demand more complete information.

So for high-investment decisions (such as purchasing or any other decision that is not easily rescinded), offer more robust mechanisms, such as reputation information, for use in decision making.

The entity has some intrinsic value worth enhancing

You can do a lot with design to "ease" the presence of reputation inputs in your application interface. Sites continue to get more and more sophisticated with incorporating explicit and implicit controls for stating an entity value. Furthermore, the web-using public is becoming more and more accepting of, and familiar with, popular voting and favoriting input mechanisms.

Neither of these facts, however, obviates this requirement: reputable entities themselves must have some intrinsic value apart from the reputation system. Ask your users to participate only in ways that are appropriate in relation to that object's intrinsic value. Don't ask users for contributions (such as reviews or other metadata) that add value to an object whose intrinsic apparent value is low.

It might be OK, for example, to ask someone to give a thumbs-up rating to someone else's blog comment (because the cost to the user providing the rating is low—basically a click). But it would be inappropriate to ask for a full-blown review of the comment. Writing the review would require more effort and thought than there was in the initial comment.

The entity should persist for some length of time

Reputable entities must remain in the community pool long enough for all members of the community to cast a vote (Figure 6-3). There's little use in asking users for metadata for an item if other users cannot come along afterward and enjoy the benefit of that metadata.

Highly ephemeral items, such as news articles that disappear after 48 or 72 hours, probably aren't good candidates for certain types of reputation inputs. For example, you wouldn't ask users to author a multi-part review of a news story destined to vanish in less than a day, but you might ask them to click a "Digg this" or "Buzz this" button.

Figure 6-3. The value of ratings increases with the time value of the content being rated.

Items with a great deal of persistence (such as real-world establishments like restaurants or businesses) make excellent candidates for reputation. Furthermore, it can be appropriate to ask users for more involved types of inputs for persistent items, because it's likely that other users will have a chance to benefit from the work that the community puts into contributing content.

Determining Inputs

Now that you have a firm grasp of the objects in your system and you've elected a handful as reputable entities, the next step is to decide what's good and what's bad. How will you decide? What inputs will you feed into the system to be tabulated and rolled up to establish relative reputations among like objects?

User Actions Make Good Inputs

Now, instead of merely listing the objects that a user might interact with in your application, we'll enumerate all the actions that she might take in relation to those objects. Again, many actions will be obvious and visible right there in your application interface, as in Figure 6-4, so let's build on the audit that you performed earlier for objects.

Explicit claims

Explicit claims represent your community's voice and opinion. They operate through interface elements you provide that solicit users' opinions about an entity, good or bad. A fundamental difference exists between explicit claims and implicit ones (discussed below), which boils down to user intent and comprehension.

With explicit claims, users should be fully aware that the action they're performing is intended as an expression of an opinion. That intent differs greatly from the ones for implicit claims, in which users mostly just go about their business, generating valuable reputation information as a side effect.

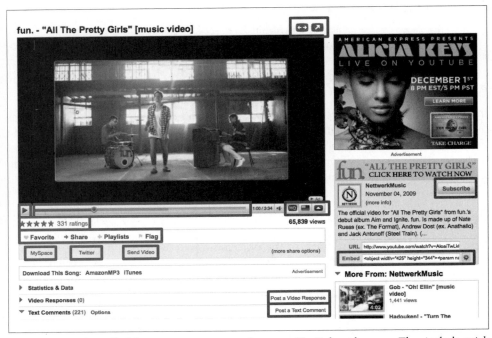

Figure 6-4. Look at all of the actions users can perform on a YouTube video page. They include a rich mix of inputs with value as explicit claims and implicit claims (and some with no real reputation value).

Provide a Primary Value

If you present explicit inputs to your users as only that—a mechanism for generating reputation information to feed the system and make your site smarter—you may be inhibiting the community from providing inputs. You are likely to see more input surrendered if the contributors get some primary value from their contributions.

The primary value can be big or small, but it probably will have some of the following characteristics:

- It provides a benefit to the user for interacting with the system: a self-evident and recognizable benefit that users themselves obtain from interacting with a widget. Comments on Digg, for instance, are hidden for a particular user when she "Diggs [thumbs] them down." This is immediately useful to the user; it cleans up her display and makes the current thread easier to read.

  Likewise, the 5-star rating system in iTunes is surpassingly useful not because of any secondary or tertiary reputation benefits it may yield, but primarily because it offers a well-articulated and extremely flexible way to manage data. iTunes users can take advantage of stars to sort track listings, build smart playlists, and get recommendations from the iTunes Store. Star rating widgets in iTunes are full of primary value.

- It provides immediate and evident feedback. Unlike reputation effects that may not be immediately evident because they happen downstream, the system should provide some quick acknowledgment that the user has expressed a claim. This just happens to reinforce good user interface principles as well. (See "Latency Reduction" in Bruce Tognazzini's *First Principles of Interaction Design*: *http://www.asktog .com/basics/firstPrinciples.html*.)

Implicit claims

Any time a user takes some action in relation to a reputation entity, it is very likely that you can derive valuable reputation information from that action. Recall the discussion of implicit and explicit reputation claims in "The Reputation Statement" on page 6. With implicit reputation claims, we watch *not what the user says* about the quality of an entity but *how they interact* with that object. For example, assume that a reputable entity in your system is a text article. You'll find valuable reputation information in the answers to the following questions:

- Does the user read the article? To completion?
- Does the user save the article for later use?
  — By bookmarking it?
  — By clipping it?
- Does the user republish the article to a wider audience?
  — By sending it to a friend?
  — By publishing to a tweet-stream?
  — By embedding it on a blog?
- Does the user copy or clone the article for use in writing another article?

You can construct any number of smart, nuanced, and effective reputation models from relevant related action-type claims. Your only real limitation is the level and refinement of instrumentation in your application: are you prepared to capture relevant actions at the right junctures and generate reputation events to share with the system?

 Don't get too clever with implicit action claims, or you may unduly influence users' behavior. If you weigh implicit actions into the formulation of an object or a person's reputation *and* you make that fact known, you're likely to actually motivate users to take those actions arbitrarily. This is one of the reasons that many reputation-intensive sites are coy about revealing the types and weightings of claims in their systems. (See the section "Keep Your Barn Door Closed (but Expect Peeking)" on page 91.)

But Other Types of Inputs Are Important, Too

A reputation system doesn't exist in a vacuum; it's part of a bigger application, which itself is part of a bigger ecosystem of applications. Relevant inputs come from many sources other than those generated directly by user actions. Be sure to build, buy, or otherwise include them in your model where needed. Here are some common examples:

- External trust databases
  —Spam IP blacklist.
  —Text scanning software that detects profanity or other abusive patterns.
  —Reputation from other applications in your ecosystem.
- Social networking relationships
  —Relationships may be used to infer positive reputation by proxy.
  —In many cases, when surfacing an evaluation of a reputable object, relationship should be a primary search criterion: "Your brother recommends this camera."
- Session data
  —Browser cookies are good for tracking additional metadata about user visits: is a user logged-out? Newly registered? Returning after some amount of time away?
  —Session cookies can be used to build up a reputation history.
  —Identity cookies allow various identities, browsers, and sessions to be linked together.
- Asynchronous activations
  —*Just-in-time inputs*. Many reputation models are real-time systems in which reputations change constantly, even when *users* aren't providing any direct input. For example, a mail antispam reputation model for IP addresses could handle irregularly timed, asynchronous inputs about mail volume received over time from an address to allow the reputation to naturally reflect traffic. In this example, the volume of incoming email that isn't marked as spam would cause the IPs reputation to improve sporadically.
  —*Time-activated inputs*. Also called cron jobs (for the Unix tool `cron` that executes them), these often are used to start a reputation process as part of periodic maintenance; for example, a timer can trigger reputation scores to decay or expire. (For one benefit of calculating reputation on a time-delay, see "Decay and delay" on page 93.) Timers may be periodic or scheduled ad hoc by an application.
  —*Customer care corrections* and *operator overrides*. When things go wrong, someone's got to fix it via a special input channel. This is a common reason that many reputation processes are required to be reversible.

Of course, the messages that each reputation process outputs also are potential inputs into other processes. Well-designed karma models don't usually take direct inputs at all—those processes always take place downstream from other processes that encode the understanding of the relationship between the objects and transform that code into a normalized score.

Good Inputs

Whether your system features explicit reputation claims, implicit ones, or a skillful combination of both, to maintain the quality of the inputs to the system, strive to follow the practices described next.

Emphasize quality, not simple activity

Don't continue to reward people or objects for performing the same action over and over; rather, try to single out events that indicate that the target of the claim is worth paying attention to. For instance, the act of bookmarking an article is probably a more significant event than a number of page views. Why? Because bookmarking something is a deliberate act—the user has assessed the object in question and decided that it's worth further action.

Rate the thing, not the person

The process of creating karma is subtly more complex and socially delicate than creating reputation for things. For a deeper explanation, see "Karma" on page 176. Yahoo! has a general community policy of soliciting explicit ratings input only for user-created content—*never* having users directly rate other users. This is a good practice for a number of reasons:

- It keeps the focus of debate on the quality of the content an author produces, which is what's of value to your community (instead of on the quality of her character, which isn't).
- It reduces ad hominem attacks and makes for a nicer culture within the community.

Reward firsts, but not repetition

It's often worthwhile to reward *firsts* for users in your system, perhaps rewarding the first user to "touch" an object (leave a review, comment on a story, or post a link). Or, conversely, you might reward a whole host of firsts for a single user (to encourage him to interact with a wide range of features, for instance).

But once a first has been acknowledged, don't continue to reward users for more of the same.

Pick events that are hard for users to replicate; this combats gaming of the system. But anticipate these patterns of behavior anyway, and build a way to deal with offenders into your system.

Use the right scale for the job

In "Ratings bias effects" on page 61, we discussed ratings distributions and why it's important to pay attention to them. If you're seeing data with poorly actionable distributions (basically, data that doesn't tell you much), it's likely that you're asking for the wrong inputs.

Pay attention to the context in which you're asking. For example, if interest in the object being rated is relatively low (perhaps it's official feed content from a staid, corporate source), 5-star ratings are probably overkill. Your users won't have such a wide range of opinions about the content that they'll need five stars to judge it.

Match user expectations

Ask for information in a way that's consistent and appropriate with how you're going to use it. For example, if your intent is to display the community average rating for a movie on a scale of 1 to 5 stars, it makes the most sense to ask users to enter movie ratings on a scale of 1 to 5 stars. Of course, you can transform reputation scores and present them back to the community in different ways (see the sidebar "What Comes in Is Not What Goes Out" on page 151), but strive to do that only when it makes sense and in a way that doesn't confuse your users.

Common Explicit Inputs

In Chapter 7, we'll focus on displaying aggregated reputation, which is partly constructed with the inputs we discuss here, and which has several output formats identical to the inputs (for example, 5 stars in, 5 stars out). But that symmetry exists only for a subset of inputs and an ever-smaller subset of the aggregated outputs. For example, an individual vote may be a yes or a no, but the result is a percentage of the total votes for each.

In this chapter, we're discussing only claims on the input side—what does a user see when she takes an action that is sent to the reputation model and transformed into a claim?

The following sections outline best practices for the use and deployment of the common explicit input types. The user experience implications of these patterns are also covered in more depth in Christian Crumlish and Erin Malone's *Designing Social Interfaces* (*http://oreilly.com/catalog/9780596154936*) (O'Reilly).

The ratings life cycle

Before we dive into all the ways in which users might provide explicit feedback about objects in a system, think about the context in which users provide feedback. Remember, this book is organized around the reputation information that users generate—usable metadata about objects and about other people. But users themselves have a different perspective, and their focus is often on other matters altogether (see Figure 6-5). Feeding *your* reputation system is likely the last thing on their mind.

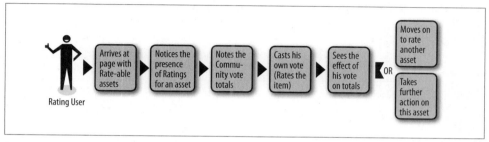

Figure 6-5. Even though this flow is idealized, it amply demonstrates that the "simple" act of rating something is actually pretty complex.

Given the other priorities, goals, and actions that your users might possibly be focused on at any given point during their interaction with your application, here are some good general guidelines for gathering explicit reputation inputs effectively.

The interface design of reputation inputs. Your application's interface design can reinforce the presence of input mechanisms in several ways:

- Place input mechanisms in comfortable and clear proximity to the target object that they modify. Don't expect users to find a ratings widget for that television episode when the widget is buried at the bottom of the page. (Or at least don't expect them to remember which episode it applies to...or why they should click it...or....)

- Don't combine too many different rateable entities on a single screen. You may have perfectly compelling reasons to want users to rate a product, a manufacturer, and a merchant all from the same page—but don't expect them to do so consistently and without becoming confused.

- Carefully strike a balance between the size and proportion of reputation-related mechanisms and any other (perhaps more important) actions that might apply to a reputable object.

    For example, in a shopping context, it's probably appropriate to make "Add to Cart" the predominant call to action and keep the Rate This button less noticeable—even *much* less noticeable. (Would you rather have a rating, or a sale?)

- Make the presentation and formatting of your input mechanisms consistent. You may be tempted to try "fun" variations like making your ratings stars different colors in different product categories, or swapping in a little Santa for your thumb-up and thumb-down icons during the holidays.

In a word: *don't*. Your users will have enough work in finding, learning, and coming to appreciate the benefits of interacting with your reputation inputs. Don't throw unnecessary variations in front of them.

Stars, bars, and letter grades

A number of different input mechanisms let users express an opinion about an object across a range of values. A very typical such mechanism is star ratings. Yahoo! Local (see Figure 6-6) allows users to rate business establishments on a scale of 1 to 5 stars.

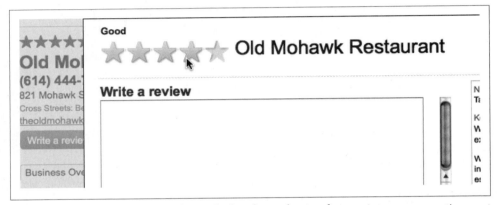

Figure 6-6. Yahoo! design standards specify that the mechanism for entering your own rating must always look different from the mechanism for displaying the community average rating.

Stars *seem* like a pretty straightforward mechanism, both for your users to consume (5-star rating systems seem to be everywhere, so users aren't unfamiliar with them) and for you, the system designer, to plan. Tread carefully, though. Here are some small behavioral and interaction "gotchas" to think about early, during the design phase.

The schizophrenic nature of stars. Star ratings often are displayed back to users in a format very similar to the one in which they're gathered from users. That arrangement need not be the case—scores generated by stars can be transformed into any number of output formats for display—but as we noted earlier (see "Match user expectations" on page 136), it's usually what is clearest to users.

As the application designer, you should be wary, however, of making the input-form for stars match *too* closely their final display presentation. The temptation is strong to design one comprehensive widget that accomplishes both: displaying the current community average rating for an object and accepting user input to cast their own vote.

Slick mouse-over effects or toggle switches that change the state of the widget are some attempts that we've seen, but this is tricky to pull off, and almost never done well. You'll either end up with a widget that does a poor job at displaying the community average or one that doesn't present a very strong call to action.

The solution that's most typically used at Yahoo! is to separate these two functions into two entirely different widgets and present them side by side on the page. The widgets are even color-coded to keep their intended uses straight. On Yahoo!, red stars are typically read-only (you can't interact with them) and always reflect the community average rating for an entity, whereas yellow stars reflect the rating that you as a user entered (or, alternately, empty yellow stars wait eagerly to record your rating).

From a design standpoint, the distinction does introduce additional interactive and visual complexity to any component that displays ratings, but the increase in clarity more than compensates for any additional clutter.

Do I like you, or do I "like" like you. Though it's a fairly trivial task to determine numerical values for selections along a 5-point scale, there's no widespread agreement among users on exactly what star ratings represent. Each user applies a subtly different interpretation (complete with biases) to star ratings. Ask yourself the following questions—they're the questions that users have to ask each time they come across a ratings system:

- What does "one star" mean on this scale? Should it express strong dislike? Apathy? Mild "like"? Many star-ratings widgets provide suggested interpretations at each point along the spectrum, such as "Dislike it," "Like it," and "Love it."

  The drawback to that approach is that it constrains the uses that individual users might find for the system. The advantage is that it brings the community interpretation of the scale into greater agreement.

- What opinion does *no* rating express? Should the interface provide an explicit option for "no rating?" Yahoo! Music's 5-star ratings widget feeds a recommender system that suggests new music according to what you've liked in the past. The site actually offers a sixth option (not presented as a star) intended to express "Don't play this track again."

- Can the user change a rating already submitted? Adding such functionality—to change a vote that's already been cast—is another reason to make an interaction design distinction between rating an item and reviewing the community average. If you support undo or change, now your super-sized universal one-size-fits-all vote *and* display widget will also need to support *that* function, too. (Good luck with that.)

- Can a rating include half-stars? Often, regardless of whether you allow half-step input for ratings, you will want to allow half-step display of community averages. In any event, notice that the possibility of half-values for stars effectively doubles the expressive range of the scale.

Two-state votes (thumb ratings)

"Thumb" voting (thumb up or thumb down) lets a user quickly rate content in a fun, engaging way (see Figure 6-7). The benefit to the user for voting is primarily related to self-expression ("I love this!" or "I hate this!"). The ratings don't need to be presented visually as thumbs (in fact, sometimes they shouldn't), but in this book, we use "thumb" as shorthand for a two-state voting mechanism.

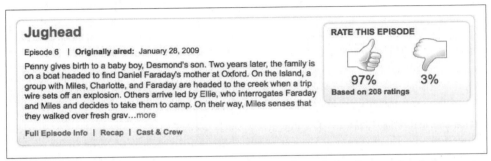

Figure 6-7. Yahoo! TV lets viewers rate their favorite episodes with thumb-up or thumb-down votes. The highly-skewed results shown in this example are typical: it turns out that only series fans go through the bother of rating individual episodes.

Thumb voting allows users to express strongly polarized opinions about assets. For example, if you can state your question as simply as "Did you like this or not?", thumb voting may be appropriate. If it seems more natural to state your question as "How much did you like this?", then star ratings seem more appropriate.

A popular and effective use of two-state voting is as a meta-moderation device for user-submitted opinions, comments, and reviews, as in Figure 6-8. Wherever you solicit user opinions about an object, also consider letting the community voice opinions about that opinion, by providing an easy control such as "Was this helpful?" or "Do you agree?"

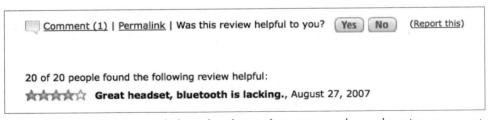

Figure 6-8. Two-state voting works best when the interface presents a clear and concise user prompt. Leave no doubt about what you're asking users to decide: "Was this review helpful to you?"

Avoid thumb voting for multiple facets of an entity. For example, don't provide multiple thumb widgets for a product review intended to record users' satisfaction with the product's price, quality, design, and features. Generally, a thumb vote should be associated with an object in a one-to-one relationship: one entity gets one thumb up or down. Think of the metaphor, after all: Emperor Nero never would have let a gladiator's arm survive while putting his leg to death. Think of thumb voting as an all-or-nothing rating.

Consider thumb voting when you want a fun, lightweight rating mechanism. The context for thumb voting should be appropriately fun and lighthearted, too; don't use thumb voting in contexts where it will appear insensitive or inappropriate.

 An upraised thumb is considered offensive in some cultures. If your site has potential international appeal, watch out.

Don't use thumb ratings when you want to compare qualitative data among assets. For example, in a long list of movies available for rental, you may want to permit sorting of the list by average rating. If you have been collecting thumb ratings, such sorting wouldn't be very useful to users. (Instead, consider a 5-star scalar rating style.)

Vote to promote: Digging, liking, and endorsing

Vote to promote fulfills a very specific niche in the world of online opinion-gathering. As users browse a collection or pool of media objects, they mark items as worthwhile using a control consisting of a simple gesture. This pattern has been popularized by social news sites such as Digg, Yahoo! Buzz, and Newsvine.

Typically, these votes accumulate and are used to change the rank of items in the community pool and present winners with more prominence or a higher status, but that's not an absolute necessity. Facebook offers an "I like this" link (Figure 6-9) that simply communicates a user's good will toward an item.

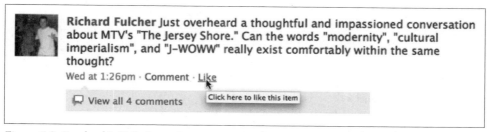

Figure 6-9. Facebook's "Like" vote is a tiny, personal vote-to-promote-style system. A large part of its value to you, the user, comes from your social connection to the voters.

The names of users who "like" an item are displayed to other users who encounter the item (until the list of vote casters becomes cumbersome, when the display switches to a sort of summary score), but highly liked items aren't promoted above other items in the news feed in any obvious or overt way.

User reviews

Writing a user review demands a lot of effort from users. It is among the most involved explicit input mechanisms that you can present, usually consisting of detailed, multi-part data entry (see Figure 6-10).

To get good, usable comparison data from user reviews, try to ensure that the objects you offer up for review meet all the criteria that we listed above for good reputable entities (see "What Makes for a Good Reputable Entity?" on page 129). Ask users to write reviews only for objects that are valuable, long-lived, and that have a high-investment decision.

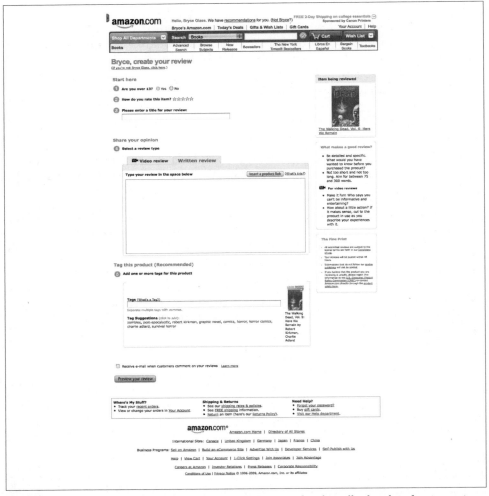

Figure 6-10. Amazon's review-writing process—while streamlined—still asks a lot of review writers. This barrier to participation may skew involvement from the community.

Reviews typically are compound reputation claims, with each review made up of a number of smaller inputs bundled together. You might consider any combination of the following for your user-generated reviews:

- You can include a freeform comment field (see "Text comments" on page 40) for users to provide their impressions of the rated object, good or bad. You may impose some standards on this field (for example, checking for profanity or requiring length in a certain character range), but generally this field is provided for users to fill in as they please.

- Optionally, the review may feature a title. Also a freeform text entry, the title lets users put their "brand" on a review or give it extra appeal and pizzazz. Users often use the title field to grab attention and summarize the tone and overall opinion of the full review.

- Consider including an explicit scalar ratings widget, such as a 5-star scale ("Stars, bars, and letter grades" on page 138). It's almost always a good idea to display one overall rating for the object in question.

  For example, even if you're asking users to rate multiple facets of, say, a movie (direction, acting, plot, and effects), you can provide one prominent rating input for the users' overall opinion. You could just derive the average from a combination of the facet reviews, but that wouldn't be as viscerally satisfying for opinionated reviewers.

- You may want to let users attach additional media to a review—for example, upload a video testimonial or attach URLs for additional resources (Flickr photos or relevant blog entries). The more participation you can solicit from reviewers, the better. And to bootstrap a review's quality reputation, you can consider each additional resource as an input.

Common Implicit Inputs

Remember, with implicit reputation inputs, we are going to pay attention to some subtle and nonobvious indicators in our interface. Actions that—when users take them—may indicate a higher level of interest (indicative of higher *quality*) in the object targeted.

It is difficult to generalize about implicit inputs because they are highly contextual. They depend on the particulars of your application: its object model, interaction styles, and screen designs. However, the following inputs represent the types of inputs you can track.

Favorites, forwarding, and adding to a collection

Any time a user saves an object or marks it for future consideration—either for himself or to pass along to someone else—that could be a reputable event.

This type of input has a lot in common with the explicit vote-to-promote input (see "Vote to promote: Digging, liking, and endorsing" on page 141), but the difference lies in user intent and perception: in a vote-to-promote system, the primary motivator for marking something as worthwhile is to publicly state a preference, and the expectation is that information will be shared with the community. It is a more extrinsic motivation.

By contrast, favorites, forwarding, and adding to a collection are more intrinsically motivated reputation inputs—actions that users take for largely private purposes.

Favorites. To mark an item as a favorite, a user activates some simple control (usually clicking an icon or a link), which adds the item to a list that she can return to later for browsing, reading, or viewing.

Some conceptual overlap exists between the favorites pattern, which can be semipublic (favorites often are displayed to the community as part of a user's profile) and the liking pattern. Both favorites and liking can be tallied and fed in almost identical ways into an object's quality reputation.

Forwarding. You might know this input pattern as "send to a friend." This pattern facilitates a largely private communication between two friends, in which one passes a reputable entity on to another for review. Yahoo! News has long promoted most emailed articles as a type of currency-of-interest proxy reputation. (See Figure 6-11.)

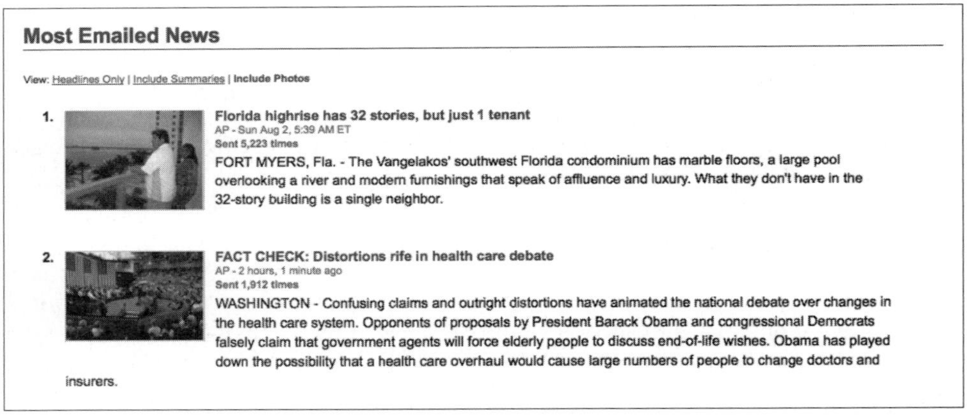

Figure 6-11. A danger with implicit inputs like send-to-a-friend is that, once the community becomes accustomed to their presence, they risk becoming a type of explicit statement. Do you suppose Yahoo! News has to battle email bots designed to artificially inflate articles' visibility on the site?

Adding to a collection. Many applications provide ordering mechanisms for users as conveniences: a way to group like items, save them for later, edit them en masse. Depending on the context of your application, and the culture of use that emerges out of how people interact with collections on your site, you may want to consider each "add to collection" action as an implicit reputation statement, akin to favoriting or sending to a friend.

Greater disclosure

Greater disclosure is a highly variable input: there's a wide range of ways to present it in an interface (and weight it in reputation processes). But if users request "more information" about an object, you might consider those requests as a measure of the interest in that object—especially if users are making the requests after having already evaluated some small component of the object, such as an excerpt, a thumbnail, or a teaser.

A common format for blogs, for instance, is to present a menu of blog entries, with excerpts for each, and "read more" links. Clicks on a link to a post may be a reasonably accurate indicator of interest in the destination article.

But beware—the limitations of a user interface can render such data misleading. In the example in Figure 6-12, the interface may not reveal enough content to allow you to infer the real level of interest from the number of clicks. (Weight such input accordingly.)

Figure 6-12. By clicking "more," a reader may be indicating a higher level of interest in this review on Yahoo! Local. (Or a click may simply indicate that the excerpt wasn't generous enough—tread carefully.)

Reactions: Comments, photos, and media

One of the very best indicators of interest in an entity is the amount of conversation, rebuttal, and response that it generates. While we've cautioned against using activity alone as a reputation input (to the detriment of good quality indicators), we certainly don't want to imply that conversational activity has no place in your system. Far from it. If an item is a topic of conversation, the item should benefit from that interest.

The operators of some popular websites realize the value of rebuttal mechanisms and have formalized the ability to attach a response to a reputable entity. YouTube's video responses feature is an example (see Figure 6-13). As with any implicit input, however, be careful; the more your site's design shows how your system uses those associations, the more tempting it will be for members of your community to misuse them.

Brilliant Woman Solves All of California's Problems

Brilliant Woman Solves All of California's Problems
2:35

It's nice to see that Miss Teen South Carolina is trying to make a difference now that she's all grown up. On the merit of her amazing plan, this woman just took over for Ben Bernanke as Chairman of t (more)

Video Responses (18 Responses)

ORIGINAL Santa
Cruz Girl video
96,548 views
sowattv
★★★★★

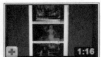

Obama Care + Miss
Teen South Car...
78 views
norriskickronpaul
no rating

The Big Picture -
Bright Eyes Cover
3,229 views
nosralkire
★★★★★

Erin Andrews video
peep show on ...
109,544 views
zennie62
★★★★★

Figure 6-13. The video responses on YouTube certainly indicate users' desire to be associated with popular videos. However, they may not actually indicate any logical thread of association.

Constraining Scope

When you're considering all the objects that your system will interact with, and all the interactions between those objects and your users, it's critical to take into account an idea that we have been reinforcing throughout this book: all reputation exists within a limited context, which is always specific to your audience and application. Try to determine the correct scope, or restrictive context, for the reputations in your system. Resist the temptation to lump all reputation-generating interactions into one score—the score will be diluted to the point of meaninglessness. The following example from Yahoo! makes our point perfectly.

Context Is King

This story tells how Yahoo! Sports unsuccessfully tried to integrate social media into its top-tier website. Even seasoned product managers and designers can fall into the trap of making the scope of an application's objects and interactions much broader than it should be.

Yahoo!'s Sports product managers believed that they should integrate user-generated content quickly *across their entire site*. They did an audit of their offering, and started to identify candidate objects, reputable entities, and some potential inputs.

The site had sports news articles, and the product team knew that it could tell a lot about what was in each article: the recognized team names, sport names, player names, cities, countries, and other important game-specific terms—in other words, the objects. It knew that users liked to respond to the articles by leaving text comments—the inputs.

It proposed an obvious intersection of the objects and the inputs: every comment on a news article would be a blog post, tagged with the keywords from the article, and optionally by user-generated tags, too. Whenever a tag appeared on another page, such as a different article mentioning the same city, the user's comment on the original article could be displayed.

At the same time, those comments would be displayed on the team- and player-detail pages for each tag attached to the comment. The product managers even had aspirations to surface comments on the sports portal, not just for the specific sport, but for all sports.

Seems very social, clever, and efficient, right?

No. It's a horrible design mistake. Consider the following detailed example from British football.

An article reports that a prominent player, Mike Brolly, who plays for the Chelsea team, has been injured and may not be able to play in an upcoming championship football match with Manchester United. Users comment on the article, and their comments are tagged with Manchester United, Chelsea, and Brolly.

Those comments would be surfaced—news feed–style—on the article page itself, the sports home page, the football home page, the team pages, and the player page. One post, six destination pages, each with a different context of use, different social norms, and different communities that they've attracted.

Nearly all these contexts are wrong, and the correct contexts aren't even considered:

- There is no all-of-Yahoo! Sports community context. At least, there's not one with any great cohesion—American tennis fans, for example, don't care about British football. When an American tennis fan is greeted on the Yahoo! Sports home page with comments about British football, they regard that about as highly as spam.

- The team pages are the wrong context for the comments because the fans of different teams don't mix. At a European football game, the fans for each team are kept on opposite sides of the field, divided by a chain link fence, with police wielding billy clubs alongside. The police are there to keep the fan communities apart.

  Online, the cross-posting of the comments on the team pages encourages conflict between fans of the opposing teams. Fans of opposing teams have completely opposite reactions to the injury of a star player, and intermixing those conversations would yield anti-social (if sometimes hilarious) results.

- The comments may or may not be relevant on the player page. It depends on whether the user actually responded to the article in the player-centric context—an input that this design didn't account for.

- Even the context of the article itself is poor, at least on Yahoo!. Its deal with the news feed companies, AP and Reuters, limits the amount of time an article may appear on the site to less than 10 days. Attaching comments (and reputation) to such transient objects tells users that their contributions don't matter in the long run. (See "The entity should persist for some length of time" on page 130.)

Comments, like reputation statements, are created in a context. In the case of comments, the context is a specific target audience for the message. Here are some possible *correct* contexts for cross-posting comments:

- Cross-post when the user has chosen a fan or team page and designated it to be a secondary destination for the comment. Your users will know, better than your system, what some legitimate related contexts are. (Though, of course, this can be abused; some decry the ascension of cross-posting to be a significant event in the devolution of the Usenet community.)

- Cross-post back to the commenter's user profile (with her permission, of course). Or allow her to post it to her personal blog, or send it to a friend—all of these approaches put an emphasis on the *user* as the context. If someone interests you enough for you to visit her user profile or blog, it's likely that you might be interested in what she has to say over on Yahoo! Sports.

- Cross-post automatically only into well-understood *and obviously related* contexts. For example, Yahoo! Sports has a completely different context that is still deeply relevant: a Fantasy Football league, where 12 to 16 people build their own virtual teams out of player-entities based on real-player stats.

    In this context—where the performance and day-to-day circumstances of real-life players affect the outcome of users' virtual teams—it might be very useful information to have cross-posted right onto a league's page.

 Don't assume that because it's safe and beneficial to cross-post in one direction, it's automatically safe to do so in the opposite direction. What if Yahoo! auto-posted comments made in a Fantasy Sports league over to the more staid Sports community site? That would be a huge mistake.

The terms of service for Fantasy Football are so much more lax than the terms of service for public-facing posts. These players swear and taunt and harass each other. A post such as "Ha, Chris— you and the Bay City Bombers are gonna suck my team's dust tomorrow while Brolly is home sobbing to his mommy!" clearly should not be automatically cross-posted to the main portal page.

Limit Scope: The Rule of Email

When thinking about your objects and user-generated inputs and how to combine them, remember the rule of email: you need a "subject" line and a "to" line (an addressee or a small number of addressees).

Tags for user-generated content act as subject identifiers, but not as addressees. Making your addressees as explicit as possible will encourage people to participate in many different ways.

Sharing content too widely discourages contributions and dilutes content quality and value.

Applying Scope to Yahoo! EuroSport Message Board Reputation

When Yahoo! EuroSport, based in the UK, wanted to revise its message board system to provide feedback on which discussions were the highest quality and incentives for users to contribute better content, it turned for help to reputation systems.

It was clear that the scope of reputation was different for each post and for all the posts in a thread and, as the American Yahoo! Sports team had initially assumed, that each user should have one posting karma: other users would flag the quality of a post and that would roll up to their all-sports-message-boards user reputation.

It did not take long for the product team to realize, however, that having Chelsea fans rate the posts of Manchester fans was folly: users would employ ratings to disagree with any comment by a fan of another team, not to honestly evaluate the quality of the posting.

The right answer, in this case, ended up being a tighter definition of scope for the context: rather than rewarding "all message boards" participation, or "everything within a particular sport," instead an effort was made to identify the most granular, cohesive units of community possible on the boards, and reward participation only within those narrow scopes.

Yahoo! EuroSport implemented a system of karma medallions (bronze, silver, and gold) rewarding both the quantity and quality of a user's participation on a *per-board* basis. This carried different repercussions for different sports on the boards.

Each UK football team has it's own dedicated message board, so theoretically an active contributor could earn medallions in any number of football contexts: a gold for participating on the Chelsea boards, a bronze for Manchester, etc.

 Bear in mind, however, that it's the community response to a contributor's posts that determines reputation accrual on the boards. We did not anticipate that many contributors would acquire reputation in many different team contexts; it's a rare personality that can freely intermix, and makes friends, among both sides of a rivalry. No, this system was intended to reward and identify good fans and encourage them to keep among themselves.

Tennis and Formula 1 Racing are different stories. Those sports have only one message board each, so contributors to those communities would be rewarded for participating in a *sport-wide* context, rather than for their team loyalty. Again, this is natural and healthy: different sports, different fans, different *contexts*.

Many users have only a single medallion, participating mostly on a single board, but some are disciplined and friendly enough to have bronze badges or better in each of multiple boards, and each badge is displayed in a little trophy case when you mouse over the user's avatar or examine the user's profile (see Figure 6-14).

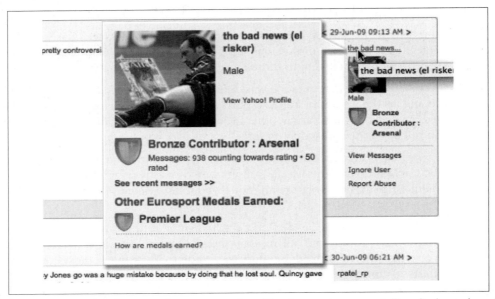

Figure 6-14. Each Yahoo! EuroSport message board has its own karma medallion display to keep reputation in a tightly bound context.

Generating Reputation: Selecting the Right Mechanisms

Now you've established your goals, listed your objects, categorized your inputs, and taken care to group the objects and inputs in appropriate contexts with appropriate scope. You're ready to create the reputation mechanisms that will help you reach your goals for the system.

Though it might be tempting to jump straight to designing the display of reputation to your users, we're going to delay that portion of the discussion until Chapter 7, where we dig into the reasons not to explicitly display some of your most valuable reputation information. Instead of focusing on presentation first, we're going to take a goal-centered approach.

The Heart of the Machine: Reputation Does Not Stand Alone

Probably the most important thing to remember when you're thinking about how to generate reputations is the context in which they will be used: your application. You might track bad-user behavior to save money in your customer care flow by prioritizing the worst cases of apparent abuse for quick review. You might also deemphasize cases involving users who are otherwise strong contributors to your bottom line. Likewise, if users evaluate your products and services with ratings and reviews, you will build significant machinery to gather users' claims and transform your application's output on the basis of their aggregated opinions.

For every reputation score you generate and display or use, expect at least 10 times as much development effort to adapt your product to accommodate it—including the user interface and coding to gather the events and transform them into reputation inputs, and all the locations that will be influenced by the aggregated results.

Common Reputation Generation Mechanisms and Patterns

Though all reputation is generated from custom-built models, we've identified certain common patterns in the course of designing reputation systems and observing systems that others have created. These few patterns are not at all comprehensive, and never could be. We provide them as a starting point for anyone whose application is similar to well-established patterns. We expand on each reputation generation pattern in the rest of this chapter.

What Comes in Is Not What Goes Out

Don't confuse the input types with the reputation generation patterns—what comes in is *not* always what goes out. In our example in the section "User Reviews with Karma" on page 75, the inputs were reviews and helpful votes, but one of the generated reputation outputs was a user quality karma score—which had no display symmetry with the inputs, since no user was asked to evaluate another user directly.

Roll-ups are often of a completely different claim type from their component parts, and sometimes, as with karma calculations, the target object of the reputation changes drastically from the evaluator's original target; for example, the author (a user-object) of a movie review gets some reputation from a helpful score given to the review that the author wrote about the movie-object.

This section focuses on calculating reputation, so the patterns don't describe the methods used to display any user's inputs back to the user. Typically, the decision to store users' actions and display them is a function of the application design—for example, users don't usually get access to a log of all of their clicks through a site, even if some of them are used in a reputation system. On the other hand, heavyweight operations, such as user-created reviews with multiple ratings and text fields, are normally at least readable by the creator, and often editable and/or deletable.

Generating personalization reputation

The desire to optimize their personal experience (see the section "Fulfillment incentives" on page 119) is often the initial driver for many users to go through the effort required to provide input to a reputation system. For example, if you tell an application what your favorite music is, it can customize your Internet radio station, making it worth the effort to teach the application your preferences. The effort required to do this also provides a wonderful side effect: it generates voluminous and accurate input into aggregated community ratings.

Personalization roll-ups are stored on a per-user basis and generally consist of preference information that is not shared publicly. Often these reputations are attached to very fine-grained contexts derived from metadata attached to the input targets and therefore can be surfaced, in aggregate, to the public (see Figure 6-15). For example, a song by the Foo Fighters may be listed in the "alternative" and "rock" music categories.

When a user marks the song as a favorite, the system would increase the personalization reputation for this user for three entities: "Foo Fighters," "alternative," and "rock." Personalization reputation can require a lot of storage, so plan accordingly, but the benefits to the user experience, and your product offering, may make it well worth the investment. See Table 6-1.

Table 6-1. Personalization reputation mechanisms

Reputation models	Vote to promote, favorites, flagging, simple ratings, and so on.
Inputs	Scalar.
Processes	Counters, accumulators.
Common uses	Site personalization and display.
	Input to predictive modeling.
	Personalized search ranking component.
Pros	A single click is as low-effort as user-generated content gets.
	Computation is trivial and speedy.
	Intended for personalization, these inputs can also be used to generate aggregated community ratings to facilitate nonpersonalized discovery of content.
Cons	It takes quite a few user inputs before personalization starts working properly, and until then the user experience can be unsatisfactory. (One method of bootstrapping is to create templates of typical user profiles and ask the user to select one to autopopulate a short list of targeted popular objects to rate quickly.)
	Data storage can be problematic. Potentially keeping a score for every target and category per user is very powerful but also very data intensive.

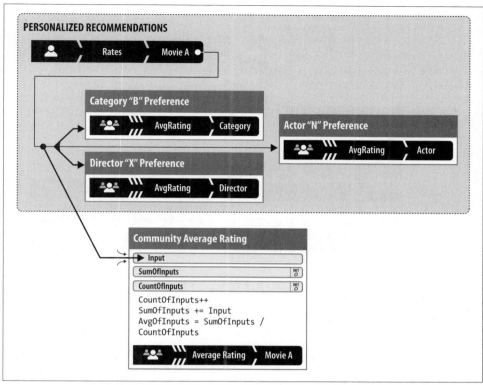

Figure 6-15. Netflix uses your movie preferences to generate recommendations for other movies that you might want to watch. It also averages your ratings against other movies you've rated in that category, or by that director, or….

Generating aggregated community ratings

Generating aggregated community ratings is the process of collecting normalized numerical ratings from multiple sources and merging them into a single score, often an average or a percentage of the total, as in Figure 6-16. See Table 6-2.

Table 6-2. Aggregated community ratings mechanisms

Reputation models	Vote to promote, favorites, flagging, simple ratings, and so on.
Inputs	Quantitative (normalized, scalar).
Processes	Counters, averages, and ratios.
Common uses	Aggregated rating display.
	Search ranking component.
	Quality ranking for moderation .
Pros	A single click is as low-effort as user-generated content gets.
	Computation is trivial and speedy.

Cons	Too many targets can cause low liquidity.
	Low liquidity limits accuracy and value of the aggregate score. See "Liquidity: You Won't Get Enough Input" on page 58.
	Danger exists of using the wrong scalar model. See "Bias, Freshness, and Decay" on page 60.

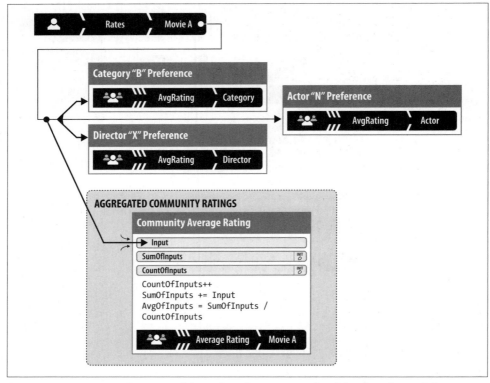

Figure 6-16. Recommendations work best when they're personalized, but how do you help someone who hasn't yet stated any preferences? You average the opinions of those who have.

Ranking large target sets (preference orders). One specific form of aggregate community ratings requires special mechanisms to get useful results: when an application needs to rank a large data set of objects completely and only a small number of evaluations can be expected from users. For example, a special mechanism would be required to rank the current year's players in each sports league of an annual fantasy sports draft. Hundreds of players would be involved, and there would be no reasonable way that each individual user could evaluate each pair against the others. Even rating one pair per second would take many times longer than the available time before the draft. The same is true for community-judged contests in which thousands of users submit content. Letting users rate randomly selected objects on a percentage or star scale doesn't help at all. (See "Bias, Freshness, and Decay" on page 60.)

This kind of ranking is called preference ordering. When this kind of ranking takes place online, users evaluate successively generated pairs of objects and choose the most appropriate one in each pair. Each participant goes through the process a small number of times, typically less than 10.

The secret sauce is in selecting the pairings. At first, the ranking engine looks for pairs that it knows nothing about, but over time it begins to select pairings that help users sort similarly ranked objects. It also generates pairs to determine whether the user's evaluations are consistent or not. Consistency is good for the system, because it indicates reliability; if a users evaluations fluctuate wildly or don't have a consistent pattern, this indicates a pattern of abuse or manipulation of the ranking.

The algorithms for this approach are beyond the scope of this book, but if you are interested, you can find out more in Appendix B. This mechanism is complex and requires expertise in statistics to build, so if a reputation model requires this functionality, we recommend using an existing platform as a model.

Generating participation points

Participation points are typically a kind of karma in which users accumulate varying amounts of publicly displayable points for taking various actions in an application. Many people see these points as a strong incentive to drive participation and the creation of content. But remember, using points as the only motivation for user actions can push out desirable contributions in favor of lower-quality content that users can submit quickly and easily (see "First-mover effects" on page 63). Also see "Leaderboards Considered Harmful" on page 192 for a discussion of the challenges associated with competitive displays of participation points.

Participation points karma is a good example of a pattern in which the inputs (various, often trivial, user actions) don't match the process of reputation generation (accumulating weighted point values) or the output (named levels or raw score); see Tables 6-3 and 6-4.

Table 6-3. ShareTV.org is one of many web applications that uses participation points karma as incentive for users to add content

Activity	Point award	Maximum/time
First participation	+10	+10
Log in	+1	+1 per day
Rate show	+1	+15 per day
Create avatar	+5	+5
Add show or character to profile	+1	+25
Add friend	+1	+20
Be friended	+1	+50
Give best answer	+3	+3 per question

Activity	Point award	Maximum/time
Have a review voted helpful	+1	+5 per review
Upload a character image	+3	+5 per show
Upload a show image	+5	+5 per show
Add show description	+3	+3 per show

Table 6-4. Participation points karma mechanisms

Reputation models	Points
Inputs	Raw point value (this type of input is risky if disparate applications provide the input; out-of-range values can do significant social damage to your community).
	An action-type index value for a table lookup of points (this type of input is safer; the points table stays with the model, where it is easier to limit damage and track data trends).
Processes	(Weighted) accumulator.
Common uses	Motivation for users to create content.
	Ranking in leaderboards to engage the most active users.
	Rewards for specific desirable actions.
	Corporate use: identification of influencers or abusers for extended support or moderation.
	In combination with quality karma in creating robust karma (see "Robust karma" on page 73).
Pros	Setup is easy.
	Incentive is easy for users to understand.
	Computation is trivial and speedy.
	Certain classes of users respond positively and voraciously to this type of incentive. See "Egocentric incentives" on page 118.
Cons	Getting the points-per-action formulation right is an ongoing process, while users continually look for the sweet spot of minimum level of effort for maximum point gain. The correct formulation takes into account the effort required as well as the value of the behavior. See "Egocentric incentives" on page 118.
	Points are a discouragement to many users with altruistic motivations. See "Altruistic or sharing incentives" on page 113 and "Leaderboards Considered Harmful" on page 192.

Points as currency. Point systems are increasingly being used as game currencies. Social games offered by developers such as Zynga generate participation points that users can spend on special benefits in the game, such as unique items or power-ups that improve the experience of the game. (See Figure 6-17.) Such systems have exploded with the introduction of the ability to purchase the points for real money.

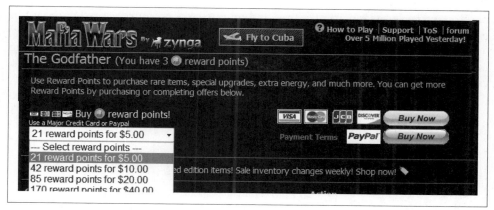

Figure 6-17. Many social games, such as Mafia Wars by Zynga, earn revenue by selling points. These points can be used to accelerate game progress or to purchase vanity items.

If you consider any points-as-currency scheme, keep in mind that because the points reflect (and may even be exchangeable for) real money, such schemes place the motivations for using your application further from altruism and more in the range of a commercial driver.

Even if you don't officially offer the points for sale and your application allows users to spend them only on virtual items in the game, a commercial market may still arise for them. A good historical example of this kind of aftermarket is the sale of game characters for popular online multiplayer games, such as *World of Warcraft*. Character levels in a game represent participation or experience points, which in turn represent real investments of time and/or money. For more than a decade, people have been power-leveling game characters and selling them on eBay for thousands of dollars.

We recommend against turning reputation points into a currency of any kind unless your application is a game and it is central to your business goals. More discussion of online economies and how they interact with reputation systems is beyond the scope of this book, but an ever-increasing amount of literature on the topic of real-money trading (RMT) is readily available on the Internet.

Generating compound community claims

Compound community claims reflect multiple separate, but related, aggregated claims about a single target and include patterns such as reviews and rated message board posts. But the power of attaching compound inputs of different types from multiple sources lets users understand multiple facets of an object's reputation.

For example, ConsumerReports.org generates two sets of reputation for objects: the scores generated as a result of the tests and criteria set forth in the labs, and the average user ratings and comments provided by customers on the website. (See Figure 6-18.) These scores can be displayed side by side to allow the site's users to evaluate a product both on numerous standard measures and on untested and unmeasured criteria. For example, user comments on front-loading clothes washers often mention odors, because former users of top-loading washers don't necessarily know that a front-loading machine needs to be hand-dried after every load. This kind of subtle feedback can't be captured in strictly quantitative measures.

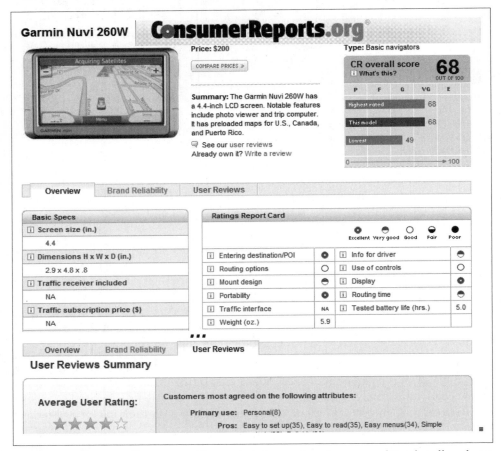

Figure 6-18. Consumer Reports combines ratings from external sources, editorial staff, and user reviews to provide a rich reputation page for products and services.

Though compound community claims can be built from diverse inputs from multiple sources, the ratings-and-reviews pattern is well established and deserves special comment here (see Table 6-5). Asking a user to create a multipart review is a very heavyweight activity—it takes time to compose a thoughtful contribution. Users' time is scarce, and research at Yahoo! and elsewhere has shown that users often abandon the process if extra steps are required, such as logging in, registration for new users, or multiple screens of input.

Even if it's necessary for business reasons, these barriers to entry will significantly increase the abandon rate for your review creation process. People need a good reason to take time out of their day to create a complex review. Be sure to understand your model (see the section "Incentives for User Participation, Quality, and Moderation" on page 111) and the effects it may have on the tone and quality of your content. For an example of the effects of incentive on compound community claims, see "Friendship incentives" on page 114.

Table 6-5. Compound community claims mechanisms

Reputation models	Ratings-and-reviews, eBay merchant feedback, and so on.
Inputs	All types from multiple sources and source types, as long as they all have the same target.
Processes	All appropriate process types apply; every compound community claim is custom built.
Common uses	User-created object reviews.
	Editor-based roll-ups, such as movie reviews by media critics.
	Side-by-side combinations of user, process, and editorial claims.
Pros	This type of input is flexible; any number of claims can be kept together.
	This type of input provides easy global access; all the claims have the same target. If you know the target ID, you can get all reputations with a single call.
	Some standard formats for this type of input—for example, the ratings-and-reviews format—are well understood by users.
Cons	If a user is explicitly asked to create too many inputs, incentive can become a serious impediment to getting a critical mass of contributions on the site.
	Straying too far from familiar formatting, either for input or output, can create confusion and user fatigue.
	There is some tension between format familiarity and choosing the correct input scale. See "Good Inputs" on page 135.

Generating inferred karma

What happens when you want to make a value judgment about a user who's new to your application? Is there an alternative to the general axiom that "no participation equals no trust"? In many scenarios, you need an inferred reputation score—a lower-confidence number that can be used to help make low-risk decisions about a user's trustworthiness until she can establish an application-specific karma score. (See Figure 6-19.)

In a web application, proxy reputations may be available even for users who have never created an object, posted a comment, or clicked a single thumb-up. The user's browser possesses session cookies that can hold simple activity counters even for logged-out users; the user is connected through an IP address that can have a reputation of its own (if it was recently or repeatedly used by a known abuser); and finally the user may have an active history with a related product that could be considered in a proxy reputation.

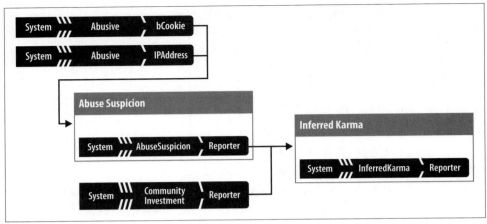

Figure 6-19. If a user comes to your application "cold" (with no prior history of interacting with it), you may be able to infer much information about him from external contexts.

Remembering that the best karma is positive karma (see the next section "Practitioner's Tips: Negative Public Karma" on page 161), when an otherwise unknown user evaluates an object in your system and you want to weight the user's input, you can use the inferences from weak reputations to boost the user's reputation from 0 to a reasonable fraction (for example, up to 25%) of the maximum value.

A weak karma score should be used only temporarily while a user is establishing robust karma, and, because it is a weak indicator, it should provide a diminishing share of the eventual, final score. (The share of karma provided by inferred karma should diminish as more trustworthy inputs become available to replace it.) One weighting method is to make the inferred share a bonus on top of the total score (the total can exceed 100%) and then clamp the value to 100% at the end. See Table 6-6.

Table 6-6. Inferred karma mechanisms

Reputation models	Models are always custom; inferred karma is known to be part of the models in the following applications:
	• Yahoo! Answers and uses inferred karma to help evaluate contributions by unknown users when their posts are flagged as abusive by other users; see the case study in Chapter 10.
	• WikiAnswers.com uses inferred karma to limit access to potentially abusive actions, such as erasing the contributions of other users.
Inputs	Application external values; examples include the following:
	• User account longevity
	• IP address abuse score
	• Browser cookie activity counter or help-disabled flag
	• External trusted karma score
Processes	Custom mixer
Common uses	Partial karma substitute: separating the partially known from the complete strangers

	Help system display, giving unknown users extra navigation help
	Lockout of potentially abused features, such as content editing, until the user has demonstrated familiarity with the application and lack of hostility to it
	Deciding when to route new contributions to customer care for moderation
Pros	Allows for a significantly lower barrier for some user contributions than otherwise possible, for example, not requiring registration or login.
	Provides for corporate (internal use) karma. No user knows this score, and the site operator can change the application's calculation method freely as the situation evolves and new proxy reputations become available.
	Helps render your application impervious to accidental damage caused by drive-by users.
Cons	Inferred karma is, by construction, unreliable. For example, since people can share an IP address over time without knowing it or each other, including it in a reputation can undervalue an otherwise excellent user by accident. However, though it might be tempting for that reason to remove IP reputation from the model, IP address is the strongest indicator of *bad* users; such users don't usually go to the trouble of getting a new IP address whenever they want to attack your site.
	Inferred karma can be expensive to generate. How often do you want to update the supporting reputations, such as IP or cookie reputation? It would be too expensive to update them at very single HTTP roundtrip, so smart design is required.
	Inferred karma is weak. Don't trust it alone for any legally or socially significant actions.

Practitioner's Tips: Negative Public Karma

Because an underlying karma score is a number, product managers often misunderstand the interaction between numerical values and online identity. The thinking goes something like this:

- In our application context, the user's value will be represented by a single karma, which is a numerical value.
- There are good, trustworthy users and bad, untrustworthy users, and everyone would like to know which is which, so we will display their karma.
- We should represent good actions as positive numbers and bad actions as negative, and we'll add them up to make karma.
- Good users will have high positive scores (and other users will interact with them), and bad users will have low negative scores (and other users will avoid them).

This thinking—though seemingly intuitive—is impoverished, and is wrong in at least two important ways:

- There can be no negative public karma—at least for establishing the trustworthiness of active users. A bad enough public score will simply lead to that user's abandoning the account and starting a new one, a process we call karma bankruptcy. This setup defeats the primary goal of karma—to publicly identify bad actors. Assuming that a karma starts at zero for a brand-new user that an application has no information about, it can never go *below* zero, since karma bankruptcy resets it. Just look at the record of eBay sellers with more than three red stars. You'll see that most haven't sold anything in months or years, either because the sellers quit or they're now doing business under different account names.

- It's not a good idea to combine positive and negative inputs in a single public karma score. Say you encounter a user with 75 karma points and another with 69 karma points. Who is more trustworthy? You can't tell; maybe the first user used to have hundreds of good points but recently accumulated a lot of negative ones, while the second user has never received a negative point at all. If you must have public negative reputation, handle it as a separate score (as in the eBay seller feedback pattern).

Even eBay, with the most well-known example of public negative karma, doesn't represent how untrustworthy an actual seller might be; it only gives buyers reasons to take specific actions to protect themselves. In general, avoid negative public karma. If you really want to know who the bad guys are, keep the score separate and restrict it to internal use by moderation staff.

The Dollhouse Mafia, or "Don't Display Negative Karma"

The Sims Online was a multiplayer version of the popular Sims games by Electronic Arts and Maxis in which the user controlled an animated character in a virtual world with houses, furniture, games, virtual currency (called Simoleans), rental property, and social activities. You could call it playing dollhouse online.

One of the features that supported user socialization in the game was the ability to declare that another user was a trusted friend. The feature involved a graphical display that showed the faces of users who had declared you trustworthy outlined in green, attached in a hub-and-spoke pattern to your face in the center.

People checked each other's hubs for help in deciding whether to take certain in-game actions, such as becoming roommates in a house. Decisions like these are costly for a new user—the ramifications of the decision stick with a newbie for a long time, and "backing out" of a bad decision is not an easy thing to do. The hub was a useful decision-making device for these purposes.

That feature was fine as far as it went, but unlike other social networks, *The Sims Online* allowed users to declare other users *untrustworthy*, too. The face of an untrustworthy user appeared circled in bright red among all the trustworthy faces in a user's hub.

It didn't take long for a group calling itself the Sims Mafia to figure out how to use this mechanism to shake down new users when they arrived in the game. The dialog would go something like this:

"Hi! I see from your hub that you're new to the area. Give me all your Simoleans or my friends and I will make it impossible to rent a house."

"What are you talking about?"

"I'm a member of the Sims Mafia, and we will all mark you as untrustworthy, turning your hub solid red (with no more room for green), and no one will play with you. You have five minutes to comply. If you think I'm kidding, look at your hub—three of us have already marked you red. Don't worry, we'll turn it green when you pay...."

If you think this is a fun game, think again. A typical response to this shakedown was for the user to decide that the game wasn't worth $10 a month. Playing dollhouse doesn't usually involve gangsters. It's hard to estimate the final cost to EA & Maxis for such a simple design decision, in terms of lost users, abandoned accounts, and cancelled subscriptions.

In your own community and application design, think twice about overtly displaying negative reputation, or putting such direct means in the hands of the community to *affect* other's reputations. You risk enabling your own mafias to flourish.

Draw Your Diagram

With your goals, objects, inputs, and reputation patterns in hand, you can draw a draft reputation model diagram and sketch out the flows in enough detail to generate the following questions: what data will I need to formulate these reputation scores correctly?; how will I collect the claims and transform them into inputs?; which of those inputs will need to be reversible, and which will be disposable?

If you're using this book as a guide, try sketching out a model now, before you consider creating screen mock-ups. One approach we've often found helpful is to start on the right side of the diagram—with the reputations you want to generate—and work your way back to the inputs. Don't worry about the calculations at first; just draw a process box with the name of the reputation inside and a short note on the general nature of the formulation, such as aggregated acting average or community player rank.

Once you've drawn the boxes, connect them with arrows where appropriate. Then consider what inputs go into which boxes, and don't forget that the arrows can split and merge as needed.

Then, after you have a good rough diagram, start to dive into the details with your development team. Many mathematical and performance-related details will affect your reputation model design. We've found that reputation systems diagrams make excellent requirements documentation and make it easier to generate the technical specification, while also making the overall design accessible to nonengineers.

Of course, your application will consist of displaying or using the reputations you've diagrammed (Chapters 7 and 8). Project engineers, architects, and operational team members may want to review Chapter 9 first, as it completes the schedule focused, development-cycle view of any reputation project.

CHAPTER 7

Displaying Reputation

In Chapter 6, we described how to create a custom reputation model by identifying the objects in your application, selecting appropriate inputs, and developing the processes you'll need to generate your reputations. But your work doesn't end there. Far from it. Now you have decisions to make about how to use the reputations that your system is tabulating.

In this chapter and the next, we discuss the many options for using reputation to improve the user experience of your site, enrich content quality, and provide incentives for your users to become better, more active participants. In this chapter specifically, we discuss options for displaying reputation, to whom to display it, how to display it, and help you decide which display forms are right for your application.

How to Use a Reputation: Three Questions

For each reputation you are creating to display or use, you should ask each of these questions before proceeding:

1. Who will be able to see the reputation?
   - Is it *personal*—hidden from other users but visible to the reputation holder?
   - Is it *public*—displayed to friends or strangers, or visible to search engines?
   - Is it *corporate*—limited to internal use—for improving the site or discreetly recognizing outliers in ways that may not be visible to the community?
2. How will the reputation be used to modify your site's output?
   - Will you use the reputation to *filter* the lowest- or highest-quality items in a set?
   - Will you use the reputation to *sort* or *rank* items?
   - And/or will this score be used to make other decisions about how the site flows or your business operates?
3. Is this reputation for a *content* item or a *person*? Each requires a fundamentally different approach.

Though you may choose multiple answers from this list for each reputation, try to keep it simple at first: don't try to do too much with a single reputation. Confounding the purposes of a reputation—by, for example, surfacing participation points in a public karma score—can encourage undesirable user behavior and may even backfire by discouraging participation. Read Chapters 7 and 8 completely for a solid understanding of the issues related to overloading a single reputation.

 Resist the temptation to treat a single reputation score as the cure-all for your user-generated content incentive ills. Remember the lesson of the FICO score in "FICO: A Study in Global Reputation and Its Challenges" on page 10.

Who Will See a Reputation?

So far, the reputation you're calculating is little more than a cold numerical score rolled up from the aggregate actions of people interacting with your site. You've carefully determined the scope of the reputation, chosen the inputs that contribute to it, and thought at length about the effect that you want the reputation to generate in the community.

Now you must decide whether it makes sense to display the reputation on your site at all and, if so, to whom. How you display reputation information—how much and how prominently—will influence the actions that users take on your site, their trust in your site and one another, and their long-term satisfaction with your community.

To Show or Not to Show?

Compelling reasons exist to keep reputations hidden from users. In fact, in some circumstances, you may want to obscure the fact that you're tracking them at all. It may sound rather Machiavellian, but the truth of the matter is this: a community under public scrutiny behaves differently (and, in many ways, less honestly) than one in blissful ignorance.

Several trade-offs are involved. Displaying reputations takes up significant page real estate, requires user interface design and testing, and can compete with your content for the user's attention and understanding. Quickly, show Digg.com (Figure 7-1) to 10 of your friends and ask them, "What kind of site is this? News? Entertainment? Community?" Odds are good that at least a few of them will answer: "This appears to be some sort of *contest*."

The impression that Digg makes is not a bad thing; it just demonstrates that Digg made a conscious decision to display content reputation prominently. In fact, the display of reputation is the central interaction mechanism on the site. It's practically impossible to interact with Digg, or get any use out of it, without some understanding of how community voting affects the selection and display of popular items on the site. (Digg

Figure 7-1. Digg's site design puts overt reputation scores front and center.

is perhaps the most well-known example of a site that employs the Vote-to-Promote pattern. See Chapter 6.)

Juxtapose Digg's approach with that of Flickr. The popular photo-sharing and discovery service also makes use of reputation to surface quality content, but it does not display explicit reputations, rather it prominently displays items that achieve a certain reputation and that can be browsed (daily, weekly, or monthly) in the "Explore" gallery (at *http://www.flickr.com/explore*); see Figure 7-2. The result is a very consistent and impressive display of high-quality photos with very little indication of how those photos were selected.

Flickr's interestingness algorithm determines which photos make it into the "Explore" gallery and which don't. The same algorithm lets users sort their own photos by interestingness.

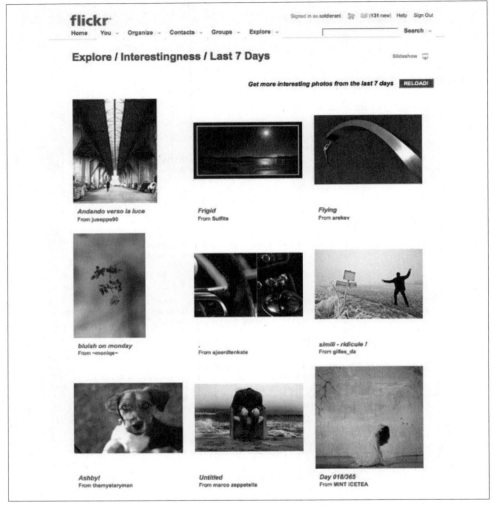

Figure 7-2. Flickr's "Explore" gallery is also based on reputation, but you never see a score associated with a photo.

Digg and Flickr represent two very different approaches to reputation display, but the results are very much the same. Theoretically, you can always glance at the front page of Digg or Flickr's "Explore" gallery to see where the good stuff is—what people are watching, commenting on, or interacting with the most on the site.

How do you decide whether to display reputations on your site? And how prominently? Generally, follow the rule of least disclosure: do not display a reputation that doesn't add specific value to the objects being evaluated.

Likewise, don't bother asking users for reputation input (see Chapter 6) that you'll never use; you'll confuse users and encourage undesired patterns of "invented significance," including abuse.

 Avoid collecting reputation for display only. Orkut allowed users to rate other users explicitly on iconic criteria like "trusty," "cool," and "sexy" for no use other than display. This use of reputation caused all kinds of social backlash.

People were either disappointed that they weren't rated "cool" by more people, or they were creeped out by people of the same gender calling them sexy. Eventually, Orkut removed the display of individual friends' ratings and kept only the aggregate scores.

Irrelevant reputations are meaningless and consume valuable resources. If you don't have a relevant use for a reputation, beware of sticking yourself later with the tough choice of either awkwardly removing a failed feature or having to support it as a costly legacy element.

Personal Reputations: For the Owner's Eyes Only

Are you tracking a reputation primarily to keep users informed about how well they or their creations are performing in the community? Consider displaying that reputation only to its owner, as a personal communication between site and user.

Personal Reputation Is Not Private

We use the word *personal* very deliberately here, distinguishing it from *private*. No reputation system is truly private; at least one other party (typically the site operator) will almost always have access to the actions, inputs, and roll-ups that formulate a user's score. In fact, you may store internally used reputations (see "Corporate Reputations Are Internal Use Only: Keep Them Hush-hush" on page 172) that are largely based on the exact same data.

In other words, reputations may be displayed in a personal context, but that's no guarantee that they're private. As a service provider, you should acknowledge that distinction and account for it in your terms of service.

Personal reputations are used extensively for applications such as social bookmarking, lists of favorites, training recommendation systems, sorting and filtering news feeds, providing content quality and feedback, fine-grained experience point tracking, and other performance metrics. Most of the same user interface patterns for displaying public reputation apply to personal ones, too, but take care to ensure that each user knows when her reputations will and will not be displayed to others.

Keep a reputation personal when its owner gains some significant benefit from it—when it either improves his experience of the site (that is, personalizes it) or provides a tool for increasing self-satisfaction. For example, by selecting news stories about various sports teams over time, a user might generate a geographic region reputation that can be used to target advertising displayed to the user. Clearly that reputation should not be public information, but it might be surfaced privately so that the user can correct it—"I'm a fan of Northern California sports teams, but I'm going to MIT and I really want ads for electronics stores in the Boston area."

Google Analytics (see Figure 7-3) is an example of rich personal reputation information. It provides detailed information about the performance of your website, across a known range of score types, and it is available only to you, the site owner (or others to whom you grant access). While that information is invaluable to you in gauging the response of a community (in this case, the entire Web) to your content, exposing it to everyone would offer very little practical benefit. In fact, it would be a horrible idea.

Figure 7-3. Google's Analytics interface shows information that is clearly best kept between you and Google. It's personal.

Personal and Public Reputations Combined

Some reputation display patterns provide both a personal and a public representation. In the named-levels display pattern "Named levels" on page 188 the personal representation of the reputation score often is numeric, showing the exact score, whereas the public representation obscures exactly where in the level the target's score actually is. Online games usually report only the level to other users and the exact experience points to the player.

Public Reputations: Widely Visible

When the whole community would benefit from knowing the reputations of either people or content, consider displaying public reputations. Public reputations may be displayed to everyone in the community or only to users who are members of a group, are connected through a social network, or have achieved status as senior, trusted members of the community by surpassing some reputation threshold.

When is it a good idea to display public reputations? Remember our original definition: reputation is *information used to make a value judgment about a person or an object in a given context for a specific time.* Consider the following questions:

- What decisions am I asking users to make on my site?
  - Compare items' quality against one another?
  - Determine someone's credibility or trustworthiness?
  - Decide whether something's worth reading?
- Am I asking users to make time-sensitive decisions or decisions in which additional, well-placed information would save them heartache?
- Can I present the reputation in a way that is fair and comprehensible and doesn't overwhelm the presentation of the content?

Public reputations are used for hundreds of purposes on the Web: to compare items in a list on the basis of community member feedback, evaluate particular targets for online transaction trustworthiness, filter and display top-rated message board posts, rank the best local Indonesian restaurants, show today's gallery of the most interesting photos, to display leaderboards of the top-scoring reputation targets, and much more.

Over time, public reputations can evolve to represent your community's understanding of its own zeitgeist. And there's the rub: depending on how you use public reputation, you can alienate users who aren't part of the in crowd. For example, Yelp is all about public ratings and reviews of local restaurants, but it isn't used extensively by people over 50. Most of the reviews are written by twentysomethings (most "Yelpers" are between the ages of 26 and 35) who seem to be mostly interested in a restaurant's potential as a dating hangout.

Public reputations are helpful for allowing users to compare like items. Public karma reputations also serve as an effective extension of a person's identity.

Corporate Reputations Are Internal Use Only: Keep Them Hush-hush

Almost every website with a large volume of user-generated content is using hidden reputation scores internally—as a means of tracking exactly who is saying what about a content item or another user:

- When users click the Spam button in a webmail application, they contribute to a database of IP addresses for abusive mail servers.
- Web crawlers constantly scan the Web to examine what sites link to what other sites and to calculate a hidden score such as Google's PageRank.
- Yahoo! Answers tracks corporate reputation for users who are particularly good at identifying bad content and gives them more power to hide bad content quickly.

And internally used reputation scores need not always be acted on immediately by scripts or bots; they can also be a very helpful tool for human decision making. Community managers often use corporate reputation reports on the most active, connected, and highest-quality user contributions and creators. They might use the information to generate high-quality best-of galleries to promote a site, or they might invite top contributors to participate in early testing of new designs, products, or features. Finally, user actions often are aggregated into reputations for behavioral targeting of advertising, customer care planning and budgeting, product feature needs assessment, and even legal compliance.

 Even if your site wouldn't benefit from any public or personal form of reputation display, you probably need to track corporate (internal) reputation scores to understand what your users are doing, tune your site development, and optimize support costs.

How Will You Use Reputation to Modify Your Site's Output?

After deciding which reputation scores to display to whom, you'll need to decide how to use the scores to change the way your application works. It's easy to think that all you need to do is display a few stars here or a few points there—but if you stopped there, you wouldn't capture the most value from reputation.

To use reputation without displaying it, focus on how to identify the outlying reputable entities (users and content) to improve the quantity and quality of interaction on your site. When you're selecting patterns, review the goals you set for your system (see Chapter 5). If you're primarily concerned about identifying abusive behavior, focus on filtering and decisions. If you're going to display a lot of public reputation over many entities, focus on ranking and sorting to help users explore your content.

We'll cover patterns for making use of the reputation of entities in Chapter 8.

Reputation Filtering

At its simplest, filtering consists of sorting by one or more reputation dimensions and looking only at the first or last entries in the list to identify the highest and lowest scoring entities for further, even automatic, action. In reality, many reputations used for filtering are often made of more numerous and complex inputs than reputations built for public display in rankings or sorted lists.

Consider Flickr's interestingness filter reputation: it is corporate (used internally and not displayed to any user), it is complex (made up of many inputs: views, favorites, comments, and more), and it is used to automatically and continuously generate a public gallery. But the score is never displayed to users; you cannot query a photo to get its interestingness score. Perhaps the easiest way to think about a filter reputation is that, if it is not ever displayed to users, they don't have to understand what it's made up of. If users can see a reputation indicator, they'll want to know what it means and how it's calculated.

 In fact, algorithm speculation has become almost a spectator sport on the Web. Name any popular reputation-heavy site (Digg, Amazon, YouTube, and many others), and odds are good that you'll find any number of threads or forums dedicated to figuring out exactly how its algorithm works.

The reputation usage patterns related to filtering are: user threshold, public gallery, guided learning, recommendations, bookmarks/favorites, similar items, content by author karma, and friends filtering.

Reputation Ranking and Sorting

By far the most common displays of reputation are in the form of explicit lists of reputable entities, such as the restaurants in the local neighborhood with the highest average overall rating, or the list of players with the highest Elo ranks for chess or even which keyword search marketing terms are generating the most clicks per dollar spent.

Typically, the reputation score is used alone or in conjunction with other metadata filters, such as geographic location, to make it easy for users to sort between multiple entities at a glance. For example, to list top-rated hotels in a five mile radius of a zip code, one would combine the distance and reputation into a rank-score before displaying the list.

The primary purpose of allowing such sorting is to enable users to select an item to examine in more detail. Note that the reputation score need not be displayed to allow sorting or ranking entities. For example, to avoid encouraging abuse, public search engines typically hide search ranking scores.

 Any time you sort or rank reputable entities, you're helping users to sort data into the good and the bad. This is creating value—and wherever value exists, people will be interested in capturing as much of it as possible using whatever means are available. The more successful your reputation ranking is, the more value it creates, and the more some people will want to game your design for their own benefit.

The lesson is a reputation-based display that may work well when a community is small may need to be modified over time, as it becomes more successful. This is a success paradox: the more popular your reputation system becomes, the more likely you'll see reputation abuse. Keep an eye out for use patterns that don't contribute to your business and community goals.

Recommender systems use reputation to make suggestions about similarities between user tastes ("People who like the same things as you do you also like…") and discover taste similarities between items ("People who liked this item also like…"). They use reputation in the form of confidence scores and typically display multiple entities in rank order when making recommendations. When the user selects a suggested item, that selection itself is also entered in the reputation system to further improve the quality of future results.

The specific reputation usage patterns related to ranking and sorting are quality-sort search results, leaderboards, related items, recommendations, search relevance (such as Google's PageRank), corporate community health metrics, and advertising performance metrics.

Reputation Decisions

This entire class of use patterns often is overlooked because it typically happens behind the scenes, out of users' sight. Though you may not be aware of it, more hidden decisions are made on the basis of reputation than are actually reflected directly to users, either with filtering or ranking.

Billions of email messages are processed daily across the world. ISPs secretly track the IP addresses of the senders; they use this reputation to decide whether the item should be dropped, put in a bulk folder, or sent on to another content-based reputation check before being delivered to your inbox. This is only one example of many patterns used by Web 2.0 site operators around the world to manage user-generated content without exposing the scores or the methods for their calculations. When used for abuse mitigation, the value of the reputation score can be directly correlated with cost savings from increased efficiency in customer care and community management, as well as in hardware and other operational costs. Each year, the IP reputation system for Yahoo! Mail saves tens of millions of dollars in real costs for servers, storage, and overhead.

When a reputation score is complex, such as karma (see the next section), it may be suitable for public display as a standalone score so that others can make specific, context-sensitive decisions. eBay's feedback and other reputation scores are a good example of a publicly shared karma. Since the transactions for items are often one of a kind, content filtering and ranking don't provide enough information for anyone to make a decision about whether to trust the seller or buyer.

Of course, some reputation is nonnumeric and can't be ranked at all—for example, comments, reviews, video responses, and personal metadata associated with source users who evaluate your entities. These forms of input must be displayed so that users can interpret the input directly. For instance, a 20-year-old single woman in Los Angeles who is looking for a new sweater might want to discount the ratings given by a 50-year-old married man living in Alaska. Nonnumeric reputation often provides just enough additional context for people to make more informed judgments about entities.

Here are the specific reputation usage patterns related to decisions: critical threshold, automatic rejection, flag for moderation, flag for promotion, and reviews and comments.

Content Reputation Is Very Different from Karma

Reputable entity refers to everything in a database, including users and content items, with one or more reputations attached to it. All kinds of reputation score types and all kinds of displays and use patterns might seem equally valid for content reputation and karma, but usually they're not. To highlight the differences between content reputation and karma, we've categorized them by the ways in which they're typically calculated:

Simple reputation
> Simple reputation is any reputation score that is generated directly by user evaluation of a reputable entity and that is subject to an elementary aggregation calculation, such as simple average. For example, simple reputation is used on most ratings-and-reviews sites. Simple reputation is direct and easy to understand.

Complex reputation
> Complex reputation is a score aggregated from multiple evaluations, including evaluations of different but related targets, calculated with an opaque method. Email IP spammer, Google PageRank, and eBay feedback reputations are examples of complex reputation. It's an indirect evaluation, and users may not understand how it was calculated, even if the score is displayed.

Content Reputation

Content reputation scores may be simple or complex. The simpler the score is—that is, the more it directly reflects the opinions or values of users—the more ways you can consider using and presenting it. You can use them for filters, sorting, ranking, and in many kinds of corporate and personalization applications. On most sites, content reputation does the heavy lifting of helping you to find the best and worst items for appropriate attention.

 When displaying content reputation, avoid putting too many different scores of different types on a page. For example, on the Yahoo! TV episode page, a user can give an overall star rating to a TV program and a thumb vote on an individual episode of the program. Examination of the data showed that many visitors to the page clicked the thumb icons when they meant to rate the entire show, not just an episode.

Karma

Content reputation is about *things*—typically inanimate objects without emotions or the ability to directly respond in any way to its reputation.

But karma represents the reputation of users, and users are *people*. They are alive, they have feelings, and they are the engine that powers your site. Karma is significantly more personal and therefore sensitive and meaningful. If a manufacturer gets a single bad product review on a website, it probably won't even notice. But if a user gets a bad rating from a friend—or feels slighted or alienated by the way your karma system works—she might abandon an identity that has become valuable to your business. Worse yet, she might abandon your site altogether and take her content with her. (Worst of all, she might take others with her.)

Take extreme care in creating a karma system. User reputation on the Web has undergone many experiments, and the primary lesson from that research is that karma should be a complex reputation and it should be displayed rarely.

Karma is complex, built of indirect inputs

Sometimes making things as simple and explicit as possible is the wrong choice for reputation:

- Rating a user directly should be avoided. Typical implementations require a user to click only once to rate another user and are therefore prone to abuse. When direct evaluation karma models are combined with the common practice of stream-lining user registration processes (on many sites *opening a new account* is an easier operation than changing the password on an existing account), they get out of hand quickly. See the example of Orkut in "Numbered levels" on page 186.

- Asking people to evaluate others directly is socially awkward. Don't put users in the position of lying about their friends.
- Using multiple inputs presents a broader picture of the target user's value.
- Economics research into "revealed preference," or what people actually do, as opposed to what they say, indicates that actions provide a more accurate picture of value than elicited ratings.

Karma calculations are often opaque

Karma calculations may be opaque because the score is valuable as status, has revenue potential, and/or unlocks privileged application features.

Display karma sparingly

There are several important things to consider when displaying karma to the public:

- Publicly displayed karma should be rare because, as with content reputation, users are easily confused by the display of many reputations on the same page or within the same context.
- Publicly displayed karma should be rare because it can create the wrong incentives for your community. Avoid sorting users by karma. See "Leaderboards Considered Harmful" on page 192.
- If you do display it publicly, make karma visually distinct from any nearby content reputation. Yahoo!'s EU message board displays the karma of a post's author as a colored medallion, with the message rated with stars. But consider this: Slashdot's message board doesn't display the karma of post authors to anyone. Even the display of a user's own karma is vague: "positive," "good," or "excellent." After originally displaying karma publicly as a number, over time Slashdot has shifted to an increasingly opaque display.
- Publicly displayed karma should be rare because it isn't expected. When Yahoo! Shopping added Top Reviewer karma to encourage review creation, it displayed a Top Reviewer badge with each review and rushed it out for the Christmas 2006 season. After the New Year had passed, user testing revealed that most users didn't even notice the badges. When they *did* notice them, many thought they meant either that the *item* was top rated or that the user was a *paid shill* for the product manufacturer or Yahoo!.

Karma caveats

Though karma should be complex, it should still be limited to as narrow a context as possible. Don't mix shopping review karma with chess rank. It may sound silly now, but you'd be surprised how many people think they can make a business out of creating an Internet-wide trustworthiness karma.

Yahoo! holds reputation for karma scores to a higher standard than reputation for content. Be very careful in applying terminology and labels to people, for a couple of reasons:

- Avoid labels that might appear as attacks. They set a hostile tone that will be amplified in users' responses. This caution applies both to overly positive labels (such as "hotshot" or "top" designations) or negative ones (such as "newbie" or "rookie").

- Avoid labels that introduce legal risks. What if a site labeled members of a health forum "experts," and these "experts" then gave out bad advice?

These are rules of thumb that may not necessarily apply to a given context. In role-playing games, for example, publicly shared simple karma is displayed in terms of experience levels, which are inherently competitive.

Reputation Display Formats

Reputation data can be displayed in numerous formats. By now, you've actually already done much of the work of selecting appropriate formats for your reputation data, so we'll simply describe pros and cons of a handful of them—the formats in most common use on the Web.

The formats you select will depend heavily on the types of inputs that you decided on Chapter 6. If, for instance, you've opted to let users make explicit judgments about a content item with 5-star ratings, it's probably appropriate to display those ratings to the community in a similar format.

However, that consistency won't work when the reputation you want to display is an aggregation or transformation of scores derived from very different input methods. For instance, Yahoo! Movies provides a critic's score as a letter grade compiled from scores from many professional critics, each of whom uses a different scale (some use 4- or 5-star ratings, some thumb votes, and still others use customized iconic scores). Such scores are all transformed into normalized scores, which can then be displayed in any form.

Here are the four primary data classes for reputation claims:

Normalized score
> Most composite reputations are represented as decimal numbers from 0.0 to 1.0, with all inputs converted, or normalized, to this range. (See Chapter 6 for more on the specific normalization functions.) Displaying a reputation in the various forms presented in the remainder of this chapter is also known as denormalization: the process of converting reputation data into a presentable format.

Summary count, raw score, and other transitional values
> Sometimes a reputation must hold other numeric values to better represent the meaning of the normalized score when it is displayed. For example, in a

simple-mean reputation, the summary count of the inputs that contribute to the reputation are also tracked, allowing a display patterns that can override or modify the score. For example, a pattern could require a minimum number of inputs (see "Liquidity: You Won't Get Enough Input" on page 58).

In cases where information may be lost during the normalization process, the original input value, or raw score, should also be stored. Finally, other related or transitional values may also be available for display, depending on the reputation statement type. For example, the *simple average* claim type keeps the rolling sum of the previous ratings along with a counter as transitional values in order to rapidly recompute the average when new ratings arrives.

Freeform content

Freeform inputs provided by users may be constrained along certain dimensions, such as format or length, but they are otherwise completely up to the users' discretion. Some examples of this class of data are user comments and video responses. Notice that items like the title of a product review (if the review writer is given the option to provide one) is also a freeform element; it gives review writers an opportunity to provide an opinion about a target. Content tags are also a type of freeform content element.

Freeform content is a notable class of data because, although deriving computable values from them is more difficult, users themselves can derive a lot of qualitative benefit from it.

 At Yahoo! study after study has shown that when users read reviews by other community members—whether the reviews cover movies, albums, or other products—it's the body of the review that users pay the most attention to. The stars and the number of favorable votes matter, but people trust others' words first and foremost. They want to trust an opinion based on shared affinity with the writer, or how well they express themselves. Only then will they give attention to the other stuff.

Metadata

Sometimes, machine-understood information about an object can yield insight into its overall quality or standing within a community. For comparative purposes, for example, you might want to know which of two different videos was available first on your site. Examples of metadata relevant to reputation include the following:

- Timestamp
- Geographical coordinates
- Format information, such as the length of audio, video, or other media files
- The number of links to an item or the number of times the item itself has been embedded in another site

Reputation Display Patterns

Once you've decided to display reputation, your decision does not end there. There are a number of possible display patterns for showing reputation (and they may even be used in combination). Some of the more common patterns are discussed in the upcoming sections.

Normalized Score to Percentage

A normalized score ranges from 0.0 to 1.0 and represents a reputation that can be compared to other reputations no matter what forms were used for input. When displaying normalized scores to users, convert them to percentages (multiply by 100.0), the numeric form most widely understood around the world. From here on, we assume this transformation when we discuss display of a percentage or normalized score to users.

The percentage may be displayed as a whole number or with fixed decimal places, depending on the statistical significance of your reputation and user interface and layout considerations. Remember to include the percent symbol (%) to avoid confusion with the display of either points or numbered levels.

Things to consider before displaying percentages:

- Use this format when the normalized reputation score is reasonably precise and accurate. For example, if hundreds or thousands of votes have been cast in an election, displaying the exact average percentage of affirmative and negative votes is easier to understand than just the total of votes cast for and against.

- Be careful how you display percentages if the input claim type isn't suitable for normalized output of the aggregated results. For example, consider displaying the results of a series of thumb votes; though you can display the thumb graphic that got the majority of votes, you'll probably still want to display either the raw votes for each or the percentages of the total up votes and down votes.

  Figure 7-4 displays content reputation as the percentage of thumbs-up ratings given on Yahoo! Television for a television episode. Notice that the simple average calculation requires that the total number of votes be included in the display to allow users to evaluate the reliability of the score.

- Consider that a graphical sliding scale or thermometer view will make the reputation easier to understand at a glance. If necessary, also display the numeric value alongside the graphic.

  Figure 7-5 shows a number of Okefarflung's karma scores as percentage bars, each representing his reputation with various political factions on *World of Warcraft*. Printed over each bar is one of the current named levels (see the next section "Named levels" on page 188) in which his current reputation falls.

Pros	Cons
• Percentage displays of normalized scores are universally understood. • Is Web 2.0 API- and spreadsheet-friendly. • Implementation is trivial. This is often the primary reason this approach is considered.	• Percentages aren't accurate for very small sample sizes and therefore can be misleading. One yes vote shouldn't be expressed as "100.00% of votes tallied are in favor...." Consider suppressing percentage display until a reasonable number of inputs have accumulated, adjusting the score, or at least displaying the number of inputs alongside the average. • As with accuracy, precision entails various challenges: displaying too many decimal digits can lead users to make unwarranted assumptions about accuracy. Also, if the input was from level-based or nonlinear normalization or irregular distributions, average scores can be skewed. • Lots of numbers on a page can seem impersonal, especially when they're associated with people.

Figure 7-4. Content example: normalized percentages with summary count.

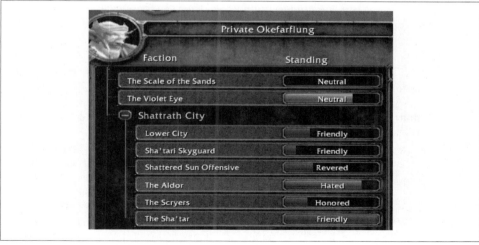

Figure 7-5. Karma example: percentage bars with named levels.

Points and Accumulators

Points are a specific example of an accumulator reputation display pattern: the score simply increases or decreases in value over time, either monotonically (one at a time) or by arbitrary amounts. Accumulator values are almost always displayed as digits, usually alongside a units designation, for example, *10,000XP* or *Posts: 1,429*. The aggregation of the Vote-to-Promote input pattern is an accumulator.

If an accumulator has a maximum value that is understood by the reputation system, an alternative is to display it using any of the display patterns for normalized scores, such as percentages and levels.

Using points and accumulators:

- Display counts of actions collected from many users, such as voting and favorites.

  Figure 7-6 shows an entry from Digg.com, which displays two different accumulators: the number of *Diggs* and *Comments*. Note the Share and Bury buttons. Though these affect the chance that an entity is displayed on the home page, the counts for these actions are not displayed to the users.

- Publicly display points when you wish to encourage users to take actions that increase or decrease the value for an entity.

  Figure 7-7 shows a typical participation-points-enabled website, in this case Yahoo! Answers. Points are granted for a very wide range of activities, including logging in, creating content, and evaluating other's contributions. Note that this miniprofile also displays a numbered level (see "Numbered levels" on page 186) to simplify comparison between users. The number of points accumulated in such systems can get pretty large.

- Alternatively, consider keeping a point value of `personal` and presenting any public display as either a numbered or a named level.

Pros	Cons
• Explicitly displayed point amounts that the user can influence can be a powerful motivator for some users to participate.	• First-mover effect. If your accumulator has no cap, awards effectively deflate over time as the leading entities continue to accumulate points and increase their lead. New users become frustrated that they can't catch up, and new—often more interesting—entities receive less attention. Consider either caps and/or decay for your point system.
• Is easy to understand in ranked lists.	• Encourages the minimum effort for the maximum benefit behavior. The system tells you exactly how many points are associated with your actions in real time. Yahoo! Answers gives 10 points for an answer chosen as the best, and 1 point each to users who rate other people's answers. Too bad that writing the best answer takes more than 10 times as long as it does to click a thumb icon 10 times.
• Implementation is trivial.	• If you do cap your points, when the most of your users reach that cap, you will need to add new activities to justify moving the cap to move higher. For example, online role-playing games typically extend the level-cap along with expanded content for the users to explore.

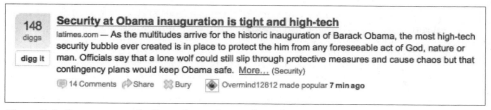

Figure 7-6. Content example: Digg shows the number of times an item has been "Dugg." Another example is the count of comments for an item.

Figure 7-7. Karma example: Yahoo! Answers awards points mostly for participation.

Statistical Evidence

One very useful strategy for reputation display is to use statistical evidence: simply include as many of the inputs in a content item's reputation as possible, without attempting to aggregate them in visible scores. Statistical evidence lets users zero in on the aspects of a content item that they consider the most telling. The evidence might consist of a series of simple accumulator scores:

- Number of views
- Number of links
- Number of comments
- Number of times marked as a favorite or voted on

Using statistical evidence:

- Use this display format when a variety of data points would provide a well-rounded view of an entity's worth or performance.

  Figure 7-8 shows YouTube.com's many different statistics associated with each video, each subject to different subjective interpretation. For example, the number of times a video is *Favorited* can be compared to the total number of *Views* to determine relative popularity.

- Use statistical evidence in displays of counts of actions collected from many users, such as voting and favorites.

Yahoo! Answers provides a categorical breakdown of statistics by contributor, as shown in Figure 7-9. This allows readers to notice whether the user is an answer-person (as shown here) or a question-person or something else.

- Optionally, you might extend statistical evidence to include even more information about how a particular score was derived.

Figure 7-10 shows how Yahoo! Answers displays not only how many people have "starred" a question (that is, found it interesting), it also shows exactly who starred it. However, displaying that information can have negative consequences: among other things, it may create an expectation of social reciprocity (for example, your friends might become upset if you opted not to endorse their contributions).

Pros	Cons
• Does not attempt to mediate or frame the experience for users. Lets them decide which reputation elements are relevant for their purposes.	• Can tend to overwhelm an interface, with a dozen factoids and statistics about every piece of content. • Giving too much prominence or weight to statistical evidence in a reputation display may overemphasize the information's importance—for example, Twitter's follower-counts encourage the hording of meaningless connections. (See "Leaderboards Considered Harmful" on page 192.)

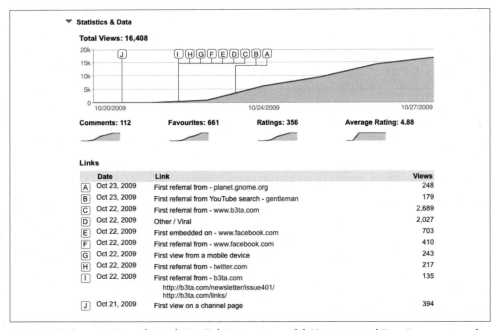

Figure 7-8. Content Example: with YouTube's very powerful "Statistics and Data" you can track a video's rise in popularity on the site. (Sociologist and researcher Cameron Marlow calls it an "Epidemiology Interface.")

Answers		Questions	
Total answers	92678	Questions asked	3
Best answers	30675	Resolved questions	3
		Stars received	194

Figure 7-9. Karma example: answers enhanced point and level information with statistical detail.

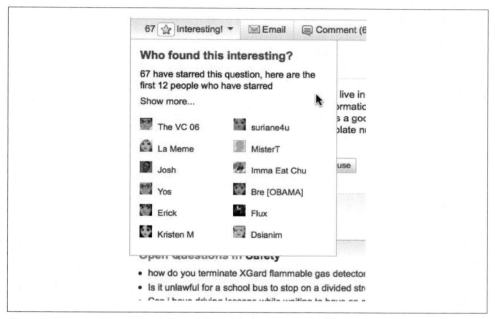

Figure 7-10. Yahoo! Answers displays the sources for statistical evidence.

Levels

Levels are reputation display patterns that remove insignificant precision from the score. Each level is a bucket holding all the scores in a range. Levels allow you to round off the results and simplify the display. Notice that the range of scores in each level need not be evenly distributed, as long as the users understand the relative difficulty of reaching each level.

Common display patterns for levels include numbered levels and named levels.

When using levels:

- Use levels when the reputation is an average and inputs are limited to a small, fixed set, such as 5 stars.

- Levels are helpful when the reputation is an average and may be calculated from a very small number of inputs. Levels will hide irrelevant precision.
- Most applications use levels when reputation accumulates at a nonlinear rate. For example, in many role-playing games, each experience level requires twice as many experience points as the previous level.
- Use levels if some features of your application are unlocked depending on the reputation score; users will want to know that they've achieved the required threshold.
- Be careful using levels when the input was gathered using a different scale. If the user clicks a thumb icon, displaying the resulting score as 5 stars will be confusing.
- Be careful when listing entities by level not to surface relative position *within* a level. Doing so can encourage undesired competition for specific page positions. Sort by the lower precision level value, not the high precision normalized value.

Numbered levels

Numbered levels are the most basic form of level display. This display pattern consists of a simple numeric value or a list of repeated icons representing the level that the reputation score falls into. Usually levels are 0 or 1 to *n*, though arbitrary ranges are possible as long as they make sense to users. The score may be an integer or a rounded fraction, such as 3½ stars. If the representation is unfamiliar to users, consider adding an element to the interface to explain the score and how it was calculated. Such an element is mandatory for reputations with nonlinear advancement rates.

Using numbered levels:

- Assign numbered levels if the reputation will be displayed in a rank-ordered sort a list of entities.

  Figure 7-11 shows a typical Stars-and-Bars display pattern for ratings and reviews. Stars and Bars are numbered levels, which happen to be displayed as graphics. In this example, each has a numbered level of 0 to 5. Though each review's ratings are useful when displayed alongside the entity, the average of the overall score is used to rank-order results on search results pages.

- It is typical to use numbered levels to display aggregate reputation if the *inputs* were also numbered levels. Did you input stars? Then output stars.

  Figure 7-12 shows the karma ratings from Orkut.com. The Fans indicator is an accumulator (see "Points and Accumulators" on page 182), and the Trusty, Cool, and Sexy ratings are numeric levels. The users simply click on the smiling faces, ice cubes, and hearts next to their friends' profiles to influence their scores. Many sites don't allow direct karma ratings such as these with good reason (see "Karma" on page 176).

- If you need to display more than 10 levels, use numbered levels. Consider using numbered levels instead of named levels if you display more than five levels.

Figure 7-13 displays two forms, out of many, of numbered levels for the game *World of Warcraft*. The user controls a character whose name is shown in the Members column. The first numbered level is labeled "Level" and ranges from 1 to 80, representing the amount of time and skill the user has dedicated to this character. The Guild Rank is a reverse-rank numbered level that represents the status of the user in the guild. This score is assigned by the guild master, who has the lowest guild rank.

Pros	Cons
• Is easy to read.	• Numeric format doesn't convey limits or global value. Is level 20 good? What about 40? Often requires "What's this?" user interface elements to explain levels to new users.
• Accommodates unlimited values. You can always add more levels at the top.	• Lots of numbers on a page can seem impersonal, especially when they're associated with people.
• In ranked lists, relative value is easy to see.	• For karma, numbered levels can be perceived as fostering an undesirable competitive spirit.

Figure 7-11. Content example: stars and bars (iconic numbered levels).

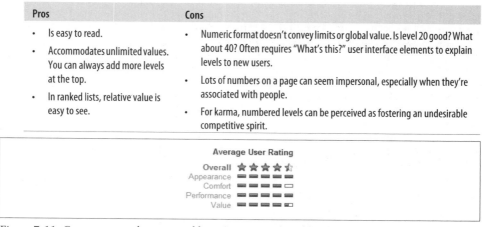

Figure 7-12. Karma example: Orkut profile with an accumulator and iconic number levels.

Figure 7-13. Karma example: Experience levels and guild rank (sortable).

Named levels

In a named levels display pattern, a short, readable string of characters is substituted for a level number.

The name adds semantic meaning to each level so that users can more easily recognize the entity's reputation when the reputation is displayed separately. Is the user a "silver contributor" or is the beef prime, choice, select, or standard?

Using named levels:

- Named levels are useful when the number of labels is five or less, so that each level can have a name that accurately expresses its meaning.

  Table 7-1 and Figure 7-14 show the meat grading levels used by the United States Department of Agriculture. The labels are descriptive, representing existing industry terms, and several are shared across different animal species—providing consumers a consistent standard for comparison.

Table 7-1. Content example: USDA meat grades

Species	Quality grades
Beef	Prime, choice, select, standard, utility, cutter, canner
Lamb and yearling mutton	Prime, choice, good, utility, cull
Mutton	Choice, good, utility, cull
Veal and calf	Prime, choice, good, standard, utility

Figure 7-14. Content example: USDA prime, choice, and select stamps.

- Named levels are particularly useful when numeric levels are too impersonal or encourage undesired competition.
- If you're considering using numeric levels but find that the top and bottom levels should feel closer together than the numeric distance between them would otherwise indicate—consider using named levels instead. This is especially useful with karma scores so that new participants don't get stuck with a demeaning level indicator, like "Level 1 of 10."

  Figure 7-15 displays the current named levels used by WikiAnswers.com for user contributions. The original three categories were Bronze, Silver, and Gold—named after competitive medals. They are granted when nonlinearly increasing thresholds are met. Over time, the system has been expanded on three separate occasions to reward the nearly compulsive contributions of a handful of users.

Figure 7-15. Karma example: The contributor levels on WikiAnswers have seen several awkward expansions.

Pros	Cons
• Hiding level numbers allows for more expressiveness.	• Care must be taken when setting up the level names if you ever expect to add more to either end of the scale.
• Level names can be thematically appropriate to, and vary by, your application(s).	• Something else for your user to learn.
• Common hierarchies work well—for example, poor, average, good, and excellent.	• Cultural bias can be a problem, especially if your site has an international audience. For example, the letter grading system of F, D, C, B, A is not internationally understood.
• This pattern is usually stronger when the named levels are displayed alongside other ratings, such as stars, points, and raw scores, to clarify them.	• Ambiguous names are more confusing than simple level numbers. Is the Ruby level better than Gold?

Ranked Lists

A ranked list is based on highest or lowest reputation scores. Ranking systems are by their very nature comparative, and—human nature being what it is—the online community is likely to perceive this design choice as an encouragement of competition between users.

Leaderboard ranking

A leaderboard is a rank-ordered listing of reputable entities within your community or content pool. Leaderboards may be displayed in a grid, with rows representing the entities and columns describing those entities across one or more characteristics (name, number of views, and so on). Leaderboards provide an easy and approachable way to display the best performers in your community.

- Use leaderboards *for content* liberally. Provide filtered views of the boards to slice and dice by time ("Popular Today/This Week/All Time") or by reputation type ("Most Viewed/Top Rated").

Figure 7-16 shows YouTube's leaderboard ranking for most viewed videos as a grid. With numbers this high, it's hard for potential reputation abusers to push inappropriate content onto the first page. Note that there are several leaderboards, one each for Today, This Week, This Month, and All Time.

- Use leaderboards *for people* sparingly, and only in contexts that are competitive by nature. Consider giving people leaderboards narrow scope (for example, only ranking me against my friends, to keep the comparisons fun and the stakes low).

Figure 7-17 displays Yahoo! Answer's leaderboard. The original version of this page was based solely on the number of points accumulated by participation, and users quickly figured out which actions produced the most points for the least effort. When the user's best-answer percentage was eventually added to the profile display, it was discovered that the top-ranked users all had quality scores of less than 10%!

Pros	Cons
• Clear and browsable way to compare items for specific qualities	• May incite unhealthy competition to reach (or stay at) the top of the leaderboard.
• Data-intensive display: leaderboards satiate demand from information junkie users	• When used with accumulators, leaderboards can get stale as a few popular items move to the top and get stuck there, since nothing makes something more popular than its appearance on the list of most popular things.

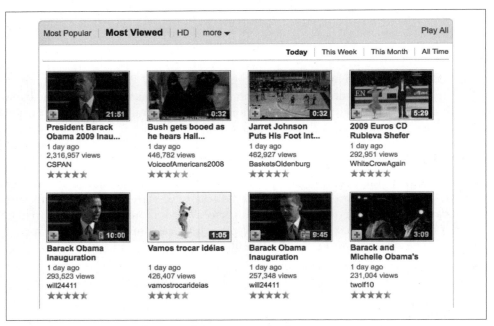

Figure 7-16. Content example: YouTube's most viewed videos.

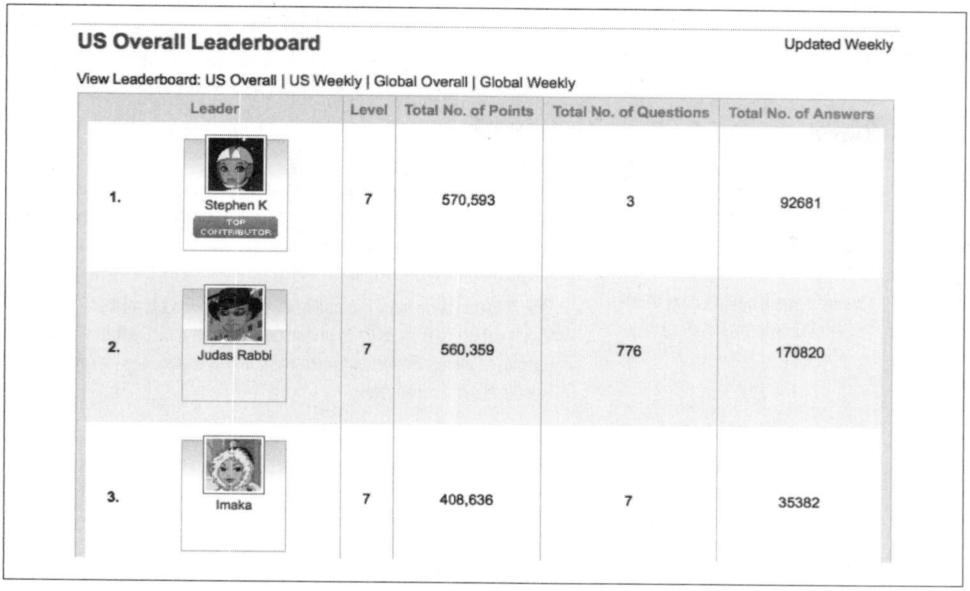

US Overall Leaderboard — Updated Weekly

View Leaderboard: US Overall | US Weekly | Global Overall | Global Weekly

	Leader	Level	Total No. of Points	Total No. of Questions	Total No. of Answers
1.	Stephen K TOP CONTRIBUTOR	7	570,593	3	92681
2.	Judas Rabbi	7	560,359	776	170820
3.	Imaka	7	408,636	7	35382

Figure 7-17. Karma example: Yahoo! Answers leaderboard.

Top-X ranking

This is a specialized type of leaderboard where top-ranking entities are grouped into numerical categories of performance. Achieving top-10 status (or even top-100) should be a rare and celebrated feat.

When using Top-X ranking:

- Use top-X leaderboards *for content* to highlight only the best of the best contributions in your community.

  Figure 7-18 shows a Top-X display for content: Billboard's Hot 100's list of top recordings. The artists themselves have very little, if any, direct influence over their song's rank on this list.

- Use top-X designations *for people* sparingly, and only in contexts that are competitive by nature. Because available categories in a top-X system are bounded, they will have greater perceived value in the community.

  Figure 7-19 displays the *new* index of Top-X karma for Amazon.com review writers. The very high number of reviews written by each of these leaders creates value both for Amazon and the reviewers themselves. Authors and publishers seek them out to review/endorse their book—sometimes for a nominal fee. The original version of this reputation system, now known as "Classic Reviewer Rank," suffered deeply from first-mover effects (see "First-mover effects" on page 63) and other problems detailed in this book. This eventually lead to the creation of the new model, as pictured.

Pros	Cons
• Highly motivating for top performers. The prestige of earning a top-10 or top-100 designation may make contributors work twice as hard to keep it. • Yields a small, bounded set of entities to promote as high quality.	• May incite unhealthy competition to reach (or stay at) the top of the ranks. • For top-X karma based on accumulators, if a user's reputation falls just below a category dividing line and the user knows his score, these categories often lead to minimum/maximum gaming, in which the user engages in a flurry of low-quality activity just to advance his top-X category. • Top-X karma badges are unfamiliar to users who don't contribute content. Don't expect passive users to understand or even notice a top-X badge displayed alongside content reputation. Top-X badges are for content producers, not consumers.

Figure 7-18. Content example: Billboard's Hot 100.

Practitioner's Tips

Leaderboards Considered Harmful

It's still too early to speak in absolutes about the design of social-media sites, but one fact is becoming abundantly clear: ranking the members of your community—and pitting them against one another in a competitive fashion—is typically a bad idea. Like the fabled *djinni* of yore, leaderboards on your site promise riches (comparisons! incentives! user engagement!!) but often lead to undesired consequences.

The thought process involved in creating leaderboards typically goes something like this: there's an activity on your site that you'd like to promote; a number of people are

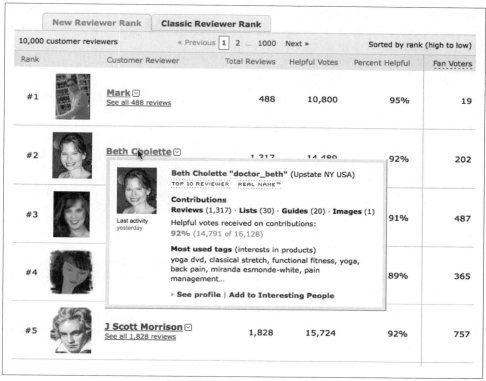

Figure 7-19. *Karma example: Amazon's top reviewer rankings.*

engaged in that activity who should be recognized; and a whole bunch of other people won't jump in without a kick in the pants. Leaderboards seem like the perfect solution. Active contributors will get their recognition: placement at the top of the ranks. The also-rans will find incentive: to emulate leaders and climb the boards.

And that activity you're trying to promote? Site usage should swell with all those earnest, motivated users plugging away, right? It's the classic win-win-win scenario. In practice, employing this pattern has rarely been this straightforward. Here are just a few reasons why leaderboards are hard to get right.

What do you measure?

Many leaderboards make the mistake of basing standings only on what is easy to measure. Unfortunately, what's easy to measure often tells you nothing at all about what is *good*. Leaderboards tend to fare well in very competitive contexts, because there's a convenient correlation between measurability and quality. (It's called "performance"—number of wins versus losses within overall attempts.)

But how do you measure quality in a user-generated video community? Or a site for ratings and reviews? It should have very little to do with the quantities of simple activity that a person generates (the number of times an action is repeated, a comment given or a review posted). But such measurements—discrete, countable, and objective—are exactly what leaderboards excel at.

Whatever you do measure will be taken way too seriously

Even if you succeed in leavening your leaderboard with metrics for quality (perhaps you weigh community votes or count send-to-a-friend actions), be aware that—because a leaderboard singles out these factors for praise and reward—your community will hold them in high esteem, too. Leaderboards have a kind of "Code of Hammurabi" effect on community values: what's written becomes the law of the land. You'll likely notice that effect in the activities that people will—and won't—engage in on your site. So tread carefully. Are you really that much smarter than your community, that you alone should dictate its character?

If it looks like a leaderboard and quacks like a leaderboard…

Even sites that don't display overt leaderboards may veer too closely into the realm of comparative statistics. Consider Twitter and its prominent display of community members' stats.

The problem may not lie with the *existence* of the stats but in the prominence of their display (see Figure 7-20). They give Twitter the appearance of a community that values popularity and the sheer size of a participant's social network. Is it any wonder, then, that a whole host of community-created leaderboards have sprung up to automate just such comparisons? Twitterholic, Twitterank, Favrd, and a whole host of others are the natural extension of this value-by-numbers approach.

Figure 7-20. You'd be completely forgiven if you signed into Twitter and mistook this dashboard for a scoreboard!

Leaderboards are powerful and capricious

In the earliest days of Orkut (Google's also-ran entry in social networking), the product managers put a fun little widget at the top of the site: a country counter, showing where members were from. Cute and harmless, right? Google had no way of knowing, however, that seemingly the entire population of Brazil would make it a point of national pride to push their country to the top of that list. Brazilian blogger Naitze Teng wrote:

Communities dedicated to raising the number of Brazilians on Orkut were following the numbers closely, planning gatherings and flash mobs to coincide with the inevitable. When it was reported that Brazilians had outnumbered Americans registered on Orkut, parties...were thrown in celebration.

Brazil has maintained its number one position on Orkut (as of this writing, 51% of Orkut users are Brazilian; the United States and India are tied for a distant second with 17% apiece). Orkut today is basically a Brazilian social network. That's not a bad "problem" for Google to have, but it's probably not an outcome that it would have expected from such a simple, small, and insignificant thing as a leaderboard widget.

Who benefits?

The most insidious artifact of a leaderboard community may be that the very presence of a leaderboard changes the community dynamic and calls into question the motivations for every action that users take. If that sounds a bit extreme, consider Twitter: friend counts and followers have become the coins of that realm. When you get a notification of a new follower, aren't you just a little more likely to believe that it's just someone fishing around for a reciprocal follow? Sad, but true. And this despite the fact that Twitter itself never has officially featured a leaderboard; it merely made the statistics known and provided an API to get at them. In doing so, it may have let the genie out of the bottle.

 "Leaderboards Considered Harmful" first appeared as an essay in *Designing Social Interfaces* (O'Reilly) by Christian Crumlish and Erin Malone, also available online at DesigningSocialInterfaces.com (*http://www.designingsocialinterfaces.com/*).

Going Beyond Displaying Reputation

This entire chapter has focused on the explicit display of reputation, usually directly to users. Though important, this isn't typically the most valuable use for this information. Chapter 8 describes using reputation to modify the utility of an application—to separate the best entities from the pack, and to help identify and destroy the most harmful ones.

Using Reputation: The Good, The Bad, and the Ugly

Reputation is a lens for filtering the content you need.

—Clay Spinuzzi, professor of rhetoric,
University of Texas at Austin

While Chapter 7 explained various patterns for displaying reputation, this chapter focuses on *using* it to improve the application's user experience by ordering and sifting your objects.

Envision your application's data splayed out across a vast surface, like a jumble of photo negatives spread out on a light table. As you approach this ill-disciplined mess of information, you might be looking for different things at different times. On a Saturday, diversion and entertainment are your goals: "Show me those awesome photos we took at the Grand Canyon last year." Come Monday morning, you're all business: "I need my corporate headshot for that speaking engagement!" Your goals may shift, but it's likely that there are some dimensions that remain fairly consistent.

It's likely, for instance, that—regardless of what you're looking for in the pile—you'd prefer to see *only the good stuff* when you approach your light table. There's some stuff that is obviously good: they're the best photos you've ever taken (all your friends agree). There's some stuff that is arguably good, and you'd like to see it to decide for yourself. And then there's some stuff that is flat-out *bad*: oops, your thumb was obscuring the lens. Or...that one was backlit. You may not want to destroy these lesser efforts, but you certainly don't want to see them every time you look at your photos.

Think of reputation as an extremely useful *lens* that you can hold up to the content of your application (or its community of contributors). A lens that reveals quality, obscures noise, and is powered by the opinions of those who've sifted through the jumble before you. In this chapter, we propose a number of strategies for employing this lens, including where to point it, how to hold it, and how to read the information that it reveals.

And, as with our light table, these strategies will approach this problem from any number of different angles. But the end goal is generally the same: to improve the quality of contributions to your application (across the dimensions that you and your community deem valuable). These strategies perform two basic functions: emphasize entities with higher, positive reputation and *deemphasize* (or hide, or remove altogether) entities with lower, negative reputation.

Up with the Good

We're positive people, by nature. We really do want to find the good in others. So let's start with some of the more affirmative strategies for using the reputations that your contributors and their contributions have earned.

Accentuate the Positive

Why is it a good idea to showcase high-quality contributions, front and center? Let's discuss the value of imprinting on your visitors and the effects it can have on their subsequent interactions with your site.

We've already discussed Dan Ariely's *Predictably Irrational* (Harper Perennial) in reference to incentives (see "Incentives for User Participation, Quality, and Moderation" on page 111). Ariely also explores the idea of *imprinting*—a phenomenon first studied in goslings, who "not only [...] make initial decisions based on what's available in their environment, but [...] stick with a decision once it has been made."

This tendency is prevalent in humans as well, and Ariely explains how imprinting can explain our somewhat-irrational tendency to fixate on *anchor* prices for goods and services. An anchor is the ideal valuation that we hold in our minds for something: it is the price that we judge all other prices against for that thing. And it is largely a function of our *first exposure* to that thing. (Maybe the old Botany Suits ads were right all along— "You'll never get a second chance to make a first impression!")

How does this matter in the Web 2.0 world of user-generated content? When someone comes to your site, there are many indicators—everything from the visual design of the site to the editorial voice presented to, heck, even the choice of domain name—that communicate to them the type of place it is, and the type of activities that people engage in there. We would argue that one indicator that speaks loudly (perhaps loudest of all) is the type of content that visitors see on display.

It is this type of evaluation, especially early on, that anchors a user's opinion of your site. And remember that anchoring and imprinting aren't just short-lived dynamics: they will persist for as long as your users have a relationship with your site. If their initial valuation of your offering is *high*, they're far more likely to become good citizens down the road—to contribute good content, with some attention payed to its creation and presentation. (And respect others who are doing so as well.)

If their valuation of your offering is low? Well...did you ever date someone that you didn't see much of a future with? You might have had other compelling reasons to stay

---

in the relationship, but you probably didn't put a lot of effort into it, right? This is what you *don't* want for your community-based website: an influx of half-hearted, lackluster nonenthusiasts. Maybe you want visitors to *come to* your video-sharing site for its generous storage limits, but you certainly don't want them stay for that reason alone. This does not make for a vibrant and engaged community.

Rank-Order Items in Lists and Search Results

Ordering items in listings always presents something of a problem. Whether the list presented is the result of a search query or just represents a natural ordering of items in a taxonomy, you generally have to wrestle with issues of scale (too many items in the list) and relevance (what do you show first?). Users are impatient and probably won't want to scroll or page through too many items in the list to find exactly what they want.

Simple ordering schemes get you only so far—take alphabetic, for instance. True, it does enjoy a certain internal logic and may appear to be imminently predictable and useful. But it's no good if your users don't know what items they're looking for. Or what those users are named. Or where, in a paginated results listing of 890 items, the "J"s might start.

Ideally, then, you'd know something about your users' desires and direct them quickly and efficiently to that exact thing in a listing. This is the type of stuff—personalization based on past habits—that Amazon does so well. But a personalized recommendation approach assumes a lot as well; users probably have to be registered with your site or at least have a cookied history with it. But more importantly, they have to have *been there before*. After all, you can't serve up recommendations based on past actions if there are no past actions to speak of.

So, once again, your reputation system can come to the rescue. Reputation-ranked ordering is available regardless of a visitor's prior relationship with your site. In fact, community-based reputation can compensate for a whole lot of contextual deficiencies in a search setting. Figure 8-1 shows a typical search result listing on Yelp.

The query provided was a fairly broad one (the term "pizza" scoped to Columbus, Ohio) and lacks a certain amount of context about what I might want to see. I might have, for instance, given a more specific search term like "bbq pizza" and gotten a very different set of results. Or I could have been more specific in neighborhood locale. And remember, I'm just any old visitor, not a registered Yelp user, so there's no real context to be gleaned from my past history.

With a bare minimum of context to scope on, Yelp does a pretty good job of showing me pizza restaurants that I might want to consider. They do this by rank-ordering search results based on establishments' reputations (their community average ratings). In fact, they present another facet by which you can order results: "Highest Rated," which is even more explicitly powered by community reputation. In an example like this—one

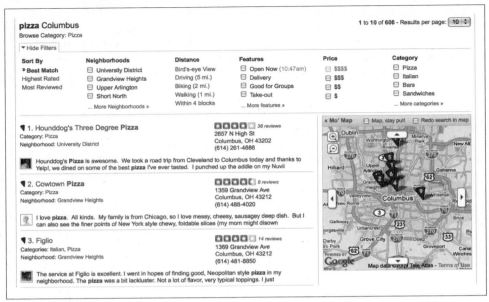

Figure 8-1. *If I want a pizza in Columbus, odds are good I want the best pizza, right? Best Match results on Yelp are flavored with reputation from user ratings.*

with a broad enough context—there's very little difference in the presentation of these two facets.

> Beware of confusing your users with an overabundance of ambiguously derived filtering mechanisms based on reputation. Most users will be hard-pressed to understand the difference between "Best Match," "Highest Rated," and "Most Popular." Either limit the number of options or make sure that you select the best default filter for users: the one most likely to reveal the highest-quality options with the *least* amount of user-provided context.

Content Showcases

One of the lowest-effort but highest-reward features you can include on your site is a gallery or a showcase that highlights excellent contributions from the community. Give this showcase a place of prominence, so that first-time visitors can't help but notice it. A handful of high-quality content should be one of the first things a new user sees on your site. (See "Accentuate the Positive" on page 198.)

Notice the view that greets you when you arrive at Vimeo (Figure 8-2), a well-designed video-sharing site. There are not one but *three* different ways to browse the site's best content—"Videos We Like," "Explore," and "Right Now." These tabs present three different types of reputation for video content: "Videos We Like" is an editor-influenced view (see "The human touch" on page 203); "Explore" appears to be quality-driven

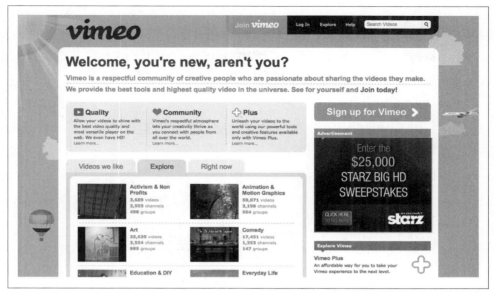

Figure 8-2. Vimeo goes out of its way to welcome new visitors, including not one but three different Greeting Galleries.

(probably based on usage patterns on the site, and the number of "Likes" that videos receive); and "Right Now" puts an emphasis on current, fresh content by incorporating decay. (See "Freshness and decay" on page 63.)

Content showcases are not only useful at the front door of your site. Smaller, contextually appropriate showcases placed at strategic locations throughout the site can continue to communicate an expectation of quality and show the best contributions within that section of the site.

Figure 8-3 features wireframe designs for a minishowcase, "Buzz on the Boards," that never went live on Yahoo! UK's sports pages. The widget was designed to pull contextually-relevant conversations out of sports message boards and surface them on daily sports news articles. The goal was to educate casual, visiting article readers about the availability of community features on the site. Hopefully, to pull them *into* the conversation—as participants—at exactly the moment when they're most opinionated and ready to engage with others.

Buzz on the Boards

What has your fellow community members hot and bothered? Here are the hot discussions right now...

In **Chelsea,** <u>arsene wenger ,Can you please resign?</u> has 134 replies in the last day

In **Cardiff City,** <u>New Stadium</u> has 48 replies in the last hour

In **Manchester United,** <u>No Sympathy!</u> has 12 replies in the last hour

In **Chelsea,** <u>Carling Cup Final</u> has received 532 Ratings!

Want more Buzz? Visit the Message Boards and stir things up!

Figure 8-3. Buzz on the Boards highlights message board threads based on activity (where are hot conversations happening), then sorts based on quality (which individual posts are highest-rated).

 There's a danger with showcases: if your design gives them too much prominence (or if your community embraces them too eagerly) then you run the risk of creating a *Leaderboard* situation. (See "Leaderboards Considered Harmful" on page 192.) Placement in the showcase will take on a certain currency with members of the community, and their desire to see their content featured there may lead to some less than ideal behaviors. See Richard's Notes on Flickr Explore (*http://www.richards notes.org/archives/2007/08/24/flickr-explore/*) for the contra-viewpoint on how reputation-based showcases may be a detriment to that community.

You can also highlight your best and brightest community members in a showcase. Figure 8-4 shows a "Community Stars" module, also planned but never released for Yahoo! UK Sports. This module first pulls active and high-quality contributors from the system based on poster reputation, and then does a secondary sort based on those

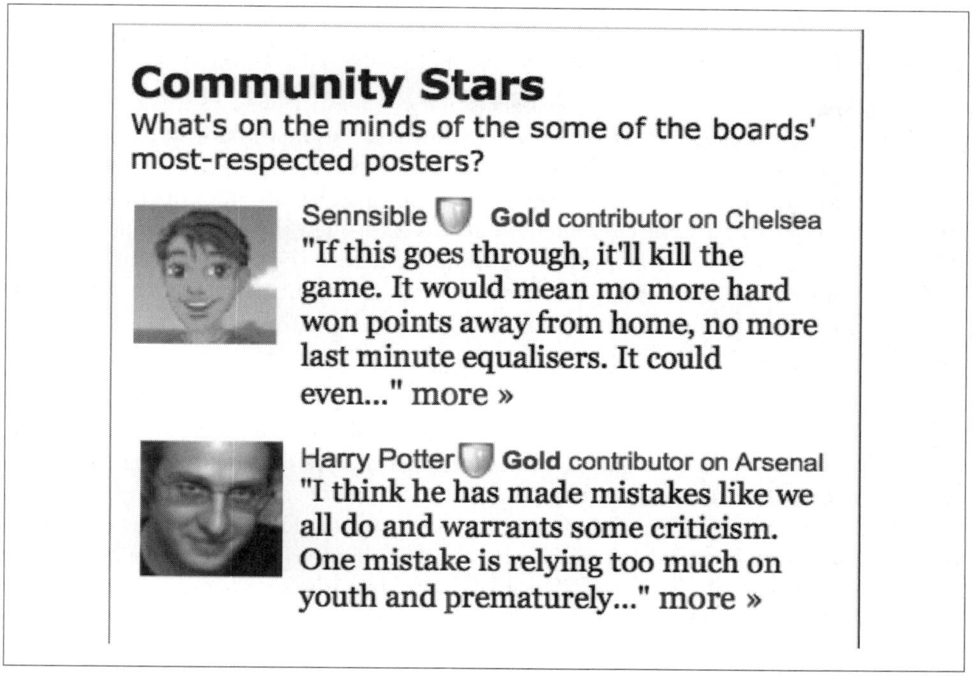

Community Stars
What's on the minds of the some of the boards' most-respected posters?
Sennsible Gold contributor on Chelsea
"If this goes through, it'll kill the game. It would mean mo more hard won points away from home, no more last minute equalisers. It could even..." more »
Harry Potter Gold contributor on Arsenal
"I think he has made mistakes like we all do and warrants some criticism. One mistake is relying too much on youth and prematurely..." more »

Figure 8-4. This module is based on contributor reputation and the quality of the posts featured, but the language downplays this. No reason to create a popularity contest, right?

users' *posts* reputation. This guarantees that—not only will the best contributors appear here—but only their *top* contributions will be considered for inclusion.

The rules for people showcases are no different than for content showcases, but you may want to alter your approach to the design and presentation of this type of showcase. Labels that apply easily and comfortably to content may invoke the wrong effects when applied to the people in your community.

Don't shower featured contributors with effusive praise—"Best & Brightest," for instance. Remember, for every person you single out for praise on your site—however well deserved that praise may be—you are simultaneously *ignoring* a much greater number of contributors. Don't dis-incent a large number of your community. No one likes to feel that they're laboring in anonymity, especially when others seem to be basking in praise.

The human touch

The idea of a *completely* algorithmically-determined showcase may give you pause. After all, you're placing these elements in high-profile, high-traffic locations on your site. They're *bound* to draw out the spammers and ne'er-do-wells , right?

You're probably right to worry. As we cautioned earlier—and throughout this book—if placement in the showcase becomes a motivation for some of your contributors, they will undoubtedly figure out ways to achieve that placement. You may want to design some safeguards.

At a minimum, the models that power your showcase should include consideration of the creator's karma, to ensure that content showcased comes primarily from long-standing and mostly reputable contributors. You should also provide controls for quick removal of abusive content that somehow makes it through the reputation filters. (See Chapter 10 for a detailed case study on community-driven abuse moderation.) And, to keep the content fresh and lively (*and* ensure that more contributors have the opportunity to be featured) also consider flavoring the model with decay. (See "Decay and delay" on page 93.)

If you're still anxious, there's no reason that a showcase gallery can't be completely editor-determined. And your reputation system can still play a big part in this workflow. Your human editors can use any combination of strategies outlined in this chapter to *find* the good stuff on the site. Perhaps they just do a search, and rank the results based on various reputations. Or maybe they have access to some internal, eyes-only tools that leverage corporate reputations you may be keeping to quickly ferret out all of the showcase-worthy content. It's still a lot of work, but it's *worlds* easier with a good reputation system in place.

Down with the Bad

Reputation is no guarantee that *all* of the content on your site will be phenomenal. Once you've employed some of the strategies just described for promoting and surfacing good content, you may still need to obscure the lesser stuff.

Remember our discussion from Chapter 1 ("There's a Whole Lotta Crap Out There" on page 13) on the levels of content quality that your site may encounter. With these strategies, we're addressing content that falls on the lower end of the spectrum—content that is at best OK, but generally tends toward the poor-to-illegal end. Different tactics are appropriate at different points along the spectrum.

You may ask yourself: do I really *need* to actively police content quality at the midpoints of the scale? Content that is OK, or even poor, certainly doesn't need to be punished, right? Isn't it enough to promote the good, and let the mediocre stuff just kind of vanish? Just let it slide into obscurity off the reputation-ranked end of the long-content tail?

Perhaps, but you may want to be mindful of the community effects of allowing poor content to pile up.

Broken Windows and Online Behavior

At the community level, disorder and crime are usually inextricably linked, in a kind of developmental sequence. Social psychologists and police officers tend to agree that if a window in a building is broken and is left unrepaired, all the rest of the windows will soon be broken. This is as true in nice neighborhoods as in rundown ones. Window-breaking does not necessarily occur on a large scale because some areas are inhabited by determined window-breakers, whereas others are populated by window-lovers; rather, one unrepaired broken window is a signal that no one cares, and so breaking more windows costs nothing.

—http://www.theatlantic.com/doc/198203/broken-windows

Does the broken windows theory apply to online spaces?

Much of the tone of discourse online is governed by the level of moderation and to what extent people are encouraged to "own" their words. When forums, message boards, and blog comment threads with more than a handful of participants are unmoderated, bad behavior follows. The appearance of one troll encourages others. Undeleted hateful or ad hominem comments are an indication that this is allowable behavior and encourages more of the same. Those commenters who are normally respectable participants are emboldened by the uptick in bad behavior and misbehave themselves. More likely, they're discouraged from helping with the community moderation process of keeping their peers in line with social pressure. Or they stop visiting the site altogether.

Unchecked comment spam signals that the owner or moderator of the forum or blog isn't paying attention, stimulating further improper conduct. Anonymity provides commenters with immunity from being associated with their speech and actions, making the whole situation worse...how does the community punish or police someone they don't know? Very quickly, the situation is out of control and your message board is the online equivalent of South Central Los Angeles in the 1980s, inhabited by roving gangs armed with hate speech, fueled by the need for attention, making things difficult for those who wish to carry on useful conversations.

—Jason Kottke

Configurable Quality Thresholds

One of the dangers inherent in controlling content display by reputation is that of being *overly presumptuous*; who's to say that the decisions you make for your community about what content they do or don't want to see are the right ones? Why not let each user decide for himself what level of conversational noise he prefers? For information-rich displays (listings, comment threads, search results), consider providing a *quality threshold* interface element that lets users "ratchet up" or "ratchet down" the signal-to-noise ratio that they're prepared to accept. Another common pattern is allowing users to reverse the sort order of the content, with worst evaluations first.

The granddaddy of reputation-based content moderation is Slashdot, and it employs this strategy to great effect. Figure 8-5 illustrates Slashdot's multiple levels of content obscurity: comments below a certain score are abbreviated in a thread—just enough content from the post is left "peeking out" to preserve context and invite those who are curious to read more. Those comments that dip below an even *lower* score are hidden altogether and no longer sully the reader's display.

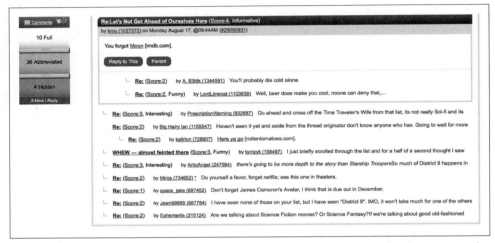

Figure 8-5. Slashdot seemingly hides more posts than it displays. It's a system that favors your rights as a discriminating information consumer over everyone else's desire to be heard.

To avoid the presumption trap, make these controls user-configurable. Let users choose the quality-level that they'd like to see. Don't bury this setting as a user-preference. Make it evident and easily accessible right in the main information display; otherwise, it will probably never be discovered or changed. (A bonus to keeping the control easily accessible: users who want to change it frequently can do so with ease.)

You may be concerned that providing a quality threshold will unfairly punish new contributors or new contributions that haven't had enough exposure to the community to surpass the level of the threshold for display. Consider pairing this strategy with Inferred Reputation (see the section "Inferred Reputation for Content Submissions" on page 210) to give those new entrants a leg up on the quality game.

Expressing Dissatisfaction

Remember *The Gong Show*? It was a popular American game show in the 1970s—contestants would come on and display a "talent" of their choosing to celebrity judges, any one of whom, at any point during the performance (OK, there were time limits, but that's beside the point), could strike an enormous gong to disqualify that contestant. Trust us, it was great entertainment.

Today's Web has a smaller, quieter (and, sadly, less satisfying) equivalent to that show's "gong." It is a judgmental little widget—the Thumbs Up/Thumbs Down vote—that often accompanies user-contributed entities as a form of participatory crowd judgment. (See the section "Two-state votes (thumb ratings)" on page 140.) Consider providing *at least* this level of explicit user voting for content on your site.

It's probably best to provide your users with *some* means of expressing an opinion about content. Otherwise, they will likely co-opt whatever other mechanisms are available to do so; either user comments (and threads) will quickly fill up with back-and-forth bickering over peoples' spelling abilities and "+1" type posts or abuse reports (discussed in the next section). And we don't want to encourage inappropriate abuse reporting. Sometimes arming the community with a simple, satisfying mechanism to say "I disagree" is enough.

Out with the Ugly

And then there's just some stuff that you don't want to keep around. At all. It's offensive and violates your TOS. Or it's *illegal* and violates common taste. This is the stuff that should *very quickly* acquire a bad reputation. You'll want your community to be able to identify this stuff swiftly and effectively, and you'll want your system to be able to act on it efficiently.

Reporting Abuse

Reporting abuse is serious business. It is an explicit input into your reputation system unlike any other: it potentially has legal repercussions. It is basically a user-to-user reputation claim (which we generally discourage; see "Good Inputs" on page 135). Users should not *think* of it as an evaluative act, i.e., is this content good or bad—rather it should feel like a straightforward act of discovery: "Whoa! This shouldn't be here!"

Your interface design should attempt to reduce the likelihood that users will conflate abuse reporting with other, more evaluative, reputation inputs. Discourage users from reporting anything that is not actual abuse. Figure 8-6 demonstrates a number of design changes that the Yahoo! Answers team enacted to clarify the intent of all the controls, and—as a side benefit—to reduce the likelihood that users would erroneously file reports against undeserving questions or answers.

In general, here are some good guidelines for maintaining the fidelity of your abuse reports, to ensure that they remain good inputs that produce high-confidence content reputations:

- Keep the Report Abuse mechanism clear and distinct from other reputation inputs that could be easily confused. Place it at a noticeable distance from the piece of content that it acts upon. (Though, of course, this is a design balance. It should be close enough that the mechanism and the entity still appear associated.)

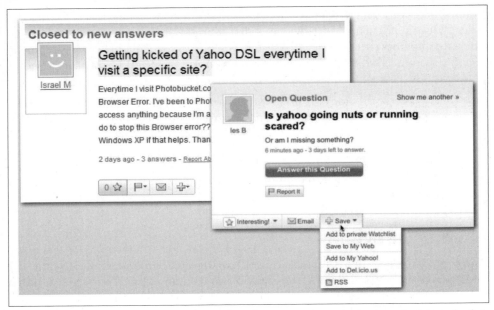

Figure 8-6. *Yahoo! Answers redesigned a number of reputation input mechanisms, both to make their semantic meanings more clear (adding labels to most of the icons, for instance) but also to remove the proximity of one of the most critical inputs, Report It.*

- Require reporters to be signed in (which, of course, requires that they be registered). You can assure reporters that their identities won't be revealed to others in the community, but they should understand that *you* will have access to it. There are two benefits to this: it will help keep folks honest, and you can use a user's history of abuse reports to track *their* reputation as well. (See the section "Who watches the watchers?" on page 209.)

- Put just enough of a "gateway" in place to discourage flippant reports. Ask for enough supporting information for staff to make a judgment, but *don't* ask for a bunch of information that your application could just capture contextually. For instance, pass along any content UIDs or user-identifying information that the report may need.

- In general, try to maintain a fine balance between ease-of-reporting and too much ease. Make it too hard, and concerned users may just opt to leave the site after viewing too much objectionable content. Make it too easy and it'll tempt the community to hurl sticks and stones unnecessarily.

 Just can't get enough abuse? The Report Abuse pattern is also covered in *Designing Social Interfaces* (O'Reilly). See its online discussion at *http://www.designingsocialinterfaces.com/patterns.wiki/index.php?title=Report_Abuse*.

Who watches the watchers?

You've probably already spotted a potential for abuse of another kind here. How can you guard against spurious and malicious use of Report Abuse mechanisms? Inevitably, some in your community will decide that tarring others' content with the suspicion of abuse is an easy path to making their own content stand out. Or they'll use abuse reports to carry out a personal vendetta, or further their own political viewpoint, or...well, you get the point.

The concern is a valid one. Depending on your abuse mitigation process, the costs can vary. If all abuse reports are vetted by staff, then—at the very least—you've lost the time and effort of a staff intervention and investigation. If your application is designed to immediately act on abuse reports and make some mechanistic determination about the content, then you run the risk of punishing content unnecessarily and unfairly. If left to persist, that situation will harm your site's credibility over time.

This is a compelling reason to keep accurate karma scores for all parties involved. Whether your mitigation process is hands-on, highly automated, or some combination of the two, swift and good judgments can only be aided by having as much information as possible about both "sides." Consider keeping a secret corporate reputation (call it *Abuse Reporter reputation*) that tracks users' past performance at finding and reporting abusive content. There are a variety of inputs that could weigh into this karma score:

- The reporter's own past contributions to the site or length of membership (or other indicators of her value to the community).
- The reporter's "success rate" at identifying abusive content: from past reports, how many were legitimate? How many ended up being overturned or denied by qualified staff?
- The volume of reports that the user files. (Note that, depending on the context, a high volume of reports can be considered a positive or a negative.)

A karma score based on these inputs will be invaluable for decision making about the accuracy of any individual report, when compared to the reputations of the reported content and/or the karma scores of the person who *posted* the disputed content.

Teach Your Users How to Fish

Up to now in this chapter, we've focused on reputation-related strategies for improving the perceived quality of content on your site. (Promote this, demote that, whoops, let's hide this one altogether....) The hope is that, by shaping the perceptions of quality, you'll influence your users' behavior and actually see *real* improvements in the quality of contributions. You'll somewhat have to take it on faith that this will work, and—to be fair—the Virtuous Circle ("The Reputation Virtuous Circle" on page 17) is, at best, an indirect and eventual method for positively influencing your community.

Aren't there some more direct ways? Why yes, there are. As it turns out, the methods and methodology of gathering reputation provide an excellent set of tools to help educate your users, and teach them how to be better contributors (or editors or readers or...). Using these techniques, you will be able to:

- Let contributors know "how they're doing" on an ongoing basis.
- Give them specific and—in some cases—quantifiable feedback on the community's response to their contributions.
- Suggest new and different strategies to them, in order to continually improve their content quality.

Inferred Reputation for Content Submissions

An approach that serves a number of different ends is the concept of *Inferred Reputation* for content submissions. With this approach, your application presumes a level of quality for a submission based on the karma of the content submitter and an appraisal of the intrinsic qualities of the submission itself. This appraisal may take any number of factors into consideration: the presence of profanity; the completeness of accompanying metadata, the length or brevity of the submission, and other community- or application-specific evaluations that make sense within the given context.

Once evaluated, the content submission is given an initial reputation. This can be displayed alongside the submission until it's garnered enough attention to display an actual, earned reputation, as in Figure 8-7. (How will you know when to switch over to display the actual reputation? When enough community members have rated the item that it's surpassed the *liquidity threshold*. See "Liquidity: You Won't Get Enough Input" on page 58.)

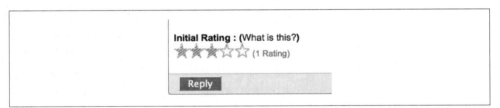

Figure 8-7. In the absence of any specific knowledge of this post (only one person has rated it), Yahoo! Message Boards assumes that it's a 3-star post.

Why would you want to use inferred reputations? For a number of reasons.

Inferred reputation is all but mandatory if your application features a Configurable Quality Threshold (see "Configurable Quality Thresholds" on page 205). When users have their threshold for content visibility set too high, then—unless you show Initial Ratings—new postings will, by default, not appear at all in content listings, which, of course, means that no one will rate those items, which means that no one will *see* those items...you can see the problem here. You will have created a self-referential *feedback loop*. (See "Beware Feedback Loops!" on page 226.)

Inferred reputations can also help influence contributor behavior in positive ways. Their simplest, but perhaps most critical, function is to educate your users that the quality of their contributions have consequences. Put simply: if they post better stuff, more people will see it. A visible and tangible initial rating makes this case more strongly than any number of admonitions or reminders would.

Just-in-time reputation calculation

A powerful enhancement to inferred reputation is the idea of showing the assumed rating *to* the content contributor even before she has contributed it. This amplifies the positive-modeling benefits mentioned earlier.

Then, you can allow the contributor to *modify* her content submission before posting it, in an effort to improve the quality, improve the initial rating assigned, and be featured more prominently on the site. The facets for improvement can be any of a number of things: simple formatting fixes, community-standards violations (e.g., SHOUTING IN ALL CAPS), or perhaps modifying a submission to be less derivative or repetitive of a submission that's come before it.

Figure 8-8 shows one such embodiment of these just-in-time principles. This draft of a design for Yahoo! Message Boards affords the person posting the message an opportunity to reflect on what he's about to post, validate it against community standards, and—if desired—change the message to improve its standing.

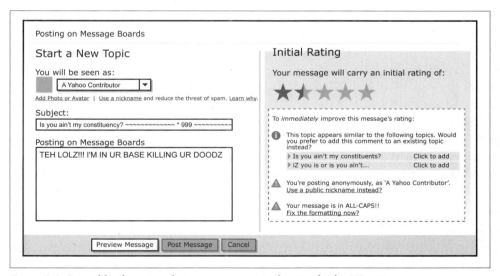

Figure 8-8. Don't like the rating that your new post is about to display? Fix it!

A Private Conversation

In the last chapter, we discussed personal reputations (see "Personal Reputations: For the Owner's Eyes Only" on page 169) and hinted at some of their utility. But you may still have questions: why keep a personal reputation? If you have no intent to display it to the community (a "public" reputation), shouldn't a completely hidden (a "corporate") reputation suffice? Why would you keep a reputation, and go to the bother of displaying it but *only* for the person to whom it applies?

Personal reputations have great utility as a type of "running internal dialog" between a site and its users, showing personal reputations to users to let them know how they're doing with respect to certain facets of their engagement with the community. Upon login, for example, you might show users the Learning Level they've achieved toward a certain task so that they may track their growth progression and understand what actions are necessary—or what skills must be mastered— to reach the next level on the scale.

LinkedIn keeps a very simple, but compelling, type of reputation that serves this end (see Figure 8-9). It shows you the degree of completeness that your LinkedIn Profile has achieved.

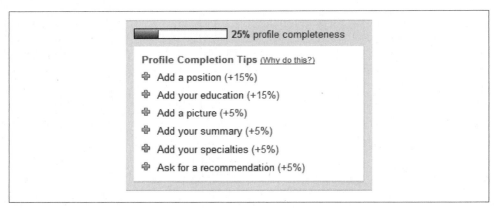

Figure 8-9. Your LinkedIn profile is only 25% complete?!? Better get crackin'!

The motivational benefits of this feature are enormous. There is a certain compulsive, game-like quality to its presence. Author and online community authority Amy Jo Kim has written and presented about the appeal of "collecting" (and the power of completing a set) in game mechanics, and the applicability of these impulses to online experience. This LinkedIn widget deftly takes advantage of these deep underlying impulses that motivate us all.

It's almost impossible to see that partially empty progress bar and *not* want to fill it up. LinkedIn takes the additional step of providing hints about the exact ways to accomplish this.

So what, then, is the advantage of handling this as a personal conversation between site and user? Notice that LinkedIn doesn't show you *other people's* profile completeness scores. Leaving this as a personal reputation means that the user is never stigmatized. She is free to advance and proceed at her own pace, but is never branded or labeled in a public fashion. Her interaction with your site remains *hers* and hers alone. Even on a largely social site, *not everything* needs to belong to the commons. Many times, reputation is better kept discrete.

Course-Correcting Feedback

Creating content to share online can be a lonely business. Sometimes it's hard to know exactly how you're doing. This is a beneficial side effect of gathering inputs for content reputation: you can package up the results of those inputs, and present them back to content contributors in educational and motivational ways. Give them detailed direction on how well the community is accepting their contributions and even suggest ways to increase that acceptance.

This, again, can function within the realm of personal, site-to-user, reputations and need not be a public affair. Of course, any reputations that *are* public will benefit contributors as well; they are free to review and compare their standings against those of their peers. But you should also feel free to give *even more* feedback to a contributor about how they're doing in a personal and confidential fashion. Flickr presents a rich dashboard of statistics about your photos, including many details of how the community has responded (see Figure 8-10).

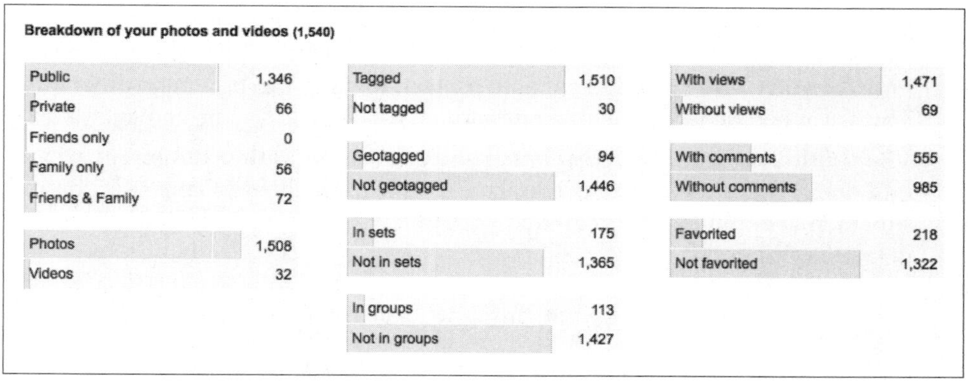

Breakdown of your photos and videos (1,540)					
Public	1,346	Tagged	1,510	With views	1,471
Private	66	Not tagged	30	Without views	69
Friends only	0				
Family only	56	Geotagged	94	With comments	555
Friends & Family	72	Not geotagged	1,446	Without comments	985
Photos	1,508	In sets	175	Favorited	218
Videos	32	Not in sets	1,365	Not favorited	1,322
		In groups	113		
		Not in groups	1,427		

Figure 8-10. Favorites, comments, and views all feed your photos reputation on Flickr. The "Stats" feature breaks them down for you.

Reputation Is Identity

Imagine you're at a party, and your friend Ted wants you to meet his friend Mary. He might very well say something like: "I want you to meet my friend Mary. She's the brunette over by the buffet line." A fine, beginning, to be sure. It helps to know who you're dealing with.

But now imagine that Ted *ended* there as well. He *doesn't* take you by the hand, walk you over to Mary, and introduce you face to face. Maybe he walks off to get another drink. Um...this does not bode well for your new friendship with Mary.

Sadly, until fairly recently, this has been the state of identity on much of the Web. When people were represented at all, they were often nothing more than a meager collection of sparse data elements: a username, maybe an avatar, just enough identifying characteristics that you might recognize them again later, but not much else.

With the advent of *social* on the Web, things have improved. Perhaps the biggest improvement has been that now people's relationships formulate a sizable component of their identity and presence on most sites. Now, mutual friends or acquaintances can act as a natural entrée to forming new relationships. So at least Ted now *will* go that extra step and walk you over to that buffet table for a proper introduction.

But, you still won't know much about Mary, will you? Once introductions are out of the way, what will you possibly have to talk about? The addition of reputation to your site will provide that much needed final dimension to your users' identities, depth. Wouldn't it be nice to review a truly rich and deep view of Mary's identity on your site *before* deciding what you and she will or won't have in common?

Here are but a few reasons why user identities on your site will be stronger *with* reputation than they would be without:

- *Reputation is based on history* and the simple act of recording those histories—a user's past actions, or voting history, or the history of their relationship to the site—provides you with a lot of content (and *context*) that you can present to other users. This is a much richer model of identity than just a display-name and an avatar.

- *Visible histories reveal shared affinities* and allow users with common interests to find one another. If you are a Top Contributor in the Board Games section of a site, then like-minded folks can find you, follow you, or invite you to participate in their activities.

 You'll find contexts where this is *not* desirable. On a question-and-answer site like Yahoo! Answers, for instance, don't be surprised to find out that many users won't *want* their questions about gonorrhea or chlamydia to appear as part of their historical record. Err on the side of giving your users control over what appears, or give them the ability to hide their participation history altogether.

- *A past is hard to fake.* Most site identities are cheap. In and of themselves, they just don't mean much. A couple of quick form fields, a Submit button, and practically anyone (or *no one*—bots welcome!) can become a full-fledged member of most sites. It is much harder, however, to fake a history of interaction with a site for any duration of time.

  We don't mean to imply that it can't be done—harvesting "deep" identities is practically an offshoot industry of the MMORPG world. (See Figure 8-11.) But it *does* provide a fairly high participatory hurdle to jump. When done properly, user karma can assure some level of commitment and engagement from your users (or at least help you to ascertain those levels quickly).

- *Reputation disambiguates identity conflicts.* Hopefully, you've moved away from publicly identifying users on your site by their unique identifier. (You *have* read the Tripartite Identity Pattern, right? See *http://habitatchronicles.com/2008/10/the -tripartite-identity-pattern/*.) But this introduces a whole new headache: identity spoofing. If your public namespace doesn't guarantee uniqueness (or even if it *does*, it'll be hard to guard against similar-appearing-speak equivalents and the like), you'll have this problem.

  Once your community is at scale, trolls will take great delight in appropriating others' identities—assuming the same display name, uploading the same avatar— purely in an effort to disrupt conversations. It's not a perfect defense, but always associate a contributor's identity with her participation history or reputation to help mitigate these occurrences. You will, at least, have armed the community with the information they need to decide who's legit and who's an interloper.

Figure 8-11. People will pay more for a developed identity on World of Warcraft than they paid for the game itself. (Even when you factor in 12 months of subscription fees!)

These are some of the reasons that extending user identities with reputation is useful. What follows is a series of considerations for *how* to do so most effectively. Some methods for surfacing reputation at the right spots in your interface to most effectively aid users in making good judgments about each other.

On the User Profile

The User Profile is an invaluable asset in your social strategy. In many ways, it provides the most "tangible" and visible presence for the users on your site. It functions as the locus of a user's identity and, as such, can accommodate a number of different reputation display patterns. Consider showing each of the following on user profiles.

My Affiliations

By now, you should be aware that reputation is earned within a context. While individual actors are probably the last person you should ask *about* their reputation, each of us does control one very important component of our reputations: the contexts we choose to affiliate ourselves with. Sometimes, the *degree* of reputation you've earned somewhere says less than the fact that you chose to frequent that context in the first place.

Surfacing the breadth and variety of reputable contexts that a user frequents can be crucial information for other users to make value judgments about that person. You should, of course, allow the profile-holder some degree of control over exactly which affiliations they choose to display or obscure. Some models allow for displaying only those associated contexts that a user has *requested* to appear on his profile.

Figure 8-12 shows a typical LinkedIn profile with group affiliations displayed. These can be considered self-selected reputable contexts; the particular combination of them can tell an evaluator a lot about a person, and provides opportunities for establishing shared interests.

Earned reputations can also provide deeper insight into a user's affiliations and interests. Figure 8-13 shows a user and the participation medals he's earned on Yahoo! Message Boards. Here, affiliation information is a powerful tool for assessing this user's competencies.

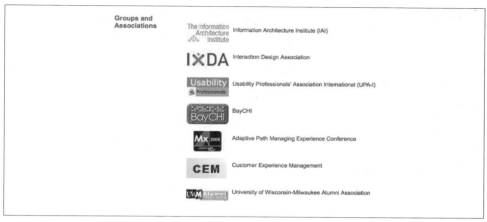

Figure 8-12. You're judged by the company you keep. Even a simple list of groups that you've joined on LinkedIn says a lot about your interests and how you choose to use your time and energy.

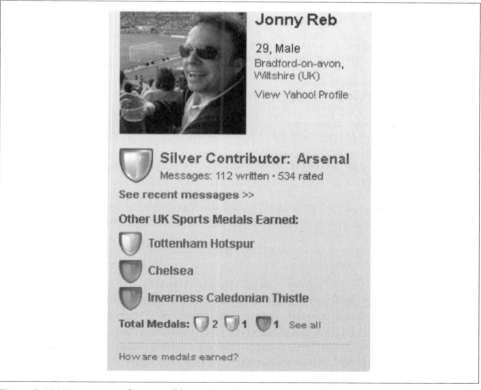

Figure 8-13. Participation history adds another dimension to your affiliations. Now you can see not only where Jonny Reb spends his time, but exactly how much he's invested in each context.

My History

An extremely popular piece of reputation information to disclose on a user profile (and a profoundly powerful one) is simple a user's "Member Since" date. Like a business establishment that boasts of its decades- or centuries-old history, once users on your site have achieved a certain seniority will want others to know and honor their status of longevity.

There are other important pieces of historical information that you should consider providing. Perhaps just a simple listing of a user's last *N* contributions to the site. Yahoo! Answers uses the user profile as a centralized, easy-access "dashboard view" into a person's history of contributions. (See Figure 8-14.)

Figure 8-14. Let your users' words speak for themselves. Yahoo! Answers lets you review a user's Questions and Answers from the profile, regardless of which context the question was originally posted in.

My Achievements

First popularized by the Xbox 360 gaming platform, the notion of rewarding specific user achievements is catching on. Figure 8-15 shows one such embodiment on the software programming Q&A site StackOverflow.com. Once they're earned, Achievements can be displayed on a users profile in perpetuity, providing a fun, engaging, and browsable history of that user's interaction with the site.

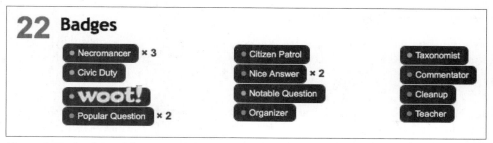

Figure 8-15. Stack Overflow awards badges for any number of user achievements; "woot!," for instance, celebrates users who have "visited the site each day for 30 days."

At the Point of Attribution

It can be very powerful to display a user's reputation directly within the context of her contribution. Amazon identifies "Top Reviewers" in situ, right at the point where you're reading one of her reviews. (See Figure 8-16.) If done discretely, this approach is useful for a couple of different reasons.

It provides some differentiation between items. In a long scrolling page of product reviews, or music playlists, or video contributions, it can be a nice, quick visual scanning aid to see certain contributors called out for special attention.

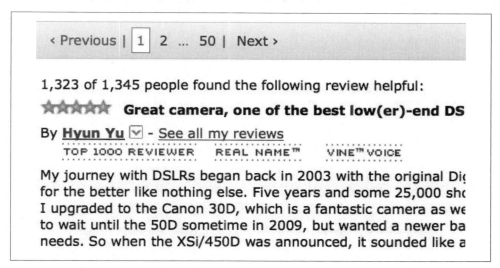

Figure 8-16. There's no need to leave the page to see this reviewer's bona fides.

To Differentiate Within Listings

In a long scannable list of user-generated content, it may be useful to visually "tag" or identify contributions that have achieved a certain level of reputation (or whose *contributors* have). The goal is to aid in scannability, so do this only if the complexity of the interface allows for it.

It helps, when doing this, if you've set reasonable boundaries for the exclusivity of reputations (see "Keep great reputations scarce" on page 239). Otherwise, everything will be tagged as special and nothing will stand out. Figure 8-17 is probably on the borderline of how much reputation information you should attempt to codify into your content listings.

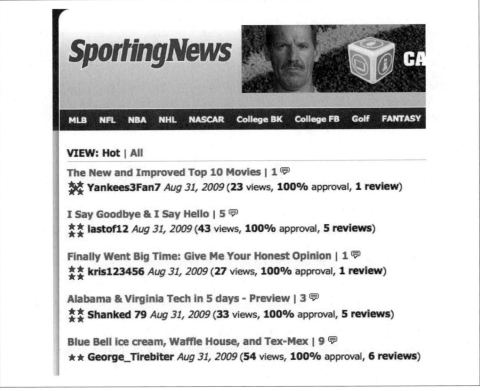

Figure 8-17. Sporting News assigns contributor ranks to each blogger, and annotates lists of blog-entries with their Star Rank. (But, boy, that's a whole lot of stars!)

Putting It All Together

We've helped you identify all of the reputation features for an application: the goals, objects, scope, inputs, outputs, processes, and the sorts filters. You're armed with a rough reputation model diagram and design patterns for displaying and using your reputation scores. These make up your reputation product requirements. In Chapter 9, we describe how to turn these plans into action: building and testing the model, integrating with your application, and performing the early reputation model turning.

Application Integration, Testing, and Tuning

If you've been following the steps provided in Chapters 5 through 8, you know your goals; have a diagram of your reputation model with initial calculations formulated; and have a handful of screen mock-ups showing how you will gather, display, and otherwise use reputation to increase the value of your application. You have ideas and plans, so now it is time to reduce it all to code and to start seeing how it all works together.

Integrating with Your Application

A reputation system does not exist in a vacuum; it is small machine in your larger application. There are a bunch of fine-grained connections between it and your various data sources, such as logs, event streams, identity db, entity db, and your high-performance data store. Connecting it will most likely require custom programming to connect the wires between your reputation engine and subsystems that were never connected before.

This step is often overlooked in scheduling, but it may take up a significant amount of your total project development time. There are usually small tuning adjustments that are required once the inputs are actually hooked up in a release environment. This chapter will help you understand how to plan for connecting the reputation engine to your application and what final decisions you will need to make about your reputation model.

Implementing Your Reputation Model

The heart of your new reputation-infused application is the reputation model. It's that important. For the sake of clarity, we refer to the software engineers that turn your model into operational code as the *reputation implementation team* and those who are going to connect the application input and output as the *application team*. In many contexts, there are some advantages to these being the same people, but consider that reputation, especially shared reputation, is so valuable to your entire product line that it might be worth having a small dedicated team for the implementation, testing, and tuning full time.

Engage Engineering Early and Often

One of the hard-learned lessons of deploying reputation systems at Yahoo! is the engineering team needs to be involved at every major milestone during the design process. Even if you have a separate reputation implementation team to build and code the model, the gathering of all the inputs and integrating the outputs is significant new work added to their already overtaxed schedule.

As the result of reputation, the very nature of your application is about to change significantly, and those on the engineering team are the ones who will turn all of this wonderful theory and the lovely screen mock-ups into code. Reputation is going to touch code all over the place.

Besides, who knows your reputable entities better than the application team? It builds the software that gives your entities meaning. Engaging these key stakeholders early allows them to contribute to the model design and prepares them for the nature of the coming changes.

Don't wait to share details about the reputation model design process until after screen mocks are distributed to engineering for scheduling estimates. There's too much happening on the reputation backend that isn't represented in those images.

Appendix A contains a deeper technical-architecture-oriented look at how to define the reputation framework: the software environment for executing your reputation model. Any plan to implement your model will require significant software engineering, so sharing that resource with the team is essential. Reviewing the framework requirements will lead to many questions from the implementation team about specific trade-offs related to issues such as scalability, reliability, and shared data. The answers will put constraints on your development schedule and the application's capabilities. One lesson is worth repeating here: the process boxes in the reputation model diagram are a notational convenience and *advisory*; they are *not* implementation requirements.

 There is no ideal programming language for implementing reputation models. In our experience, what matters most is for the team to be able to create, review, and test the model code rigorously. Keeping each reputation process's code tight, clean, and well documented is the best defense against bugs and vastly simplifies testing and tuning the model.

Rigging Inputs

A typical complex reputation model, such as those described in Chapters 4 and 10, can have dozens of inputs, spread throughout the four corners of your application. Often implementors think only of the explicit user-entered inputs, when many models also include nonuser or implicit inputs from places such as logfiles or customer care agents. As such, rigging inputs often involves engineers from differing engineering teams, each with their own prioritized development schedule. This means that the inputs will be attached to the model incrementally.

This challenge requires that the reputation model implementation be resilient in the face of missing inputs. One simple strategy is to have the reputation processes that handle inputs have reasonable default values for every input. Inferred karma is an example (see "Generating inferred karma" on page 159). This approach also copes well if a previously reliable source of inputs becomes inactive, either through a network outage or simply a localized application change.

Explicit inputs, such as ratings and reviews, take much longer to implement as they have significant user-interface components. Consider the overhead with something as simple as a thumbs-up/thumbs-down voting model. What does it look like if the user hasn't voted? What if he wants to change his vote? What if he wants to remove his vote altogether?

For models with many explicit reputation inputs, all of this work can cause a waterfall effect on testing the model. Waiting until the user interface is done to test the model causes the testing period to be very short because of management pressure to deliver new features—"The application *looks* ready, so why haven't we shipped?"

We found that getting a primitive user interface in place quickly for testing is essential. Our voting example can be quickly represented in a web application as two text-links: "Vote Yes," "Vote No," and text next to it that represented the tester's previous vote: "(You [haven't] voted [Yes|No].)" Trivial to implement, no art requirements, no mouse-overs, no compatibility testing, no accessibility review, no pressure to ship early, but completely functional. This approach allows the reputation team to test the input flow and the functionality of model. This sort of development interface is also amenable to robotic regression testing.

Applied Outputs

The simplest output is reflecting explicit reputation back to users—showing their star-rating for a camera back to them when they visit the camera again in the future, or on their profile for others to see. The next level of output is the display of roll-ups, such as the average rating from all users about that camera. The specific patterns for these are discussed in detail in Chapter 7. Unlike the case with integrating inputs, these outputs can be simulated easily by the reputation implementation team on its own, so there isn't a dependency on other application teams to determine if a roll-up result is accurate. One practice during debugging a model is to simply log every input with the changes to the roll-ups that were generated, giving a historical view of the model's state over time.

But, as we detailed in Chapter 8, these explicit displays of reputation aren't usually the most interesting or valuable; using reputation to identify and filter the best (and worst) reputable entities in your application is. Using reputation output to perform these tasks is more deeply integrated with the application. For example, search results may be ranked by a combination of a keyword search and reputation score. A user's report of TOS-violating content might want to compare the karma of the author of the content to the reporter. These context-specific uses require tight integration with the application.

This leads to an unusual suggested implementation strategy—code the complex reputation uses *first*. Get the skeleton reputation-influenced search results page working even before the real inputs are built. Inputs are easy to simulate, the reputation model needs to be debugged as well as the application-side weights used for the search will need tuning. This approach will also quickly expose the scaling sensitivities in the system—in web applications, search tends to consume the most resources by far. Save the fiddling over the screen presentation of roll-ups for last.

Beware Feedback Loops!

Remember our discussion of credit scores, way back in Chapter 1? Though over-reliance on a global reputation like FICO is generally bad policy, some particular uses are especially problematic. The *New York Times* recently pointed out a truly insidious problem that has arisen as employers have begun to base hiring determinations on job applicants' credit scores. Matthew W. Finkin, law professor at the University of Illinois, who fears that the unemployed and debt-ridden could form a luckless class said:

> How do you get out from under it [a bad credit rating]? You can't re-establish your credit if you can't get a job, and you can't get a job if you've got bad credit.

This mis-application of your credit rating creates a *feedback loop*. This is a situation in which the inputs into the system (in this case, your employment) are dependent in some part upon the output from the system.

Why are feedback loops bad? Well, as the *Times* points out, feedback loops are self-perpetuating and, once started, nigh-impossible to break. Much like in music production (Jimi Hendrix notwithstanding), feedback loops are generally to be avoided because they muddy the fidelity of the signal.

Plan for Change

Change may be good, but your community's reaction to change won't always be positive. We are, indeed, advocating for a certain amount of architected flexibility in the design and implementation of your system. We are *not* encouraging you to actually make such changes lightly or liberally. Or without some level of deliberation and scrutiny before each input-tweak or badge addition.

Don't overwhelm your community with changes. The more established the community is, the greater the social inertia that will set in. People get used to "the way things work" and may not embrace frequent and (seemingly random) changes to the system. This is a good argument for obscuring some of its details. (See "Keep Your Barn Door Closed (but Expect Peeking)" on page 91.)

Also pay some heed to the manner in which you introduce new reputation-related features to your community:

- Have your community manager announce the features on your product blog, along with a solicitation for public feedback and input. That last part is important because, though these may be feature additions or changes like any other, oftentimes they are fundamentally transformative to the experience of engaging with your application. Make sure that people know they have a voice in the process and their opinion counts.

- Be careful to be simultaneously clear—in describing what the new features are—and vague in describing exactly how they work. You want the community to become familiar with these fundamental changes to their experience, so that they're not surprised or, worse, offended when they first encounter them in the wild. But you *don't* want everyone immediately running out to "kick the tires" of the new system, poking prodding and trying to earn reputation to satisfy their "thirst for first." (See "Personal or private incentives: The quest for mastery" on page 119.)

- There is a certain class of changes that you probably shouldn't announce at all. Low-level tweaking of your system—the addition of a new input, readjusting the weightings of factors in a reputation model—can usually be done on an ongoing basis and, for the most part, silently. (This is not to say that your community won't notice, however; do a web search on "YouTube most popular algorithm" to see just how passionately and closely that community scrutinizes every reputation-related tweak.)

Testing Your System

As with all new software deployment, there are several phases of testing recommended: bench testing, environmental testing (aka alpha), and predeployment testing (aka beta). Note that we don't mean web-beta, which has come to mean deployed applications that can be assumed, by the users, to be unreliable; we mean pre- or limited deployment.

Bench Testing Reputation Models

A well-coded reputation model should function with simulated inputs. This allows the reputation implementation team to confirm that the messages flow through the model correctly and provides a means to test the accuracy of the calculations and the performance of the system.

Rushed development budgets often cause project staff to skip this step to save time and to instead focus the extra engineering resources on rigging the inputs or implementing a new output—after all, nothing like real data to let you know if everything's working properly, right? In the case of reputation model implementations, this assumption has been proven both false and costly every single time we've seen it deployed. Bench testing would have saved hundreds of thousands of dollars in effort on the Yahoo! Shopping Top Reviewer karma project.

Bench Test Your Model with the Data You Already Have. Always.

The first reputation team project at Yahoo! was intended to encourage Yahoo! Shopping users to write more product reviews for the upcoming fall online shopping season.

It decided to create a karma that would appeal to people who already write reviews and respond to ego-based rewards: Top Reviewer karma. A small badge would appear next to the name of users who wrote many reviews, especially those that received a large number of helpful votes. This was intended to be a combination of quantitative and qualitative karma. The badges would read Top 100, Top 500, and Top 1000 reviewers. There would also be a leaderboard for each badge, where the members of each group were randomized before display to discourage people trying to abuse the system. (See "Flickr Interestingness Scores for Content Quality" on page 88.)

Over several weeks and dozens of meetings, the team defined the model using a prototype of the graphical grammar presented in this book. The final version was very similar to that presented in "User Reviews with Karma" on page 75 in Chapter 5. The weighting constants were carefully debated and set to favor quality with a score four times higher than the value of writing a review. The team also planned to give users backdated credit to reviewers by writing an input simulator by reading the current ratings-and-reviews database and running them through the reputation model.

The planning took so long that the implementation schedule was crushed—the only way to get it to deployment on time was to code it quickly and enable it immediately. No bench testing, no analysis of the model or the backdated input simulator. The application team made sure the pages loaded and the inputs all got sent, and then pushed it live in early October.

The good news was that everything was working. The bad news? It was *really* bad: every single user on the Top Reviewer 100 list had something in common. They all wrote dozens or hundreds of CD reviews. All music users, all the time. Most of the reviews were "I liked it" or "SUX0RZ," and the helpful scores almost didn't figure into the calculation at all. It was too late to change anything significant in the model and so the project failed to accomplish its goal.

> A simple bench test with the currently available data would have revealed the fatal flaw in the model. The presumed reputation context was just plain *wrong*—there is no such thing as a global "Yahoo! Shopping" context for karma. The team should have implemented per-product category reviewer karma: who writes the best digital camera reviews? Who contributes the classical CD reviews that others regard as the most helpful?

Besides accuracy and determining suitability of the model for its intended purposes, one of the most important benefits of bench testing is stress testing of performance. Almost by definition, initial deployment of a model will be incremental—smaller amounts of data are easier to track and debug and there are less people to disappoint if the new feature doesn't always work or is a bit messy. In fact, bench testing is the only time the reputation team will be able to accurately predict the performance of the model under stress until long after deployment, when some peak usage brings it to the breaking point, potentially disabling your application.

Do not count on the next two testing phases to stress test your model. They won't, because that isn't what they are for.

Professional-grade testing methodologies, usually using scripting languages such as JavaScript or PHP, are available as open source and as commercial packages. Use one to automate simulated inputs to your reputation model code as well as to simulate the reputation output events of a typical application, such as searches, profile displays, and leaderboards. Establish target performance metrics and test various normal- and peak-operational load scenarios. Run it until it breaks and either tune the system and/or establish operational contingency plans with the application engineers. For example, say that hitting the reputation database for a large number of search results is limited to 100 requests per second and the application team expects that to be sufficient for the next few months—after which either another database request processor will be deployed, or the application will get more performance by caching common searches in memory.

Environmental (Alpha) Testing Reputation Models

After bench testing has begun and there is some confidence that the reputation model code is stable enough for the application team to develop against, crude integration can begin in earnest. As suggested in "Rigging Inputs" on page 225, application developers should go for breadth (getting all the inputs/outputs quickly inserted) instead of depth (getting a single reputation score input/output working well). Once this reputation scaffolding is in place, both the application team and the reputation team can test the characteristics of the model in it's actual operating environment.

Also, any formal or informal testing staff that are available can start using the new reputation features while they are still in development allowing for feedback about calculation and presentation. This is when the fruits of the reputation designer's labor begin to manifest: an input leads to a calculation leads to some valuable change in the application's output. It is most likely that this phase will find minor problems in calculation and presentation, while it is still inexpensive to fix them.

Depending on the size and duration of this testing phase, initial reputation model tuning may be possible. One word of warning though: testers at this phase, even if they are from outside your formal organization, are not usually representative of your post-deployment users, so be careful what conclusions you draw about their reputation behavior. Someone who is drawing a paycheck or was given special-status access is *not* a typical user, unless your application is for a corporate intranet.

Once the input rigging is complete and placeholder outputs are working, the reputation team should adjust its user-simulation testing scripts to better match the actual use behavior they are seeing from the testers. Typically this means adjusting assumptions about the number and types of inputs versus the volume and composition of the reputation read requests. Once done, rerun the bench tests, especially the stress tests, to see how the results have changed.

Predeployment (Beta) Testing Reputation Models

The transformation the predeployment stage of testing is marked by at least two important milestones:

- The application/user interface is now nominally complete (meets specification); it's no longer embarrassing to allow noninsiders to use it.
- The reputation model is fully functional, stable, performing within specifications, and is outputting reasonable reputation statement claim values, which implies that your system has sufficient instrumentation to evaluate the results of a larger scale test.

A predeployment testing phase is important when introducing a new reputation system to an application as it enables a very different and largely unpredictable class of user interactions driven by diverse and potentially conflicting motivations. See "Incentives for User Participation, Quality, and Moderation" on page 111. The good news is that most of the goals typical for this testing phase also apply to testing reputation models, with a few minor additions.

Performance: Testing scale

Although the maximum throughput of the reputation system should have been determined during the bench-testing phase, engaging a large number of users during the beta test will reveal a much more realistic picture of the expected use patterns in deployment. The shapes of peak usage, the distribution of inputs, and especially the reputation query rates should be measured and the bench tests should be rerun using these observations. This should be done at least twice: halfway through the beta, and a week or two before deployment, especially as more testers are added over time.

Confidence: Testing computation accuracy

As beta users contribute to the reputation system, an increasingly accurate picture of the nature of their evaluations will emerge. Early during this phase the accuracy of the model calculations should be manually confirmed, especially double-checking an independently logged input stream against the resulting reputation claim values. This is an end-to-end validation process, and particular attention should be paid to reputation statements that contain inputs that were reversed or manually changed (due to abuse mitigation or other circumstances). Once a reputation model is in full deployment, this verification process will become significantly more expensive, so the beta test is usually the last chance to cheaply find bugs and conversely reinforce confidence in the system.

Application optimization: Measuring use patterns

Reputation systems change the way applications display content. Those changes add elements to the user interface that require additional space and new user behavior learning, and change the flow of the application significantly. A good example of this effect is when search URL reputation (page ranking) replaced hand-built directories as the primary method for finding content on the Web.

When a reputation-enabled application enters predeployment testing, tracking the actions of users—their clicks, evaluations, content contributions, and even their eye movements—provides important information to optimize the effectiveness of the model and the application as a whole.

Feedback: Evaluating customer's satisfaction

Despite our focus on measuring the performance and flow of user interaction, we'd like to caution that pure quantitative testing can lead to faulty conclusions about the effectiveness of your application, especially if the metrics are not as positive as you expected. Everyone knows that when metrics are bad, all the tell you is that you've done something wrong, not what it is. But that is also often true for good metrics—a lot of page-views doesn't always mean you have a healthy or profitable product. Sometimes it's quite the contrary, controversial objects generate a lot of heat (in the form of online discussion) but can create negative value to the provider.

In the beta phase, explicit feedback is required to help understand how users perceive the application, especially the reputation system. Besides multiple opt-in feedback channels, such as email or a message boards, guided surveys are strongly recommended. In our experience, opt-in message formats don't accurately represent the opinions of the largest group of users—the *lurkers*—those that only consume reputation and never explicitly evaluate anything. At least in applications that are primarily advertising supported, the lurkers actually produce the largest chunk of revenue.

Value: Measuring ROI

During the predeployment phase the instrumentation is used to regularly measure the effect on revenue and/or other critical success metrics, such as engagement and customer satisfaction. After deployment the daily, weekly, and monthly reports of these business metrics will become the bible for driving the application and model designs forward, so getting them established during this phase is critical to getting management to understand why the investment in reputation is worthwhile. The beta test phase *will not* demonstrate that reputation has been successful/profitable, but it will establish the means for determining when it becomes so.

Tuning Your System

Sometime in the latter half of the testing phase, the reputation system begins to operate sufficiently well enough to gauge the general effect it will have on the application and early indications of its likely success against the original goals. This is when the ongoing process of reputation model tuning can begin.

Tuning for ROI: Metrics

The most important thing the reputation team can do when implementing and deploying a reputation system is to define the key metrics for success. What are the numerical measures that a reputation-enabled application is contributing to the goals set out for it? For each measure, what are the target values? Is there a predicted lift in user contributions? Should there be more page-views? Is there an expected direct effect on product revenues? Is the model expected to decrease customer care costs? By how much? All of these metrics allow both the application and reputation teams to identify areas for tuning. Sometimes just the application will need to be adjusted, other times just the model will, and (especially early on) sometimes it will all need tuning.

Certainly the reputation team should have metrics for performance, such as the number of reputation statement writes per second and a maximum latency of such-and-such milliseconds for 95% of all reputation queries, but those are internal metrics for the system and do not represent the value of the reputation itself to the applications that use it.

Every change to the reputation model and application should be measured against all corporate and success-related metrics. Resist the desire to tune things unless you have a specific goal to change one or more of your most important metrics.

Beware Excessive Tuning: The Hawthorne Effect

In 1924, the Western Electric company commissioned a multiyear study for their Hawthorne Works facility to see whether its workers would become more productive in higher or lower levels of light. In 1955, Henry A. Landsberger analyzed the data gathered and observed an interesting pattern, now known as the Hawthorne effect.

He noticed that the employees provided short-lived productivity increases *in response to the fact that they were being studied*. It did not seem to matter if the lighting was raised or lowered. He concluded that the fact that the study was communicated to the workers made it clear that management was paying attention had a greater morale effect than particular changes to the environment. Other changes that showed similar effects also included moving workstations, clearing the floors, and maintaining work areas.

On this insight alone, it should be clear that reputation model tuning should not only be judged by goal-centric objectives, but also that any model changes should be given ample time to stabilize. A spike in activity immediately after the release of a reputation change is not, necessarily, an indication that the change is working as intended. It is good to assume the Hawthorne effect is in play until things stabilize.

But, the story of this effect gets even more interesting and relevant.

The Wikipedia entry for the Hawthorne Effect has a rather large section entitled *Interpretations and criticisms of the Hawthorne studies* that quotes many modern scholars challenging many of the details in Landsberger's two decades delayed analysis. From that entry: "A psychology professor at the University of Michigan, Dr. Richard Nisbett, calls the Hawthorne Effect 'a glorified anecdote.' 'Once you've got the anecdote,' he said, 'you can throw away the data.'"

The existence of significant questions surrounding this effect reinforces the fact that, when it comes to human behavior, there is a tendency to over-extrapolate from the available data, while ignoring all of the factors that aren't even quantitative measured or even measurable.

This problematic simplified extrapolation can also happen while tuning reputation models. It's easy to say, "Oh! I know what they're doing." That's fine as far as it goes, but the school of hard knocks has taught us that for every behavior we posit, there are at least two more we are missing. If you really want to know how your model is working, you'll have to do both qualitative and quantitative research. Use your metrics to create groups based on similar activity patterns and then reach out and *ask* them why they do what they do.

Model tuning

Initially any moderately complex reputation model will need tuning. Plan for it in the first weeks of the post-deployment period. Best guesses at weighting constants used in reputation calculations, even when based on historical data, will prove to be inaccurate in the light of real-user interaction.

Tune *public* reputation, especially karma, as early as possible.

This does two useful things:

- If the changes required are significant, such as making large adjustment to incentive weights, the change will have the smallest impact on your community as possible.

- Establishing the pattern that reputation can, and will, be changing over time helps set expectations with the early adopters. Getting them used to changes will make future tuning cause less of a community disruption.

End users won't see much of the tuning to the reputation models. For example, corporate reputations (internal-only) such as Spammer-IP can be tuned and returned with impunity—actually it should be tuned regularly to compensate for improved knowledge and as abusers learn to work their way around the system.

When tuning, an A-B test where the proposed changes and the old model can be tested side by side would be ideal, but most application and metrics environments make this cost-prohibitive. Alternatively, when tuning a reputation model, keep a backup snapshot of both the model code *and* the values of the critical metrics of the original for comparison. If after a few days or weeks, the tuned model under-performs against the previous version, it will be less painful to return to the backup.

Application tuning

There are a number of application- and reputation-system related problems that will probably come to light only once a community of real users has been using the application for an extended duration of time. You might see hints of these misunderstandings or mis-comprehensions during early-stage user testing, but you'll have little means of gauging their severity until you analyze the data in bulk. Forgive us an extended example, again from the world of Yahoo! Answers. But it illustrates the kind of back-and-forth tune-observe-tune rhythm that you may need to fall into to improve the performance of the reputation-related elements of your application.

Once upon a time, the Yahoo! Answers interface featured a simple, plain "Star" mechanism associated with a question. The original design intent for the star was to act as a sort of lightweight endorsement of an item, somewhat akin to Facebook's "Like" control. Star-vote totals were to be displayed next to questions in listings, and also feed into a "Most Starred" widget (actually, a tab on a widget, displayed alongside Recent and Popular questions) at the top of the site. When viewing a particular question, you could see a listing of all other users that had "starred" that question.

As a convenience for users, there was one more feature: Answers would keep a list of all the questions that *you* had "starred," and display those on your Profile for others to see (or, you could opt to keep them private, for your eyes only). It was this final feature that may have tipped the utility for some users away from seeing stars primarily as a voting mechanism and instead toward seeing them as a kind of quasi-bookmark for questions.

Up to this point, a user's profile had only ever displayed questions that she'd asked or answered. There was no facility for saving an arbitrary question posed by anyone on the site. Stars finally gave this functionality to Answers users. One might think that this shouldn't be a problem, right? It's just a convenient and emergent use of the Star feature. As William Gibson said, "The street finds it own use for things." (See more about emergence in "Emergent effects and emergent defects" on page 236.)

But the ancillary, downstream reputation effects of those star-votes were still being compiled, and still being applied to some very prominent listings on the site. Remember, those stars votes completely determined the placement of questions in the Most Starred listing. Over time, a disconcerting effect started to take place: users who were, in good faith, reporting bad content as *abusive* (see "Reporting Abuse" on page 207) would subsequently Star those very same questions, to save them for later review. (Probably to come back later and determine whether their complaints had been acted upon by Yahoo! moderators.)

As a result, the Most Starred tab, featured at a high and prominent level of the site, was—with alarming regularity—filling up with the absolute *worst* content on the site! In fact, the worst of the worst, this was the stuff that users felt strongly enough about to report it to Yahoo!. And, given the unbearable time-lags between reporting and moderation on Answers in those days, these horrible questions were actually being *rewarded* with higher visibility on the site for a prolonged period of time.

The Star feature had backfired entirely. When measured against the original metrics laid out for the project (to encourage easier identification of high-quality content on the site), it was evident that a redesign was called for.

In response, the Answers team put some features in place to actually facilitate this report-then-save behavior that it was noticing, but in a way that did not have downstream reputation ramifications. The approach was two-pronged: first, they clarified the purpose and intent of the star-vote (adding the simple label "Interesting!" to the Star button was a huge improvement); second, they provided a different facility for saving a question—one intended to be personal-only, and not displayed back to the community. (And with no observable downstream reputation ramifications.) "Watchlists" on Answers now let a user mark something for future reference, but doesn't assume any specific judgment about the quality of the question being watched (Figure 9-1).

Conditions like these are unlikely to be uncovered during early-stage design and planning, nor will their gravity be easily assessed from small-scale user testing. These are truly application tweaks that will only start to come to light under the load of a public beta. (Though they may crop up again at any time once the application is in production!) Stay nimble, keep an eye on metrics, and pay attention to how folks are actually using the features you've provided.

Figure 9-1. By giving users a simple, private "Watchlist," the Answers designers responded to the needs of Abuse Reporters who wanted to check back in on bad content.

See Chapter 10 for an in-depth case study on a more comprehensive project to not only keep bad content on Answers subdued, but actually *clean it up* and remove it altogether, with much greater accuracy and speed.

Tuning for Behavior

There are many useful sources for reputation input, but source stands out among all others: the user. The vast majority of content on the Web is user-generated, and user feedback generates the reputation that powers the Web. Even every search engine is built on evaluations in the form of links provided not by algorithms, but by people.

In an effort to optimize all of this people-powered value, reputation systems have come to play a large part in creating incentives for user behavior: participation points, top contributor awards, etc. Users then respond to these incentives, changing their behavior, which then requires the reputation systems to be tuned to optimize newer and more sophisticated behavior (including adjustments for undesirable side effects: aka abuse). The cycle then repeats, if you're lucky.

Emergent effects and emergent defects

It's quite possible that—even during the beta period of your deployment—you're noticing some strange effects starting to take hold. Perhaps content items are rising in the ranks that don't entirely seem…deserving somehow. Or maybe you're noticing a predominance of a certain kind of content at the expense of other types. What you're seeing is the character of your community shaking itself out, finding its edges, and defining itself. Tread carefully before deciding how (and if) to intervene.

Check out Delicious's *Popular Bookmarks* ranking for any given week; we bet you'll see a whole lot of "Top N" blog articles (see Figure 9-2). Why might this be? Technology essayist Paul Graham posits that it may be the users of the service, and their motivational mindset, that explain it: "Delicious users are collectors, and a list of N things seems particularly collectible because it's a collection itself." (Graham explores the "List of N Things" phenomenon to some depth at *http://www.paulgraham.com/nthings.html*.) The preponderance of lists on Delicious is a natural offshoot of its context of

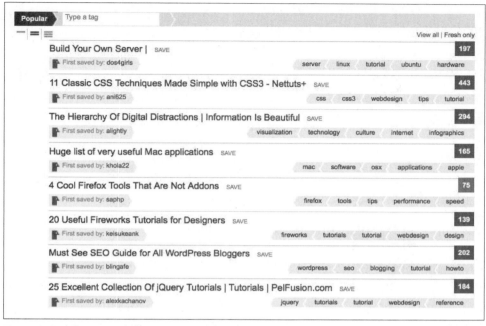

Figure 9-2. What are people saving on Delicious? Lists, lists and more lists…(and there's nothing wrong with that).

use—an emergent effect—and is probably *not* one that you would worry about, nor try to control in any way.

But you may also be seeing the effects of some design decisions that you've made, and you may want to tweak those designs now before wider deployment. Blogger and social media maven Muhammad Saleem noticed one such problem with voting on socially driven news sites such as Digg:

> We are beginning to see a trend where people make assumptions about the contents of an article based on the meta-data associated with the submission rather than reading the article itself. Based on these (oft-flawed) assumptions, people then vote for or against the stories, and even comment on the stories without having read the stories themselves.

> *—http://web.archive.org/web/20061127130645/http://themulife.com/?p=256*

We've noticed a similar tendency on some community-voting sites we've worked on at Yahoo! and have come to consider behavior like this to be a type of emergent *defect*: behavior that is homegrown within the community and may even become a de facto standard for interacting, but is not necessarily valued. In fact, it's basically a *bug* and a failing of your system or—more likely—user interface design.

In instances like these, you should consider tweaking your design, to encourage the proper and appropriate use of the controls you're providing. In some ways, it's not surprising that Digg users are voting on articles based on only surface appraisals; the application's very design in fact encourages this (see Figure 9-3).

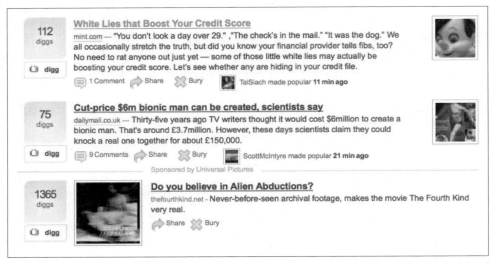

Figure 9-3. The design of Digg enables (one might argue, encourages) voting for articles at a high level of the site. This excerpted screen is the front page of Digg—users can vote for (Digg) an article, or against (bury) it, with no need to read further.

Of course, one should not presuppose that the Digg folks think of this behavior (if it's even as widespread as Saleem indicates) as a defect. Again, it's a careful balance between the actual observed behavior of users and your own predetermined goals and aspirations for the application.

It's quite possible that Digg feels that high voting levels—even if some percentage of those votes are from uninformed users—are important enough to promote voting at higher and higher levels of the site. From a brand perspective alone, it certainly would be odd to visit Digg.com, and not see a single place to Digg something up, right?

Defending against emergent defects. It's hard to anticipate all emergent defects until they... well...emerge. But there are certainly some good principles of design that you can follow that may defend your system against some of the most common ones:

Encourage consumption

If your system's reputations are intended to capture the quality of a piece of content, you should make a good-faith attempt to ensure that users are qualified to make that assessment. Some examples:

- Early on in its lifetime, Apple's iPhone App Store allowed *any* visitor to rate an application, whether they'd purchased it or not! You can probably see the potential for bad data to arise from this situation. A subsequent release addressed this problem, ensuring that only users who'd installed the program would have a voice. It doesn't guarantee perfection, but a gating mechanism for rating does help dampen noise.

- Digg and other social voting sites provide a toolbar that follows logged-in users out to external sites, encouraging them to actually read linked articles before clicking the toolbar-provided voting mechanism. Your application could even *require* an interaction like this for a vote to be counted. (More likely, you'll simply want to weight votes more heavily when they're cast in a guaranteed-better fashion like this.)

- Think of ways to check for consumption in a media-specific way. With videos, for example, perhaps you should give more weight to opinions cast about a video only once the user has passed a certain time-threshold of viewing (or, perhaps, disable voting mechanisms altogether until that time).

Avoid ambiguous controls

Try not to lard too much input overhead onto reputable entities, and try to keep the purpose and primary value of each clear, concise, and nonconflicting. If your design already calls for a Bookmarking or Favorites features, carefully consider whether you also need a Thumbs Up or "I Like It."

In any event, provide some cues to users about the utility of those controls. Are they strictly for expressing an opinion? Sharing with a friend? Saving for later? The downstream effects may, in fact, be that one control does *all three* of these things, but sometimes it's better to suggest clear and consistent uses for controls than let the community muddle along, inventing its own utilities and rationales for things. If a secondary or tertiary use for a control emerges, consider formalizing that function as a new feature.

Keep great reputations scarce

Many of the benefits that we've discussed for tracking reputation (the ability to highlight good contributions and contributors, the ability to "tag" user profiles with awards or recognition, even the simple ability to motivate contributors to excel) can be undermined if you make one simple mistake with your reputation system: being *too generous* with positive reputations. Particularly, if you hand out reputations at the higher end of the spectrum too widely, they will no longer be seen as valuable and rare achievements. You'll also lose the ability to call out great content in long listings; if everything is marked as special, nothing will stand out.

It's probably OK to wait until the tuning phase to address the question of distribution thresholds. You'll need to make some calculations—based on available data for current use of the application—to determine how heavily or lightly to weight certain inputs into the system. A good example is the Gold/Silver/Bronze medal system that we developed at Yahoo! to reward active, quality contributors to UK Sports Message Boards.

We knew that we wanted certain inputs to factor into users' badge-holder reputations: the number of posts posted, how well the community received the posts (i.e., how highly the posts were rated, and so on. But, at first, our guesses at the appropriate thresholds for these activities were just that—guesses.

Take, for instance, one input that was included to indicate dedication to the community: the number of posts that a user had rated. (In general, we caution against simple activity-level indicators for karma, but remember—this is but one input into the model—weighted appropriately against other quality-indicators like community response to your own postings.) We arbitrarily settled on the following minimum thresholds for badge-earners:

- *Bronze Badge*—5 posts rated
- *Silver Badge*—20 posts rated
- *Gold Badge*—100 posts rated

These were simply stabs in the dark—placeholders, really—that we fully expected to tune as we got closer to deployment.

And, in fact, once we'd done an in-depth calculation of project badge numbers in the community (based on Message Board activity levels that were already evident *before* the addition of badges), we realized that these estimates were way too low. We would be giving out millions of Bronze badges, and, heck, still thousands of Golds. This felt way too liberal, given the goals of the project: to identify and reward *only* the most active and valued contributors to boards.

By the time the feature went into production, these minimum thresholds for rating others postings were made *much* higher (orders of magnitude higher) and, in fact, it was several months before the first message board Gold badge actually surfaced in the wild! We considered that a good thing, and perfectly in-line with the business and community metrics we'd laid out at the project's outset.

So...How Much Is Enough?

When you're trying to plan out these distribution thresholds for reputations, your calculations will (of course!) vary with the context of use.

Is this karma (people reputation) or content reputation?
> Be more mindful of the distribution of karma. It's probably OK to have an overabundance of "Trophy-winning videos" floating around your site, but too many top-flight experts risks devaluing the reward altogether.

Honor the presentation pattern
> Some distribution thresholds will be super easy to calibrate; if you're honoring the Top 100 Reviewers on your site, for example, the number of users awarded *should* be fairly self-evident. It's only with more ambiguous patterns that thresholds will need to be actively tuned and massaged to get the desired distributions.

Power-law is your friend
> When in doubt, try to award reputations along a power-law distribution. (Go to *http://en.wikipedia.org/wiki/Power_law*.) Great reputations should be rare, good

---

ones scarce, and mediocre ones should be the norm. This will naturally mimic the natural properties of most networks, so—really—your reputations should reflect those values also.

Tuning for the Future

There are sometimes pleasant surprises when implementing reputation systems for the first time. When users begin to interact with reputation-powered applications, the very nature of the application can change significantly; it often becomes communal—control of the reputable entities shifts from the company to the people.

This shift from a content-centric to a community-centric application often leads to inspirational application designs to be built on the lessons drawn from the existing reputation system. Simply put, if reputation works well for one application, all of the other related applications will want to integrate it, yesterday!

Though new reputation models can be added only as fast as they can be developed, tested, integrated, and deployed, the application team can release new uses for *existing* reputations without coordination and almost instantaneously—it already has access to the reputation API calls. This suggests that the reputation team should continuously optimize for performance against its internal metrics. Expect significant growth, especially in the number of reputation queries. Even if the primary application, as originally implemented, doesn't grow daily users by an unexpected rate, expect the application team to add new types of uses, such as more reputation-weighted searches, or to add more pages that display a reputation score.

Tuning reputation systems for ROI, behavior, and future improvements is a never-ending process. If you stop this required maintenance, the entire system *will* lose value as it becomes abused, slow, noncompetitive, broken, and eventually irrelevant.

Learning by Example

It's one thing to describe and critique currently deployed reputation systems—after they've already been deployed. It's another to prescribe a detailed set of steps that are recommended for new practitioners, as we have done in this book.

> Talk is easy; action is difficult. But, action is easy; true understanding is difficult!
>
> —Warrior Proverb

The lessons we presented here are the direct result of many attempts—some succeeded, some failed—at reputation system development and deployment. The book is the result of successive refinement of those lessons, especially as we refined it at Yahoo!. Chapter 10 is our proof-in-the-pudding that this methodology works in practice; it covers each step as we applied them during the development of a community moderation reputation model for Yahoo! Answers.

Case Study: Yahoo! Answers Community Content Moderation

This chapter is a real-life case study applying many of the theories and practical advice presented in this book. The lessons learned on this project had a significant impact on our thinking about reputation systems, the power of social media moderation, and the need to publish these results in order to share our findings with the greater web application development community.

In the summer of 2007, Yahoo! tried to address some moderation challenges with one of its flagship community products: Yahoo! Answers (*http://answers.yahoo.com*). The service had fallen victim to its own success and drawn the attention of trolls and spammers in a big way. The Yahoo! Answers team was struggling to keep up with harmful, abusive content that flooded the service, most of which originated with a small number of bad actors on the site.

Ultimately, a clever (but simple) system that was rich in reputation provided the answer to these woes: it was designed to identify bad actors, indemnify honest contributors, and take the overwhelming load off of the customer care team. Here's how that system came about.

What Is Yahoo! Answers?

Yahoo! Answers debuted in December of 2005 and almost immediately enjoyed massive popularity as a community driven website and a source of shared knowledge.

Yahoo! Answers provides a very simple interface to do, chiefly, two things: pose questions to a large community (potentially, any active, registered Yahoo! user—that's roughly a half-billion people worldwide); or answer questions that others have asked. Yahoo! Answers was modeled, in part, from similar question-and-answer sites like Korea's Naver.com Knowledge Search.

The appeal of this format was undeniable. By June of 2006, according to *Business 2.0*, Yahoo! Answers had already become "the second most popular Internet reference site after Wikipedia and had more than 90% of the domestic question-and-answer market share, as measured by comScore." Its popularity continues and, owing partly to excellent search engine optimization (SEO), Yahoo! Answers pages frequently appear very near the top of search results pages on Google and Yahoo! for a wide variety of topics.

Yahoo! Answers is by far the most active community site on the Yahoo! network. It logs more than 1.2 million user contributions (questions and answers combined) each day.

A Marketplace for Questions and Yahoo! Answers

Yahoo! Answers is a unique kind of marketplace—one not based on the transfer of goods for monetary reward. No, Yahoo! Answers is a knowledge marketplace, where the currency of exchange is ideas. Furthermore, Yahoo! Answers focuses on a specific kind of knowledge.

Micah Alpern was the user experience lead for early releases of Yahoo! Answers. He refers to the unique focus of Yahoo! Answers as "experiential knowledge"—the exchange of opinions and sharing of common experiences and advice (see Figure 10-1). While verifiable, factual information is indeed exchanged on Yahoo! Answers, a lot of the conversations that take place there are intended to be social in nature.

 Micah has published a detailed presentation that covers this project in some depth. You can find it at *http://www.slideshare.net/malpern/wiki mania-2009-yahoo-answers-community-moderation*.

Yahoo! Answers is not a reference site in the sense that Wikipedia is; it is not based on the ambition to provide objective, verifiable information. Rather, its goal is to encourage participation from a wide variety of contributors. That goal is important to keep in mind as we delve further into the problems that Yahoo! Answers was undergoing and the steps needed to solve them. Specifically, keep the following in mind:

- The answers on Yahoo! Answers are subjective. It is the community that determines what responses are ultimately "right." It should *not* be a goal of any metamoderation system to distinguish right answers from wrong or otherwise place any importance on the objective truth of answers.

- In a marketplace for opinions such as Yahoo! Answers, it's in the best interest of everyone (askers, answerers, and the site operator) to encourage *more* opinions, not fewer. So the designer of a moderation system intended to weed out abusive content should make every attempt to avoid punishing legitimate questions and

Figure 10-1. The questions asked and answers shared on Yahoo! Answers are often based on experiential knowledge rather than authoritative, fact-based information.

answers. False positives can't be tolerated, and the system must include an appeals process.

Attack of the Trolls

So, exactly what problems was Yahoo! Answers suffering from? Two factors—the time lines with which Yahoo! Answers displayed new content and the overwhelming number of contributions it received—had combined to create an unfortunate environment that was almost irresistible to trolls. Dealing with offensive and antagonistic user content had become the number one feature request from the Yahoo! Answers community.

The Yahoo! Answers team first attempted a machine-learning approach, developing a black-box abuse classifier (lovingly named the "Junk Detector") to prefilter abuse reports coming in. It was intended to classify the worst of the worst content and put it into a prioritized queue for the attention of customer care agents.

The Junk Detector was mostly a bust. It was moderately successful at detecting obvious spam, but it failed altogether to identify the subtler, more insidious contributions of trolls.

Do Trolls Eat Spam?

What's the difference between trolling behavior and plain old spam? The distinction is subtle, but understanding it is critical when you're combating either one. We classify communications that are unwanted, make overtly commercial appeals, and are broadcast to a large audience as *spam*.

Fortunately, the same characteristics that mark a communication as spam also make it stand out. You probably can easily identify spam after just a quick inspection. We can teach these same tricks to machines. Although spammers constantly change their tactics to evade detection, spam generally can be detected by machine methods.

Trollish behavior, however, is another matter altogether. Trolls may not have financial motives—more likely, they crave attention and are motivated by a desire to disrupt the larger conversation in a community. Trolls quickly realize that nonobvious means are the best way to accomplish these goals. An extremely effective means of trolling, in fact, is to disguise your trollish intentions as real conversation.

Accomplished trolls can be so subtle that even human agents are hard pressed to detect them. In the section "Applying Scope to Yahoo! EuroSport Message Board Reputation" on page 149, we discussed a kind of subtle trolling in a sports context: a troll masquerading as a fan of the opposing team. For these trolls, pretending to be faithful fans is part of the fun, and it renders them all the more disruptive when they start to trash-talk the home team.

How do you detect for *that*? It's hard for *any single* human—and near impossible for a machine—but it's possible with *a number* of humans. Adding consensus and reputation-enabled methods makes it easier to reliably discern trollish behavior from sincere contributions. Because a reputation system to some degree reflects the tastes of a community, it also has a better than average chance at catching behavior that transgresses those tastes.

Engineering manager Ori Zaltzman recalls the exact moment he knew for certain that something had to be done about trolls: when he logged onto Yahoo! Answers to see the following question highlighted on the home page: "What is the best sauce to eat with my fried dead baby?" (And, yes, we apologize for the citation—but it certainly illustrates the distasteful effects of letting trolls go unchallenged in your community.)

That question got through the Junk Detector easily. Even though it's an obviously unwelcome contribution, on the surface, to a machine, it looked like a perfectly legitimate question: grammatically well formed, no SHOUTING, i.e., ALL CAPS. So abusive content could sit on the site with impunity for hours before the staff could respond to abuse reports.

Time was a factor

Because the currency of Yahoo! Answers is the free exchange of opinions, a critical component of "free" in this context is *timely*. Yahoo! Answers functions best as a near-real-time communication system, and—as a design principle—erred on the side of timely delivery of users' questions and answers. User contributions are not subject to any type of editorial approval before being pushed to the site.

 Early on, the Yahoo! Answers product plan *did* call for editor approval of all questions before publishing. This was an early attempt to influence the content quality level by modeling good user behavior. The almost immediate, skyrocketing popularity of the site quickly rendered that part of the plan moot. There simply was no way that any team of Yahoo! content moderators was going to keep up with the levels of use on Yahoo! Answers.

Location, location, location

One particular area of the site became a highly sought-after target for abusers: the high-profile front page of Yahoo! Answers. (See Figure 10-2.)

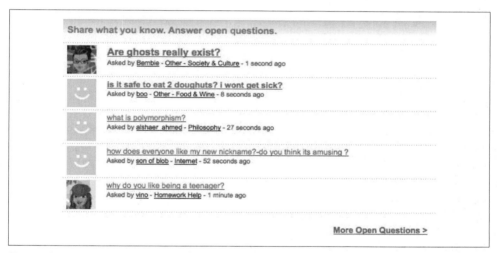

Figure 10-2. Because questions on Yahoo! Answers could appear on the front page of the site with no verification that the content was appropriate, spammers and trolls flocked to this high-value real estate.

Any newly asked question could potentially appear in highly trafficked areas, including the following:

- The index of open (answerable) questions (*http://answers.yahoo.com/dir/index*)
- The index of the category in which a question was listed
- Communities such as Yahoo! Groups, Sports, or Music, where Yahoo! Answers content was syndicated

Built with Reputation

Yahoo! Answers, somewhat famously, already featured a reputation system—a very visible one, designed to encourage and reward ever-greater levels of user participation. On Yahoo! Answers, user activity is rewarded with a detailed point system. (See "Points and Accumulators" on page 182.)

We say "famously" because the Yahoo! Answers point system is somewhat notorious in reputation system circles, and debate continues to rage over its effectiveness.

At the heart of the debate is this question: does the existence of these points—and the incentive of rewarding people for participation—actually improve the experience of using Yahoo! Answers? Does it make the site a better source of information? Or are the system's game-like elements promoted too heavily, turning what could be a valuable, informative site into a game for the easily distracted?

We're mostly steering clear of that discussion here. (We touched on aspects of it in Chapter 7.) This case study deals only with combating obviously abusive content, not with judging good content from bad.

Yahoo! Answers decided to solve the problem through community moderation based on a reputation system that would be completely separate from the existing public participation point system. However, it would have been foolish to ignore the point system; it was a potentially rich source of inputs into any additional system. The new system clearly would have to be influenced by the existence of the point system, but it would have to use the point system input in very specific ways, while the point system continued to function.

Avengers Assemble!

The crew fielded to tackle this problem was a combination of two teams.

The Yahoo! Answers product team had ultimate responsibility for the application. It was made up of domain experts on questions and answers, from the rationale behind the service, to the smallest details of user experience, to building the high-volume scalable systems that supported it. These were the folks who best understood the service, and they were held accountable for preserving the integrity of the user experience. Ori Zaltzman was the engineering manager, Quy Le was product manager, Anirudh Koul was the engineer leading the troll hunt and optimizing the model, and Micah Alpern was the lead user experience designer.

The members of the product team were the primary customers for the technology and advice of another team at Yahoo!, the reputation platform team. The reputation platform was a tier of technology (detailed in Appendix A) that was the basis for many of the concepts and models we have discussed in this book (this book is largely documentation of that experience). Yvonne French was the product manager for the reputation platform, and Randy Farmer, coauthor of this book, was the platform's primary designer and advised on reputation model and system deployment. A small engineering team built the platform and implemented the reputation models.

 Yahoo! enjoyed an advantage in this situation that many organizations may not: considerable resources and, perhaps more important, *specialized* resources. For example, it is unlikely that your organization will feature an engineering team specifically dedicated to architecting a reputation platform. However, you might consider drafting one or more members of your team to develop deep knowledge in that area.

Here's how these combined teams tackled the problem of taming abuse on Yahoo! Answers.

Initial Project Planning

As you'll recall from Chapter 5, we recommend starting any reputation system project by asking these fundamental questions:

1. What are your goals for your application?
2. What is your content control pattern?
3. Given your goals and the content models, what types of incentives are likely to work well for you?

Setting Goals

As is often the case on community-driven websites, what is good for the community— good content and the freedom to have meaningful, interruption-free exchanges—also just happens to make for good business value for the site owners. This project was no different, but it's worth discussing the project's specific goals.

Cutting costs

The first motivation for cleaning up abuse on Yahoo! Answers was cost. The existing system for dealing with abuse was expensive, relying as it did on heavy human-operator intervention. Each and every report of abuse had to be verified by a human operator before action could be taken on it.

Randy Farmer, at the time the community strategy analyst for Yahoo!, pointed out the financial foolhardiness of continuing down the path where the system was leading: "the cost of generating abuse is *zero*, while we're spending a million dollars a year on customer care to combat it—and it *isn't even working*." Any new system would have to fight abuse at a cost that was orders of magnitude lower than that of the manual-intervention approach.

Cleaning up the neighborhood

The monetary cost of dealing with abuse on Yahoo! Answers was considerable, but the community cost of *not* dealing with it would have been far higher. Bad behavior begets bad behavior, and leaving obviously abusive content in high-profile locations on the site would over time absolutely erode the perceived value of social interactions on Yahoo! Answers. (For more, see the sidebar "Broken Windows and Online Behavior" on page 205.)

Of course, Yahoo! hoped that the inverse would also prove true: if Yahoo! Answers addressed the problem forcefully and with great vigor, the community would notice the effort and respond in kind. (See the sidebar "Beware Excessive Tuning: The Hawthorne Effect" on page 233.)

The goals for content quality were twofold:

- Reduce the overall amount of abusive content on the site.
- Reduce the amount of time it took for content reported as abusive to be pulled down.

Who Controls the Content?

In Chapter 5, we proposed a number of content control patterns as useful models for thinking about the ways in which your content is created, disseminated, and moderated. Let's revisit those patterns briefly for this project.

Before the community content moderation project, Yahoo! Answers fit nicely in the basic social media pattern. (See "Basic social media: Users create and evaluate, staff removes" on page 109.) While users were given responsibility of creating and editing (voting for or reporting as abusive) questions and answers, final determination for removing content was left up to the staff.

The team's goal was to move Yahoo! Answers closer to The Full Monty (see "The Full Monty: Users create, evaluate, and remove" on page 110) and put the responsibility of removing or hiding content right into the hands of the community. That responsibility would be mediated by the reputation system, but staff intervention in content quality issues would be necessary only in cases where content contributors appealed the systems' decisions.

Incentives

We discussed some ways to think about the incentives that could drive community participation on your site in the section "Incentives for User Participation, Quality, and

Moderation" on page 111. For Yahoo! Answers, the team decided to devise incentives that took into account a couple of primary motivations:

- Some community members would report abuse for altruistic reasons: out of a desire to keep the community clean. (See the section "Altruistic or sharing incentives" on page 113.) Downplaying the contributions of such users would be critical; the more public their deeds became, the less likely they would continue acting out of sheer altruism.

- Some community members had egocentric motivations for reporting abuse. The team appealed to those motivations by giving those users an increasingly greater voice in the community.

The High-Level Project Model

The team devised this plan for the new model: a reputation model would sit between the two existing systems—a report mechanism that permitted any user on Yahoo! Answers to flag any other user's contribution and the (human) customer care system that acted on those reports. (See Figure 10-3.)

This approach was based on two insights:

1. Customer care could be removed from the loop—in most cases—by shifting the content removal process into the application and giving it to the users, who were already the source of the abuse reports, and then optimizing it to cut the amount of time and offensive posting by 90%.

2. Customer care could then handle just the exceptions—undoing the removal of content mistakenly identified as abusive. At the time, such false positives made up 10% of all content removal. Even if the exception rate stayed the same, customer care costs would decrease by 90%.

The team would accomplish item 1, removing customer care from the loop, by implementing a new way to remove content from the site—"hiding." Hiding involved trusting the community members themselves to vote to hide the abusive content. The reputation platform would manage the details of the voting mechanism and any related karma. Because this design required no external authority to remove abusive content from view, it was probably the fastest way to cut display time for abusive content.

As for item 2, dealing with exceptions, the team devised an ingenious mechanism—an appeals process. In the new system, when the community voted to hide a user's content, the system sent the author an email explaining why, with an invitation to appeal the decision. Customer care would get involved only if the user appealed. The team predicted that this process would limit abuse of the ability to hide content; it would provide an opportunity to inform users about how to use the feature; and, because trolls often don't give valid email addresses when registering an account, they would simply be unable to appeal because they'd never receive the notices.

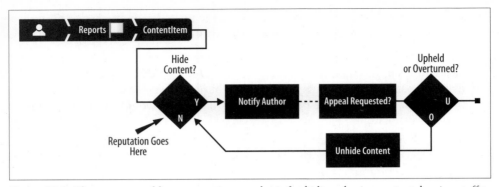

Figure 10-3. The system would use reputation as a basis for hiding abusive content, leaving staff to handle only appeals.

Most of the rest of this chapter details the reputation model designated by the Hide Content? diamond in Figure 10-3. See the patent application for more details about the other (nonreputation) portions of the diagram, such as the Notify Author and Appeals process boxes.

 Yahoo! has applied for a patent on this reputation model, and that application has been published: Trust Based Moderation (*http://www.goo gle.com/patents?q=TRUST+BASED+MODERATION*)—Inventors: Ori Zaltzman and Quy Dinh Le. Please consider the patent if you are even thinking about copying this design.

We are grateful to both the Yahoo! Answers and the reputation product teams for sharing their design insights and their continued assistance in preparing this case study.

Objects, Inputs, Scope, and Mechanism

Yahoo! Answers was already a well-established service at the time that the community content moderation model was being designed, with all of the objects and most of the available inputs already well defined. The final model includes dozens of inputs to more than a dozen processes. Out of respect for intellectual property and the need for brevity, we have not detailed every object and input here. But, thanks to the Yahoo! Answers team's willingness to share, we're able to provide an accurate overall picture of the reputation system and its application.

The Objects

Here are the objects of interest for designing a community-powered content moderation system:

User contributions

User contributions are the objects that users make by either adding or evaluating content:

Questions

Arriving at a rate of almost 100 per minute, questions are the starting point of all Yahoo! Answers activity. New questions are displayed on the home page and on category pages.

Answers

Answers arrive 6 to 10 times faster than questions and make up the bulk of the reputable entities in the application. All answers are associated with a single question and are displayed in chronological order, oldest first.

Ratings

After a user makes several contributions, the application encourages the user to rate answers with a simple thumb-up or thumb-down vote. The author of the question is also allowed to select the best answer and give it a rating on a 5-star scale. If the question author does not select a best answer in the allotted time, the community vote is used to determine the best answer.

Users may also mark a question with a star, indicating that the question is a favorite.

Each of these rating schemes already existed at the time the community content moderation system was designed, so for each scheme, the inputs and outputs were both available for the designers' consideration.

Users

All users in this application have two data records that can hold and supply information for reputation calculations: an all-Yahoo! global user record, which includes fields for items such as registration data and connection information, and a record for Yahoo! Answers, which stores only application-specific fields.

Developing this model required considering at least two different classifications of users:

Authors

Authors create the items (questions and answers) that the community can moderate.

Reporters

Reporters determine that an item (a question or an answer) breaks the rules and should be removed.

Customer care staff

The customer care staff is the target of the model. The goal is to reduce the staff's participation in the content moderation process as much as possible but not to zero. Any community content moderation process can be abused: trusted users may decide to abuse their power, or they may simply make a mistake. Customer care would still evaluate appeals in those cases, but the number of such cases would be far less than the total number of abuses.

Customer care agents also have a reputation—for accuracy—though it isn't calculated by this model. At the start of the Yahoo! Answers community content moderation project, the accuracy of a customer care agent's evaluation of questions was about 90%. That rate meant that 1 in 10 submissions was either incorrectly deleted or incorrectly allowed to remain on the site. An important measure of the model's effectiveness was whether users' evaluations were more accurate than the staff's.

The design included two noteworthy documents, though they were not formal objects (that is, they neither provided input nor were reputable entities). The Yahoo! Terms of Service and the Yahoo! Answers Community Guidelines (Figure 10-4) are the written standards for questions and answers. Users are supposed to apply these rules in evaluating content.

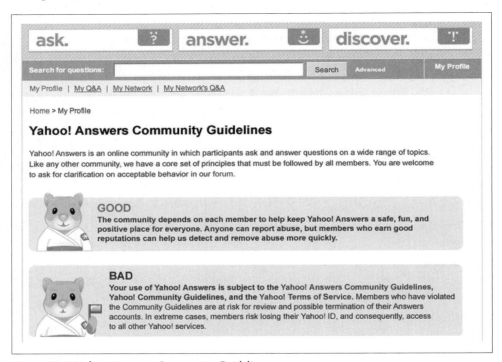

Figure 10-4. Yahoo! Answers Community Guidelines.

Limiting Scope

When a reputation model is introduced, users often are confused at first about what the reputation score means. The design of the community content moderation model for Yahoo! Answers is only intended to identify abusive *content*, not abusive *users*. Remember that many reasons exist for removing content, and some content items are removed as a result of behaviors that authors are willing to change, if gently instructed to do so.

The inclusion of an appeals process in the application not only provides a way to catch false-positive classification by reporters, it also gives Yahoo! a chance to inform authors of the requirements for participating in Yahoo! Answers, allowing users to learn more about expected behavior.

An Evolving Model

Ideally, in designing a reputation system, you'd start with as comprehensive a list of potential inputs as possible. In practice, when the Yahoo! Answers team was designing the community content moderation model, they used a more incremental approach. As the model evolved, the designers added more subtle objects and inputs. Next, to illustrate an actual model development process, we'll roughly follow the historical path of the Yahoo! Answers design.

Iteration 1: Abuse reporting

When you develop a reputation model, it's good practice to start simple; focus only on the main objects, inputs, decisions, and uses. Assume a universe in which the model works exactly as intended. Don't focus too much on performance or abuse at first; you'll get to those issues in later iterations. Trying to solve this kind of complex equation in all dimensions simultaneously will just lead to confusion and impede your progress.

For the Yahoo! Answers community content moderation system, the designers started with a very basic model: abuse reports would accumulate against a content item, and when some threshold was reached, the item would be hidden. This model, sometimes called "X-strikes-and-you're-out," is quite common in social web applications. Craigslist is a well-known example.

Despite the apparent complexity of the final application, the model's simple core design remained unchanged: accumulated abuse reports automatically hide content. Having that core design to keep in mind as the key goal helped eliminate complications in the design.

Inputs. From the beginning, the team planned for the primary input to the model to be a user-generated abuse report explicitly about a content item (a question or an answer). This user interface device was the same one already in place for alerting customer care to abuse. Though many other inputs were possible, initially the team considered a model with abuse reports as the only input.

Abuse reports (user input)
> Users could report content that violated the community guidelines or the terms of service. The user interface consisted of a button next to all questions and answers.

The button was labeled with a flag icon, and sometimes the action of clicking the button was referred to as "flagging an item." In the case of questions, the button label also included the phrase "Report Abuse." The interface then led the user through a short series of pages to explain the process and narrow down the reason for the report.

The abuse report was the only input in the first iteration of the model.

Mechanism and diagram. At the core of the model was a simple, binary decision: should a content item that has just been reported as abusive be hidden? How does the model make the decision, and, if the result is positive, how should the application be notified?

In the first iteration, the model for this decision was "three strikes and you're out." (See Figure 10-5.) Abuse reports fed into a simple accumulator (see "Simple Accumulator" on page 48). Each report about a content item was given equal weight; all reports were added together and stored as `AbusiveScore`. That score was sent on to a simple evaluator, which tested it against a threshold (3) and either terminated it (if the threshold had not been reached) or alerted the application to hide the item.

Given that performance was a key requirement for this model, the abuse reports were delivered asynchronously, and the outgoing alert to the application used an application-level messaging system.

This iteration of the model did not include karma.

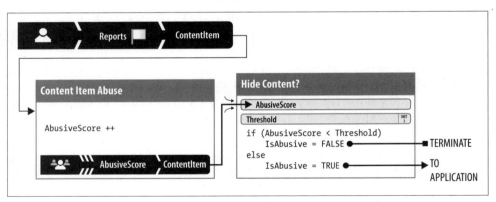

Figure 10-5. Iteration 1: A not-very-forgiving model. Three strikes and your content is out!

Analysis. This very simple model didn't really meet the minimum requirement for the application—the fastest possible removal of abusive content. Three strikes is often too many, but one or two is sometimes too few, giving too much power to bad actors.

The model's main weakness was to give every abuse report equal weight. By giving trusted users more power to hide content and giving unknown users or bad actors less power, the model could improve the speed and accuracy with which abusive content was removed.

The next iteration of the model introduced karma for reporters of abuse.

Iteration 2: Karma for abuse reporters

Ideally, the more abuse a user reports accurately, the greater the trust the system should place in that user's reports. In the second iteration of the model, shown in Figure 10-6, when a trusted reporter flagged an item, it was hidden immediately. Trusted reporters had proven, over time, that their motivations were pure, their comprehension of community standards was good, and their word could be taken at face value.

Reports by users who had never previously reported an item, with unknown reputation, were all given equal weight, but it was significantly lower than reports by users with a positive history. In this model, individual unknown reporters had less influence on any one content item, but the votes of different individuals could accrue quickly. (At the same time, the individuals accrued their own reporting histories, so unknown reporters didn't stay unknown for long.)

Though you might think that "bad" reporters (those whose reports were later overturned on appeal) should have less say than unknown users, the model gave equal weight to reports from bad reporters and unknown reporters. (See "Practitioner's Tips: Negative Public Karma" on page 161.)

Inputs. To the inputs from the previous iteration, the designers added three events related to flagging questions and answers accurately:

Item hidden (moderation model feedback)
> The system sent this input message when the reputation process determined that a question or answer should be hidden, which represented that all users who reported the content item agreed that the item was in violation of either the TOS or the community guidelines.

Appeal Result: Upheld (customer care input)
> After the system hid an item, it contacted the content author via email and enabled the author to start an appeal process, requesting customer care staff to review the decision. If a customer care agent determined that the content was appropriately hidden, the system sent the event `Appeal Result: Upheld` to the reputation model.

Appeal Result: Overturned (customer care input)
> If a customer care agent determined that the content was inappropriately hidden, the system displayed the content again and sent the event `Appeal Result: Overturned` to the reputation model for corrective adjustments.

Mechanism and diagram. The designers transformed the overly simple "strikes"-based model to account for a user's abuse report history.

The goals were to decrease the time required to hide abusive content, and reduce the risk of inexperienced or bad actors hiding content inappropriately.

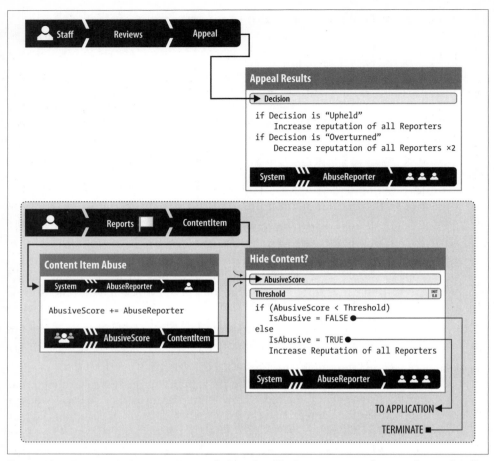

Figure 10-6. Iteration 2: A reporter's record of good and bad reports now influences the weight of his opinion on other content items.

The solution was to add **AbuseReporter** karma to record the user's accuracy in hiding abusive content. Use **AbuseReporter** to give greater weight to reports by users with a history of accurate abuse reporting.

To accommodate the varying weight of abuse reports, the designers changed the calculation of **AbusiveScore** from strikes to a normalized value, where 0.0 represented no abuse information known and 1.0 represented the maximum abuse value. The evaluator now compared the **AbusiveScore** to a normalized value representing the certainty required before hiding an item.

The designers added an **AbuseReporter** reputation claim, a normalized value, where 0.0 represented a user with no history of abuse reporting and 1.0 represented a user with a completely accurate abuse reporting history. A user with a perfect score of 1.0 could hide any item immediately.

The inputs that increased `AbuseReporter` were `Item Hidden` and `Appeal Result: Upheld`. The input `Abuse Result: Overturned` had a disproportionately large negative effect on `AbuseReporter`, providing an incentive for reporters not to use their power indiscriminately.

Unlike the first process, the new version of the Content Item Abuse process did not treat each input the same way. It read the reporter's `AbuseReporter` karma, added a small constant to `AbusiveScore` (so that users with no karma made at least a small contribution to the result), and capped the result at the maximum. If the result was 1.0, the system hid the item but, in addition to alerting the application, it updated the `AbuseReporter` karma for each user that flagged the item. This reflected community consensus and, since the vast majority of hidden items would never be reviewed by customer care, was often the only opportunity the system had to reinforce the karma of those users. Very few appeals were anticipated given that trolls were known to give bogus email addresses when registering. The incentives for both the legitimate authors and good abuse reporters discourage abusing the community moderation model.

The system sent appeal results messages asynchronously as part of the customer care application; the messages could come in at anytime. After `AbuseReporter` was adjusted, the system did not attempt to update other `AbusiveScore`s the reporter may have contributed to.

Analysis. The second iteration of the model did exactly what it was supposed to do: it allowed trusted reporters to hide abusive content immediately. However, it ignored the value of contributions by *authors* who might themselves be established, trusted members of the community. As a result, a single *mistaken* abuse report against a top contributor led to a higher appeal rate, which not only increased costs but generated bad feelings about the site. Furthermore, even before the first iteration of the model had been implemented, trolls already had been using the abuse reporting mechanism to harass top contributors. So in the second iteration, treating all authors equally allowed malicious users (trolls or even just rivals of top contributors) to take down the content of top contributors with just a few puppet accounts.

The designers found that the model needed to account for the understanding that in cases of alleged abuse, some authors always deserve a second opinion. In addition, the designers knew that to hide content posted by casual regular users, the `AbusiveScore` required by the model should be lower—and for content by unknown authors, lower still.

In other words, the model needed karma for author contributions.

Iteration 3: Karma for authors

The third iteration of the model introduced `QuestionAuthor` karma and `AnswerAuthor` karma, which reflected the quality and quantity of author contributions. The system compared `AbusiveScore` to those two reputations instead of a constant. This change raised the threshold for hiding content for active, trusted authors and lowered the threshold for unknown authors and authors known to have contributed abusive content.

Inputs. The new inputs to the model fell into two groups: inputs that indicated the quantity and community reputation of the questions and answers contributed by an author and evidence of any previous abusive contributions.

Inputs contributing to positive reputation for a question

Numerous events could indicate that a question was valuable to the community. When a reader took any of the following actions on a question, the author's `QuestionQuality` reputation score increased:

- Added the question to his watch list
- Shared the question with a friend
- Gave the question a star (marked it as a favorite)

Inputs contributing to negative reputation for a question

When customer care staff deleted a question, the system set the author's `Question Quality` reputation score to 0.0 and adjusted the author's karma appropriately.

Another negative input was the Junk Detector score, which acted as an initial guess about the level of abusive content in the question. Note that a high Junk Detector score would have prevented the question from ever being displayed at all.

Inputs related to content creation

When an author posted a question, the system increased the total number of questions submitted by that author by 1 (`QuestionsAskedCount`). This configuration allowed new contributors to start with a reputation score based on the average quality of all previous contributions to the site, by all authors (`AuthorAverageQues tionQuality`).

When other users answered the question, the question itself inherited the `AverageAnswererQuality` reputation score for all users who answered it. (If a lot of good people answer your question, it must be a good question.)

Inputs contributing to positive reputation for an answer

As with a question, several events could indicate that an answer was valuable to the community. When a reader took any of the following actions on an answer, the author's `AnswerQuality` reputation score increased:

- The author of the original question selected the answer as Best Answer
- The community voted the answer Best Answer
- The average community rating given for the answer

Inputs contributing to negative reputation for an answer

If the number of negative ratings of an answer rose significantly higher than the number of positive ratings, the system hid the answer from display, except to users who asked to see all items regardless of rating. The system lowered the `AnswerQual ity` reputation score of answers that fell below this display threshold. This choked off further negative ratings simply because the item was no longer displayed to most users.

When customer care staff deleted an answer, the system reset the `AnswerQuality` reputation to 0.0 and adjusted the author's karma appropriately.

Another negative input was the Junk Detector rating, which acted as a rough guess at the level of abusive content in the answer. Note that if the Junk Detector rating was high, the system would already have hidden the answer before even sending it through the reputation process.

New-answer input

When a user posted an answer, the system increased the total number of answers submitted by that user by 1 (`QuestionsAnsweredCount`). In that configuration, each time an author posted a new answer, the system assigned a starting reputation based on the average quality of all answers previously submitted by that author (`AuthorAverageAnswerQuality`).

Previous abusive history

As part of the revisions accounting for the content author's reputation when determining whether to hide a flagged contribution, the model needed to calculate and consider the history of previously hidden items (`AbusiveContent` karma). All previously hidden questions or answers had a negative effect on all contributor karmas.

Mechanism and diagram. In the third iteration of the model, the designers created several new reputation scores for questions and answers and a new user role with a karma—that of *author* of the flagged content. Those additions more than doubled the complexity compared to the previous iteration, as illustrated in Figure 10-7. But if you consider each iteration as a separate reputation model (which is logical because each addition stands alone), each one is simple. By integrating separable small models, the combination made up a full-blown reputation system. For example, the karmas introduced by the new models—`QuestionAuthor` karma, `AnswerAuthor` karma, and `Abusive Content` karma—could find uses in contexts other than hiding abusive content.

In this iteration the designers added two new main karma tracks, represented by the parallel messaging tracks for question karma and answer karma. The calculations are so similar that we present the description only once, using *item* to represent either *answer* or *question*.

The system gave each item a quality reputation [`QuestionQuality` | `AnswerQuality`], which started as the average of the quality reputations of the previously contributed items [`AuthorAverageQuestionQuality` | `AuthorAverageAnswerQuality`] and a bit of the Junk Detector score. As either positive (stars, ratings, shares) or negative inputs (items hidden by customer care staff) changed, the scores, the averages, and karmas in turn were immediately affected. Each positive input was restricted by weights and limits; for example, only the first 10 users marking an item as a favorite were considered, and

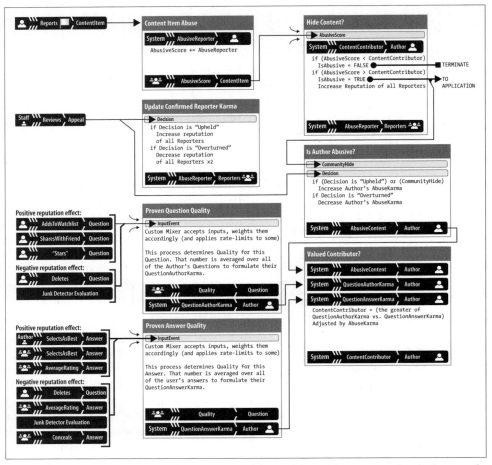

Figure 10-7. Iteration 3: This improved iteration of the model now also accounts for the history of a content author. When users flag a question or answer, the system gives extra consideration to authors with a history of posting good content.

each could contribute a maximum of 0.5 to the final quality score. This meant that increasing the item quality reputation required many different types of positive inputs.

Once the system had assigned a new quality score to an item and then calculated and stored the item's overall average quality score, it sent the process a message with the average score to calculate the individual item's quality karma [`QuestionAuthor` | `Answer Author`], subtracting the user's overall `AbusiveContent` karma to generate the final result.

The system then combined the `QuestionAuthor` and `AnswerAuthor` karmas into `ContentAuthor` karma, using the best (the larger) of the two values. That approach reflected the insight of Yahoo! Answers staff that people who ask good questions are not the same as people who give good answers.

The designers once again changed the Hide Content? process, now comparing `AbusiveScore` to the new `ContentContributor` karma to determine whether the content should be hidden. When an item was hidden, that information was sent as an input into a new process that updated the `AbusiveContent` karma.

The new process for updating `AbusiveContent` karma also incorporated the inputs from customer care staff that were included in iteration 2—appeal results and content removals—which affected the karma either positively or negatively, as appropriate. Whenever an input entered that process, the system sent a message with the updated score to each of the processes for updating question and answer karma.

Analysis. By adding positive and negative karma scores for authors and effectively requiring a second or third opinion before hiding their content, the designers added protection for established, trusted authors. It also shortened the amount of time that bad content from historically abusive users would appear on the site by allowing single-strike hiding by only lightly experienced abuse reporters. The team was very close to finished.

But it still had a cold-start problem. How could the model protect authors who weren't abusive but didn't have a strong history of posting contributions or reporting abuse? They were still too vulnerable to flagging by other users—especially inexperienced or malicious reporters.

The team needed as much outside information as it could get its hands on to provide some protection to new users who deserved it and to expose malicious users from the start.

Final design: Adding inferred karma

The team could have stopped here, but it wanted the system to be as effective as possible as soon as it was deployed. Even before abuse reporters can build up a history of accurately reporting abuse, the team wanted to give the best users a leg up over trolls and spammers, who almost always create accounts solely for the purpose of manipulating content for profit or malice.

In other words, the team wanted to magnify any reasons for trusting or being suspicious of a user from the very beginning, before the user started to develop a history with the reputation system.

To that end, the designers added a model of inferred karma (see "Generating inferred karma" on page 159).

Fortunately, Yahoo! Answers had access to a wealth of data—inferred karma inputs—about users from other contexts.

Inputs. Many of the inferred inputs came from Yahoo! site security features. To maintain that security, some of the inputs have been omitted, and the descriptions of others have been altered to protect proprietary features.

IP is suspect

More objects are accessible to web applications at the system level. One available object is the IP address for the user's current connection. Yahoo!, like many large sites, keeps a list of addresses that it doesn't trust for various reasons. Obviously, any user connected through one of those addresses is suspect.

Browser cookie is suspect

Yahoo! maintains security information in browser cookies. Cookies may raise suspicion for several reasons—for example, when the same cookie is reused by multiple IP addresses in different ranges in a short period of time.

Browser cookie age

A new browser cookie reveals nothing, but a valid, long-lived cookie that isn't suspect may slightly boost trust of a user.

Junk detector score (for rejected content)

In the final iteration of the model, the model captures the history of Junk Detector scores that caused an item to be *automatically* hidden as soon as a user posted it. In earlier iterations, only questions and answers that passed the detector were included in reputation calculations.

Negative evaluations by others

The final iteration of the model included several different evaluations of a user's content in calculations of inferred karma: poor ratings, abuse reports, and the number of times a user was blocked by others.

Best-answer percentage

On the positive side, the model included inputs such as the average number of best answers that a user submitted (subject to liquidity limits). See "Liquidity: You Won't Get Enough Input" on page 58.

User points level

The level of a user's participation in Yahoo! provided a significant indicator of the user's investment in the community. Yahoo! Answers already displayed user participation on the site—a public karma for every user.

User longevity

Absent any previous participation in Yahoo!, a user's Yahoo! account registration date provided a minimum indicator of community investment, along with the date of a user's first interaction with Yahoo! Answers.

Customer care action

Finally, certain events were a sure sign of abusive behavior. When customer care staff removed content or suspended accounts, those events were tracked as strongly negative inputs to bootstrap karma.

Appeal results upheld

Whenever an appeal to hide content was upheld, that event was tracked as an additional indicator of possible abuse.

Mechanism and diagram. In the final iteration of the model, shown in Figure 10-8, the designers implemented this simple idea: until the user had a detailed history in the reputation model, use a `TrustBootstrap` reputation as reasonably trustworthy placeholder. As the number of a user's abuse reports increased, the share of `TrustBootstrap` used in calculating the user's reporter and author karmas was decreased. Over time, the user's bootstrap reputation faded in significance until it became computationally irrelevant.

The scores for `AbusiveContent` karma and `AbuseReporter` karma now took the various inferred karma inputs into account.

`AbusiveContent` karma was calculated by mixing what we knew about a user's karma reporting history (`ConfirmedRerporterKarma`) with what could be inferred about the user's behavior from other inputs (`TrustBootstrap`).

`TrustBootstrap` was itself made up of three other new reputations: `SuspectedAbuser` karma, which reflected any evidence of abusive behavior; `CommunityInvestment` karma, which represented the user's contributions to Yahoo! Answers and other communities; and `AbusiveContent` karma, which held an author's record of submitting abusive content.

There were risks in getting the constants wrong—too much power too early could lead to abuse. Depending on the bootstrap too long could lead to distrust when reporters don't see the effects of their reputation quickly enough.

We detail each new process:

Process: Calculate Suspicious Connection
> When a user takes an action of value, such as asking a question, giving an answer, or evaluating content on the site, the application stores the user's connection information. If the user's IP address or browser cookie differed from the one used in a previous session, the application activates this process by sending it the IP and/or browser cookie related inputs. The system updated the `SuspectedAbuser` karma using those values and the history of previous values for the user. Then it sent the value in a message to the Abuse Reporter Bootstrap process.

Process: Calculate User Community Investment
> Three different application events triggered this process:

- A change (usually upward) in the user's points
- Selection of a best answer to a question—whether or not the user wrote the answer that was selected
- The first time the user flags any item as abusive content

> This process generated `CommunityInvestment` karma by accounting for the longevity of the user's participation in Yahoo! Answers and the age of the user's Yahoo! account, along with a simple participation value calculation (the user's level) and an approximation of answer quality—the best answer percentage. Each time this value was changed, the system sent the new value to the Abuse Reporter Bootstrap process.

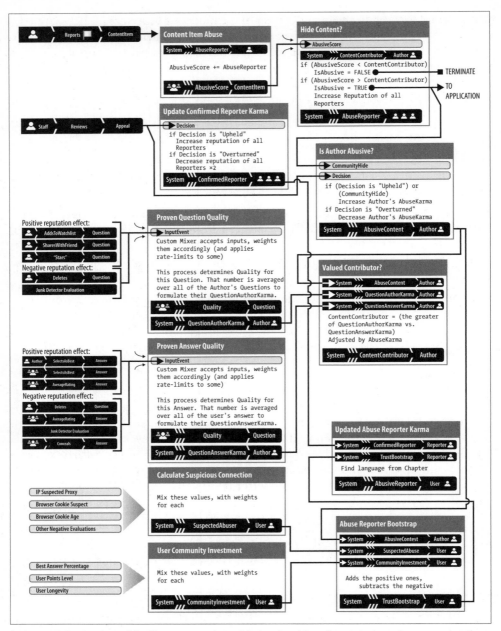

Figure 10-8. Final model: Eliminating the cold-start problem by giving good users an upfront advantage as abuse reporters.

Process: Is Author Abusive?

The inputs and calculations for this process were the same as in the third iteration of the model—the process remained a repository for all confirmed and nonappealed user content violations. The only difference was that every time the system executed the process and updated `AbusiveContent` karma, it now sent an additional message to the Abuse Reporter Bootstrap process.

Process: Abuse Reporter Bootstrap

This process was the centerpiece of the final iteration of the model. The `TrustBootstrap` reputation represented the system's best guess at the reputation of users without a long history of transactions with the service. It was a weighted mixer process, taking positive input from `CommunityInvestment` karma and weighing that against two negative scores: the weaker score was the connection-based `SuspectedAbuser` karma, and the stronger score was the user history–based `AbusiveContent` karma. Even though a high value for the `TrustBootstrap` reputation implied a high level of certainty that a user would violate the rules, `AbusiveContent` karma made up only a share of the bootstrap and not all of it. The reason was that the context for the score was content quality, and the context of the bootstrap was reporter reliability; someone who is great at evaluating content might suck at creating it. Each time the bootstrap process was updated, it was passed along to the final process in the model: Update Abuse Reporter Karma.

Process: Valued Contributor?

The input and calculations for this process were the same as in the second iteration of the model—the process updated `ConfirmedRerporter` karma to reflect the accuracy of the user's abuse reports. The only difference was that the system now sent a message for each reporter to the Update Abuse Reporter Karma process, where the claim value was incorporated into the bootstrap reputation.

Process: Update Abuse Reporter Karma

This process calculated `AbuseReporter` karma, which was used to weight the value of a user's abuse reports. To determine the value, it combined `TrustBootstrap` inferred karma with a verified abuse report accuracy rate as represented by `ConfirmedRerporter`. As a user reported more items, the share of `TrustBootstrap` in the calculation decreased. Eventually, `AbuseReporter` karma became equal to `ConfirmedRerporter` karma. Once the calculations were complete, the reputation statement was updated and the model was terminated.

Analysis. With the final iteration, the designers had incorporated all the desired features, giving historically trusted users the power to hide spam and troll-generated content almost instantly while preventing abusive users from hiding content posted by legitimate users. This model was projected to reduce the load on customer care by at least 90% and maybe even as much as 99%. There was little doubt that the worst content would be removed from the site significantly faster than the typical 12+ hour response time. How much faster was difficult to estimate.

In a system with over a dozen processes, more than 20 unproven formulas, and about 50 best-guess constant values, a lot could go wrong. But iteration provided a roadmap for implementation and testing. The team started with one model, developed test data and testing suites for it, made sure it worked as planned, and then built outward from there—one iteration at a time.

Displaying Reputation

The Yahoo! Answers example provides clear answers to many of the questions raised in Chapter 7, where we discussed the visible display of reputation.

Who Will See the Reputation?

All interested parties (content authors, abuse reporters, and other users) certainly could see the *effects* of the reputations generated by the system at work: content was hidden or reappeared, and appeals and their results generated email notifications. But the designers made no attempt to roll up the reputations and display them back to the community. The reputations definitely were not public reputations.

In fact, even showing the reputations only to the interested parties as personal reputations likely would only have given actual those intending harm more information about how to assault the system. These reputations were best reserved for use as *corporate* reputations only.

How Will the Reputation Be Used to Modify Your Site's Output?

The Yahoo! Answers system used the reputation information that it gathered for one purpose only: to make a decision about whether to hide or show content. Some of the other purposes discussed in "How Will You Use Reputation to Modify Your Site's Output?" on page 172 do not apply to this example. Yahoo! Answers already used other, application-specific methods for ordering and promoting content, and the community content moderation system was not intended to interfere with those aspects of the application.

Is This Reputation for a Content Item or a Person?

This question has a simple answer, with a somewhat more complicated clarification. As we mentioned earlier in "Limiting Scope" on page 254, the ultimate target for reputations in this system is content: questions and answers.

It just so happened that in targeting those objects, the model resulted in generation of a number of proven and assumed reputations that pertained to people: the authors of the content in question, and the reporters who flagged it. But judging the character the users of Yahoo! Answers was not the purpose of the moderation system, and the data

---

on those users should never be extended in that way without careful deliberation and design.

Using Reputation: The…Ugly

In Chapter 8, we detailed three main uses for reputation (other than displaying scores directly to users). We only half-jokingly referred to them as the good, the bad, and the ugly. Since the Yahoo! Answers community content moderation model says nothing about the quality of the content itself—only about the users who generate and interact with it—it can't really rank content from best to worst. These first two use categories—the good and the bad—don't apply to this moderation model.

The Yahoo! Answers system dealt exclusively with the last category—the ugly—by allowing users to rid the site of content that violated the terms of service or the community guidelines.

The primary result of this system was to hide content as rapidly as possible so that customer support staff could focus on the exceptions (borderline cases and bad calls). After all, at the start of the project, even customer care staff had an error rate as high as 10%.

This single use of the model, if effective, would save the company over $1 million in customer care costs per year. That savings alone made the investment profitable in the first few months after deployment, so any additional uses for the other reputations in the model would be an added bonus.

For example, when a user was confirmed as a content abuser, with a high value for `AbusiveContent` karma, Yahoo! Answers could share that information with the Yahoo! systems that maintained the trustworthiness of IP addresses and browser cookies, raising the `SuspectedAbuser` karma score for that user's IP address and browser. That exchange of data made it harder for a spammer or a troll to create a new account. Users who are technically sophisticated can circumvent such measures, but the measures have been very effective against those who aren't—and who make up the vast majority of Yahoo! users.

When customer care agents reviewed appeals, the system displayed `ConfirmedRe porter` karma for each abuse reporter, which acted as a set of confidence values. An agent could see that several reports from low-karma users were less reliable than one or two reports from abuse reporters with higher karma scores. A large enough army of sock puppets, with no reputation to lose, could still get a nonabusive item hidden, even if only briefly.

Application Integration, Testing, and Tuning

The approach to rolling out a new reputation-enabled application detailed in Chapter 9 is derived from the one used to deploy all reputation systems at Yahoo!, including the community content moderation system. No matter how many times reputation models had been successfully integrated into applications, the product teams were always nervous about the possible effects of such sweeping changes on their communities, product, and ultimately the bottom line. Given the size of the Yahoo! Answers community, and earlier interactions with community members, the team was even more cautious than most others at Yahoo!. Whereas we've previously warned about the danger of over-compressing the integration, testing, and tuning stages to meet a tight deadline, the product team didn't have that problem. Quite the reverse—they spent more time in testing than was required, which created some challenges with interpreting reputation testing results, and which we will cover in detail.

Application Integration

The full model as shown in Figure 10-8 has dozens of possible inputs, and many different programmers managed the different sections of the application. The designers had to perform a comprehensive review of all of the pages to determine where the new "Report Abuse" buttons should appear. More important, the application had to account for a new internal database status—"hidden"—for every question and answer on every page that displayed content. Hiding an item had important side effects on the application: it had to adjust total counts and revoke points granted, and a policy had to be devised and followed on handling any answers (and associated points) attached to any hidden questions.

Integrating the new model required entirely new flows on the site for reporting abuse and handling appeals. The appeals part of the model required that the application send email to users, functionality previously reserved for opt-in watch lists and marketing-related mailings—appeals mailings were neither. Last, the customer care management application would need to be altered.

Application integration was a very large task that would have to take place in parallel with the testing of the reputation model. Reputation inputs and outputs would need to be completed or at least simulated early on. Some project tasks didn't generate reputation input and therefore didn't conflict with testing—for example, functions in the new abuse reporting flows such as informing users about how a new system worked and screens confirming receipt of an abuse report.

Testing Is Harder Than You Think

Just as the design was iterative, so too were the implementation and testing. In "Testing Your System" on page 227, we suggested building and testing a model in pieces. The Yahoo! Answers team did just that, using constant values for the missing processes and inputs. The most important thing to get working was the basic input flow: when a user clicked Report Abuse, that action was tested against a threshold (initially a constant), and when it was exceeded, the reputation system sent a message back to the application to hide the item—effectively removing it from the site.

Once the basic input flow had been stabilized, the engineers added other features and connected additional inputs.

The engineers bench tested the model by inserting a logical test probe into the existing abuse reporting flow and using those reports to feed the reputation system, which they ran in parallel. The system wouldn't take any action that users would see just yet, but the model would be put through its paces as each change was made to the application.

But the iterative bench-testing approach had a weakness that the team didn't understand clearly until much later: the output of the reputation process—the hiding of content posted by other users—had a huge and critical influence on the effectiveness of the model. The rapid disappearance of content items changed the site completely, so real-time abuse reporting data from the current application turned out to be nearly useless for drawing conclusions about the behavior of the model.

In the existing application, several users would click on an abusive question in the first few minutes after it appeared on the home page. But once the reputation system was working, few, if any, users would ever even see the item before it was hidden. The shape of inputs to the system was radically altered by the system's very operation.

 Whenever a reputation system is designed to change user behavior significantly, any simulated input should be based on the assumption that the model accomplishes its goal; in other words, the team should use simulated input, not input from the existing application (in the Yahoo! Answers case, the live event stream from the prereputation version of the application).

The best testing it was possible to perform before the actual integration of the reputation model was stress testing the messaging channels and update rates, and testing using handmade simulated input that approximated the team's best guess at possible scenarios, legitimate and abusive.

Lessons in Tuning: Users Protecting Their Power

Still unaware that the source of abuse reports was inappropriate, the team inferred from early calculations that the reputation system would be significantly faster and at least as accurate as customer care staff had been to date. It became clear that the nature of the application precluded any significant tuning before release—so release required a significant leap of faith. The code was solid, the performance was good, and the web side of the application was finally ready—but the keys to the kingdom were about to be turned over to the users.

The model was turned on provisionally, but every single abuse report was still sent on to customer care staff to be reviewed, just in case.

> I couldn't sleep the first few nights. I was so afraid that I would come in the next morning to find all of the questions and answers gone, hidden by rogue users! It was like giving the readers of the *New York Times* the power to delete news stories.
>
> —Ori Zaltzman, Yahoo! community content moderation architect

Ori watched the numbers closely and made numerous adjustments to the various weights in the model. Inputs were added, revised, even eliminated.

For example, the model registered the act of "starring" (marking an item as a favorite) as a positive indicator of content quality. Seems natural, no? It turned out that a high correlation existed between an item being "starred" by a user and that same item eventually being hidden. Digging further, Ori found that many reporters of hidden items also "starred" an item soon before or after reporting it as abuse! Reporters were using the favorites feature to track when an item that they reported was hidden, and consequently they were abusing the favorites feature. As a result, "starring" was removed from the model.

At this time, the folly of evaluating the effectiveness of the model during the testing phase became clear. The results were striking and obvious. *Users were much more effective than customer care staff at identifying inappropriate content; not only were they faster, they were more accurate!* Having customer care double-check every report was actually decreasing the accuracy rate because they were introducing error by reversing user reports inappropriately.

Users definitely were hiding the worst of the worst content. All the content that violated the terms of service was getting hidden (along with quite a bit of the backlog of older items). But not all the content that violated the community guidelines was getting reported. It seemed that users weren't reporting items that might be considered borderline violations or disputable. For example, answers with no content related to the question, such as chatty messages or jokes, were not being reported. No matter how Ori tweaked the model, that didn't change.

In hindsight, the situation is easy to understand. The reputation model penalized disputes (in the form of appeals): if a user hid an item but the decision was overturned on appeal, the user would lose more reputation than he'd gained by hiding the item. That was the correct design, but it had the side effect of nurturing risk avoidance in abuse reporters. Another lesson in the difference between the bad (low-quality content) and the ugly (content that violates the rules)—they each require different tools to mitigate.

Deployment and Results

The final phase of testing and tuning of the Yahoo! Answers community content moderation system was itself a partial deployment—all abuse reports were temporarily verified post-reputation by customer care agents. Full deployment consisted mostly of shutting off the customer care verification feed and completing the few missing pieces of the appeals system. This was all completed within a few weeks of the initial beta-test release.

While the beta-test results were positive, in full deployment the system exceeded all expectations.

Note that we've omitted the technical performance metrics in Table 10-1. Without meeting those requirements, the system would never have left the testing phase.

Table 10-1. Yahoo! Answers community content moderation system results

Metric	Baseline	Goal	Result	Improvement
Average time before reported content is removed	18 hours	1 hour	30 *seconds*	120 times the goal >2000 times the baseline
Abuse report evaluation error rate	10%	10%	<0.1% (appeal result: overturned)	100× the goal or baseline
Customer care costs	100% $1 million per year	10% $100,000 per year	<0.1% <$10,000 per year	10 times the goal 100 times the baseline Saved >$990,000 per year

Every goal was shattered, and over time the results improved even further. As Yahoo! Answers product designer Micah Alpern put it: "Things got better because things were getting better!"

That phenomenon was perhaps best illustrated by another unexpected result about a month after the full system was deployed: both the number of abuse reports and requests for appeal dropped drastically over a few weeks. At first the team wondered if something was broken—but it didn't appear so, since a recent quality audit of the service showed that overall quality was still on the rise. User abuse reports resulted in hiding hundreds of items each day, but the total appeals dropped to a single-digit number, usually just 1 or 2, per day. What had happened?

The trolls and many spammers had left. They had simply given up and moved on.

The broken windows theory (see the sidebar "Broken Windows and Online Behavior" on page 205) clearly applied in this context—trolls found that the questions and answers they placed on the service were removed by vigilant reporters *faster than they could create the content.* Just as graffiti artists in New York stopped vandalizing trains because no one saw their handiwork, the Yahoo! Answers trolls either reformed or moved on to some other social media neighborhood to find their jollies.

Another important characteristic of the design was that, except for a small amount of localized text, the model was not language-dependent. The product team was able to deploy the moderation system to dozens of countries in only a few months, with similar results.

Reputation models fundamentally change the applications into which they're integrated. You might think of them as coevolving with the needs and community of your site. They may drive some users away. Often, that is exactly what you want.

Operational and Community Adjustments

This system required major adjustments to the Yahoo! Answers operational model, including the following:

- The customer care workload for reviewing Yahoo! Answers abuse reports decreased by 99%, resulting in significant staff resource reallocations to other Yahoo! products and some staff reductions. The workload dropped so low that Yahoo! Answers no longer required even a single full-time employee for customer care. (Good thing the customer care tool measured productivity in terms of events processed, not person-days.)

- The team changed the customer care tool to provide access to reputation scores for all of the users and items involved in an appeal. The tool can unhide content, and it always sends a message to the reputation model when the agent determines the appeal result. The reputation system was so effective at finding and hiding abusive content that agents had to go through a special training program to learn how to handle appeals, because the items in the Yahoo! Answers customer care event queues were qualitatively so different from those in other Yahoo! services. They were much more likely to be borderline cases requiring a subtle understanding of the terms of service and community guidelines.

- Before the reputation system was introduced, the report abuse rate had been used as a crude approximation of the quality of content on the site. With the reputation system in place and the worst of the worst not a factor, that rate was no longer a very strong indicator of quality, and the team had to devise other metrics.

There was little doubt that driving spammers and trolls from the site had a significantly positive effect on the community at large. Again, abuse reporters became very protective of their reputations so that they could instantly take down abusive content. But it took users some time to understand the new model and adapt their behavior. The following are a few best practices for facilitating the transformation from a company-moderated site to full user moderation:

- Explain what abuse means in your application.

  In the case of Yahoo! Answers, content must obey two different sets of rules: the Terms of Service and the Community Guidelines. Clearly describing each category and teaching the community what is (and isn't) reportable is critical to getting users to succeed as reporters as well as content creators (see Figure 10-9).

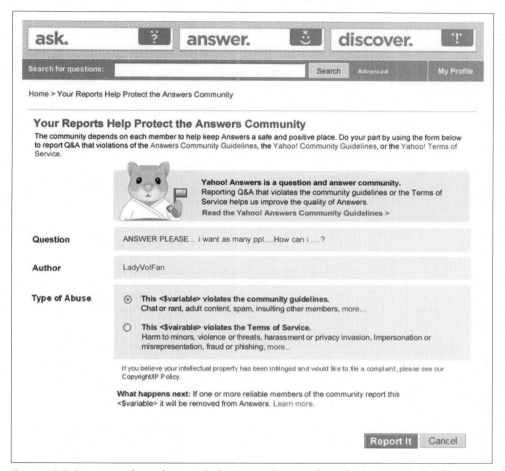

Figure 10-9. Reporting abuse: distinguish the Terms of Service from the Community Guidelines.

- Explain the reputation effects of an abuse report.

  Abuse reporter reputation was not displayed. Reporters didn't even know their own reputation score. But active users knew the effects of having a good abuse reporter reputation—most content that they reported was hidden instantly. What they didn't understand was what specific actions would increase or decrease it. As shown in Figure 10-10, the Yahoo! Answers site clearly explained that the site rewarded accuracy of reports, not volume. That was an important distinction because Yahoo! Answers points (and levels) were based mostly on participation karma—where doing more things gets you more karma. Active users understood that relationship. The new abuse reporter karma didn't work that way. In fact, reporting abuse was one of the few actions the user could take on the site that *didn't* generate Yahoo! Answers points.

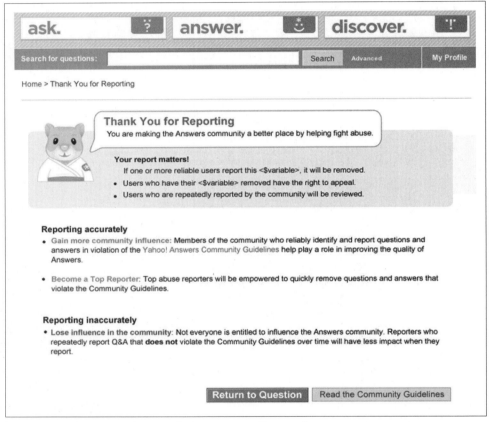

Figure 10-10. Reporting abuse: explain reputation effects to abuse reporters.

Adieu

We've arrived at the end of the Yahoo! Answers tale and the end of *Building Web Reputation Systems*. With this case study and with this book we've tried to paint as complete and real-world a picture as possible of the process of designing, architecting, and implementing a reputation system.

We covered the real and practical questions that you're likely to face as you add reputation-enhanced decision making to your own product. We showed you a graphical grammar for representing entities and reputation processes in your own models. Our hope is that you now have a whole new way to think about reputation on the Web.

We encourage you to continue the conversation with us at this book's companion website (*http://buildingreputation.com*).

The Reputation Framework

The reputation framework is the software that forms the execution environment for reputation models. This appendix takes a deeper and much more technical look at the framework. The first section is intended for software architects and technically minded product managers to generate appropriate requirements for implementation and possible reuse by other applications.

The second section of this appendix describes two different reputation frameworks with very different sets of requirements in detail: the Invisible Reputation Framework and the Yahoo! Reputation Platform.

This appendix talks about messaging systems, databases, performance, scale, reliability, etc., and you can safely skip it if you are not interested in such gory internals.

Reputation Framework Requirements

This section helps you identify the requirements for your reputation framework. As with all projects, the toughest requirements can be stated as a series of trade-offs. When selecting the requirements for your framework, be certain that they consider its total lifetime, meeting the needs at the beginning of your project and going forward, as your application grows and becomes successful.

Keep in mind that your first reputation model may be just one of several to utilize your reputation framework. Also, your reputation system is only a small part of an application...it shouldn't be the only part.

- Are your reputation *calculations* static or dynamic? Static means that you can compute your claim values on a go-forward basis, without having to access all previous inputs. Dynamic means the opposite...that each input and/or each query will regenerate the values from scratch.
- What is the *scale* of your reputation system...small or huge? What is the rate of inputs per minute? How many times will reputation scores be accessed for display or use by your application?

- How *reliable* must the reputation scores be...transactional or best-effort?
- How *portable* is the data? Should the scores be shared with other applications or integrated with their native application only?
- How *complex* is the reputation model...complicated or simple? If it is currently simple, will it stay that way?
- Which is more important, getting the best possible response immediately, or a perfectly accurate response as soon as possible? Or, more technically phrased: What is the most appropriate *messaging* method...Optimistic/Fire-and-Forget or Request-Response/Call-Return?

Calculations: Static Versus Dynamic

There are significant trade-offs in the domain of performance and accuracy when considering how to record, calculate, store, and retrieve reputation events and scores. Some static models have scores that need to be continuous and real-time; they need to be as accurate as possible at any given moment. An example would be spammer IP reputation for industrial and scale email providers. Others may be calculated in batch-mode, because a large amount of data will be consulted for each score calculation.

Dynamic reputation models have constantly changing constraints:

Variable contexts
> The data considered for each calculation is constrained differently for each display context. This use is common in social applications, such as Zynga's popular *Texas HoldEmPoker*, which displays friends-only leaderboards.

Complex multielement relationships
> The data calculations affect one another in a nonlinear way, such as search relevance calculations like Google's PageRank. Recommender systems are also dynamic data models...typically a large portion of the data set is considered to put every element in a multidimensional space for nearest-neighbor determination. This allows the display of "People like you also bought..." entities.

Static: Performance, performance, performance

Very large applications require up-to-the-second reputation statements available to any reading applications at incredibly high rates. For example, a top email provider might need to know a spammer reputation for every IP address for email messages entering the service in real time! Even if that's cached in memory, when that reputation changes state, say from *nonspammer* to *spammer*, instant notification is crucial. There's just no time to use the traditional database method of recalculating the reputation over and over again from mostly unchanged data. By static we mean roll-forward calculations, in which every reputation input modifies the roll-ups in such a way that they contain the correct value at the moment and contain enough state to continue the process for the next input.

Dynamic: Reputation within social networks

Given the description of static, you might be tempted to select the dynamic requirement for a framework because it provides the greatest range of reputation models possible. There is a serious cost to this option...it increases the cost of implementing, testing, and most importantly scaling your framework. Static reputations are easier to understand, implement, and test, and they scale better. Look at the history of Twitter.com's Fail Whale, a direct result of the requirement for a dynamic custom display of tweets for each and every user. Dynanism is costing them a fortune.

When possible, find ways to simplify your model, either by adding more specific contexts or by reducing dimensions through some clever math. This book won't cover the many forms of dynamic systems in any depth, as many of the algorithms are well covered in academic literature. See Appendix B for pointers to various document archives.

Scale: Large Versus Small

Scale—or the number of inputs (and the database writes they ultimately generate) and reputation claim value reads—is probably the most important factor when considering any reputation system implementation.

Small scale is any transaction rate such that a single instance of a database can handle all reputation-related reads and writes without becoming overloaded and falling behind.

Large scale requires additional software services to support reading and storing reputation statements. At the point where your reputation system grows large enough to require multiple databases (or distributing the processing of inputs to multiple machines), then you probably need a distinct reputation framework. It becomes just too complicated for the high-level application to manage the reputation data model.

At a low enough volume, say less than thousands of reads per minute and only hundreds of writes, it is easy to think that simple database API calls mixed directly into the application code as needed would be the best approach for speed of development. Why bother adding a layer to isolate the reputation system access to the database? Consider that your application may not always stay small. What if it is a hit and suddenly you need multiple databases or more reputation frameworks to process all the inputs? This has happened to more than a few web databases over the years, and on occasion—such as when Ma.gnolia ended up losing all its users' data—it can be fatal to the business.

So, even for small-scale applications, we recommend a clean, modular boundary between the application and the reputation system: all inputs should use a class or call a library that encapsulates the reputation process code and the database operations. That way, the calculations are centralized and the framework can be incrementally scaled. See the section "The Invisible Reputation Framework: Fast, Cheap, and Out of Control" on page 287 for a specific example of this practice.

Reliability: Transactional Versus Best-Effort

Reputation claims are often *critical* to the success of an application, commercial or otherwise. So it would seem to follow naturally that it should be a requirement that the value of the claims should be 100% reliable. This means that every input's effect on the reputation model should be reflected in the calculations. There's nothing more valuable than the application's contributions to the bottom line, right?

There's another reason you'd like reputation roll-ups to be reliable, especially when users provide the claims that are combined to create them: sometimes users abuse the system, and often this abuse comes in great volume if the scores have financial value to the end users themselves. (See "eBay Seller Feedback Karma" on page 78.) If scores are reliable and tracked on a *transactional* basis, the effects of the abuse can be reversed. If a user is determined to abuse the reputation system, often the correct action is to reverse all of his inputs on *every target that he ever evaluated*. This is the *Undo* anything feature and requires a reputation framework that is optimized to support reversible inputs and a database that is indelible by source identifier only.

So, if it's good for business and it's good for abuse mitigation, why shouldn't my reputation system require transactional-style reliability throughout? The answer: performance.

Every reversible input adds at least one additional database read-modify-write to store the event. If the database is locked for each input, high-transaction rate systems can create a severe bottleneck waiting for resources to become available. Not only that, it at least doubles the size of the database and messaging network load, and depending on the input-to-output ratio, may increase it by an order magnitude or more.

For some applications, say Ratings and Reviews (see the section "User Reviews with Karma" on page 75), storing all the inputs is already a part of the application design, so these costs must be met. But when you look at top-100 website or online game transaction rates, you see that it quickly becomes cost-prohibitive to store everything everyone does in an indexed database. As Mammad Zadeh, chief architect of Yahoo!'s Reputation Platform, said about best-effort volume data inputs for spammer reputation:

> Approximate can be good enough!

For applications that have continuous input, the reputation model can be designed to deal with best-effort message delivery. Yahoo!'s reputation model for identifying spammer IP addresses takes user inputs in the form of "This Is Spam" votes and also receives a continuous stream of volume data: the total email received per IP address per minute. There are hundreds of thousands of mail server IP addresses, and at any moment tens of thousands of them are sending mail to Yahoo! mailboxes. The user inputs are several orders of magnitude less common than the incoming traffic data.

It was clear immediately that the internal messaging infrastructure would quickly get overwhelmed if every reputation input message had to be sent with guaranteed delivery.

Instead, the much lighter overhead and much quicker protocol was selected to make best-effort delivery for these messages, while the user actions were sent using a slower but more reliable channel. The model was designed so that it would keep a windowed history of traffic data for each target IP address and a floating average volume for calculations. This allowed the model to have a sense of time as well as make it insensitive to the occasional dropout of traffic data. Likewise, the inputs never had to be reversed, so were never stored in deployment. During the testing, tuning, and debugging phase, the traffic data was stored in order to verify the model's results.

Why not just design all of the models to be compatible with best-effort delivery then? Because it becomes a much more difficult task with user inputs. In many applications, the user evaluations took considerable effort to construct (i.e., Reviews) or are a part of the user's identity (i.e., Favorites) and can't just disappear; if this ever approaches becoming a common occurrence, you risk driving the customer away. This is also true for roll-up reputation that is attached to users' objects: their karma scores or ratings for their eBay shop or reviews of their favorite objects. People track their scores like hawks and get upset if ratings are incorrectly calculated.

Best-effort message delivery also makes reversible reputation math very messy...because of lost messages, counters can go negative; go out of range; and scores can get stuck with inappropriate values given the number of reported inputs, for example, "0 users say this movie is 5-stars!"

Finally, losing inputs in a time-critical application, such as the one described in Chapter 10, could increase operational costs.

There is a compromise: if you build a reputation framework that supports reversible transactions, and use that feature only *judiciously* in your models, you can have the best of both worlds.

Model Complexity: Complex Versus Simple

Reputation models often start out very simple: store a number, starting at 0, and periodically add 1 to it and update the record. It seems there is no need for a reputation framework in this case beyond that provided by the current application environment and that of the database.

In practice, however, reputation systems either evolve or fail. Reputation is used to increase the value of your entities. So, either the model succeeds at increasing value or it needs to be abandoned or changed to reflect the actual use pattern that will achieve this goal. This usually involves making the system more complex, for example, tweaking it to include a more subtle set of inputs. On the other hand, if it is successful, it may well become the target of manipulation by those who directly benefit from such actions. For instance, the business owners on Yelp formed collectives to cross-review each other's businesses and increase their rankings (see "Merchants angry over getting yanked by Yelp" by Ellen Lee and Anastasia Ustinova in the July 4, 2008, edition of the

San Francisco Chronicle). Even when successful, reputation models must constantly evolve.

So, whether a reputation model starts as complex or succeeds sufficiently to become complex, the reputation framework should be designed to assume that models may contain several, perhaps dozens of reputation processes—and more importantly that the model will change over time. This suggests that version control for both the framework and the models that execute within.

As the number of processes in a model increases, there are performance trade-offs based on other requirements on the framework. If the entire framework is transactional—say by wrapping a complex process chain with a database lock—though reliable, this will lead to increased lock contention and may significantly decrease throughput.

It may also be possible to do static graph analysis of reputation models to combine processes and parallelize execution, in effect reducing the complexity before execution to improve performance.

Data Portability: Shared Versus Integrated

Should reputation statements be kept separate on a per-application or per-context basis or be made more available for other uses? Intuitively, from both a simplified security view and an incremental development approach, the answer would be *yes*: isolate the data and integrate the reputation framework in-line with the application code, which has appropriate access to the database as well has a code-level understanding of the source and target objects. For single-application environments, data portability seems like a *nice-to-have* feature, something that the team will get to in version 1.x.

Although it is true that reputation claims are always most valuable in the context in which they were generated, sometimes the context stretches across multiple applications. For example, Yahoo! Shopping and Yahoo! Music both benefit from users evaluating new music releases, either at the time of purchase or even when listening to them via real-time stream.

Shared context is the primary reason reputation frameworks should treat targets as foreign keys: identifiers in an external database. But it also means that the reputation statement store should be accessible by multiple applications. This exact situation comes up more often than you might think, and one-off solutions for sharing or duplicating data across applications quickly become cost prohibitive. When Yahoo! Local and Yahoo! Travel decided that they should share their hotel and restaurant reviews between the applications, they incurred a large cost to merge the data, since they each used different target identifiers for the same real-world business.

Even if you don't yet have multiple applications in development, plan for success. Create sharable object identifiers that new applications can use, and make the schema portable. It doesn't take any longer and keeps your options open.

Even with shared source and target identifiers, you might be tempted to think that the reputation framework should be developed all in-line with the initial application. For example, you might presume that a *master* application would be the only one that would want to calculate the reputations and store them; all ancillary apps would be *read-only*. Many systems are structured this way. This sounds great, but it creates a dependency on the master application development team whenever the reputation model needs to change to accommodate a new input or new interim score or to retune based on anomalous behavior perhaps introduced as the result of a new use pattern.

In the section "Generating inferred karma" on page 159, we discussed the pattern of *inferred karma*, where reputation is borrowed from other contexts to create an interim reputation that can be used in the case where no context-specific claim is available or yet trustworthy. As detailed in Chapter 10, when Yahoo! Answers borrowed membership reputation, IP reputation, and browser cookie reputation to use as a reason to trust someone's report of abusive content, the creators of those component reputations had no inkling that they'd be used this way.

This mixing of external scores may seem to be a contradiction of the "reputation is always in context" rule, but it doesn't have to be, as long as each reuse *maintains* all, or most, of the original context's meaning. The fact that a Yahoo! account is months or years old has more reputation value when compared to one created today. The same thing goes for the age of a browser cookie, or abuse history on an IP address. None of these components is reliable alone, nor should any of them be used to make serious decisions about the reliability of a user, but combined they might just give you enough information to make the user's experience a little better.

A reputation framework that allows multiple applications to read and write reputation statements to each other's contexts can lead to serious data problems; a bug in one model can damage the execution of another. For such environments, a security model and/or a disciplined development process is strongly suggested.

See the detailed example in "The Yahoo! Reputation Platform: Shared, Reliable Reputation at Scale" on page 289 for a description of a specific implementation.

Optimistic Messaging Versus Request-Reply

The reputation framework really has only two interfaces to the application environment: a channel for routing inputs to an executing model and a method for sending a signal that something interesting happened in the model. In the vast majority of cases, reputation scores are not output in the classical sense, but they are stored for the application code to retrieve later.

This approach means that the reputation framework *can* be isolated from the application for performance and security reasons. One way to think of it is like a special database preprocessor for turning inputs into database records.

Given the narrow input channel, the framework implementor may choose between several messaging models. Certainly programmers are most familiar with request-reply messaging—most everything works that way: programs call functions that return results when complete, and even the Web can make your computer wait up to a minute for the server to reply to a HTTP GET request. It seems logical for an application to send a reputation input, such as a star-rating for a movie to the reputation model, and wait for confirmation of the new average score to return. Why bother with any other messaging model?

Performance at scale

Many inputs, especially those that are not reflected back to the user, should be sent without waiting for acknowledgment. This is called optimistic (or asynchronous) messaging, colloquially known as *fire-and-forget*. This makes the application much faster, as the application no longer has to wait for network round trip plus all of the database accesses required by the reputation model. The load instead shifts the burden to the messaging infrastructure and the machines that process the messages. This is how large-scale applications work: send messages into a cloud of computers that can be expanded and reconfigured to handle increasing traffic.

Note that request-reply can be added as a lightweight library on top of an optimistic messaging service: pass a callback handle to the model, which will get triggered when the result is complete. Application developers would use this wrapper sparingly, only when they needed an immediate new result. Generally, this is rare. For example, when a user writes a review for a hair dryer, he doesn't see the effects on the roll-up score immediately; instead he's looking at the review he just submitted. In fact, delaying the display of the roll-up might be a good idea for abuse mitigation reasons.

Even if it seems that you will never need optimistic messaging because you'll never have that many inputs, we urge that your reputation framework (even if it is just a local library) provide the *semantics* of messaging (i.e., `SendReputationEvent()` and `SendReputationEventAndWait()`), even if it is implemented as a straightforward function call underneath. This is low cost and will allow your applications to run even if you significantly change the operational characteristics of your framework.

Framework Designs

Each trade-off made when selecting framework design requirements has implementation impacts for the framework itself and constrains the reputation models and applications that utilize it. In order to more clearly illustrate the costs and benefits of various configurations, we now present two reputation sandbox designs: the minimalist *Invisible Framework* and the full-scalable *Yahoo! Reputation Platform*. Table A-1 shows the framework requirements for each.

Table A-1. Example reputation framework requirements

Framework design	Calculations	Scale	Reliability	Portability	Messaging	Model complexity
Invisible Reputation Framework	Dynamic (option)	Small	Best-effort	Embedded	Request-reply	Simple
Yahoo! Reputation Platform	Static	Huge	Transactional (option)	Shared	Optimistic	Complex

The Invisible Reputation Framework: Fast, Cheap, and Out of Control

When most applications start implementing social media, including the gathering of user evaluations or reputation, they just place all input, processing, and output as code in-line with their application. Need a thumbs-up? Just add it to the page, create a votes table to store an entry for everyone who votes, and do a database query to count the number of entries at display time. It is quick and easy. Then they start using a score like this for ranking search results, and they quickly realize that they can't afford to do that many queries dynamically, so they create a background or timed process to recalculate the reputation for each entity and attach it to that entities record.

And so it goes, feature after feature, one new-use optimization after another, until either the application becomes too successful and scaling breaks or the cost-benefit of another integration exceeds the business pain threshold.

Everyone starts this way. It is completely normal.

Requirements

"Time to market is everything...we need reputation (ratings, reviews, or karma) and we need it now. We can fix it later." This summarizes the typical implementation plan for legions of application developers. Get something—*anything*—working, ship alpha-quality code, and promise yourself you will fix it later. This is a surprisingly tight constraint on the design of the invisible reputation framework, which is actually no framework at all!

Mostly dynamic calculations with static results cache as optimization
> When first implementing a reputation system, it seems obvious and trivial: store some ratings and when you need to display the roll-up, do a database query to calculate the average just in time. This is the dynamic calculation method, and it allows for some interesting reputation scores, such as *Your Friends Rated this 4.5 Stars*. When reputation gets used for things such as influencing the search rank of

entities, this approach becomes too expensive. Running hundreds of just-in-time averages against the database when only the top 10 results are going to be displayed 90% of the time is cost-prohibitive. The typical approach is a dynamic-static hybrid: at a fixed interval, say daily, calculate a dynamic database average for each and every entity and store the roll-up value in a search index for speedy searches tomorrow. When you need a new index for some new calculation, repeat the process. Clearly this can quickly become unwieldy.

Small Scale: 100 transactions/minute or less
At a small scale, no more than one transaction per second or so, the database is not a bottleneck, and even if it becomes one, many commercial scaling solutions are available.

Best-effort reliability with ad-hoc cleanup
Reliability is a secondary consideration when time to market is the main driver. Code developed in Internet time will be buggy and revised often. It's simply impractical to consider that reputation would be completely accurate. This requires that reputation models themselves will be built to auto-correct obvious errors, such as a roll-up going negative or out-of range, since it *will* happen.

Application bound reputation data
The temptation will be to store reputation statements as claim values as closely bound to the target data records as possible. After all, it will make it easier for search ranking and other similar uses. Only one application will read and write the reputation, so there is no need to be worried about future uses, right?

Request-reply messaging direct to database
When coding in a hurry, why introduce a new and potentially unfamiliar optimistic messaging system? It adds cognitive, implementation, and messaging overhead. The invisible reputation framework trusts the engineer to code up the database action in-line in the application: the SQL Query requests are sent using the vendor-supplied interface, and the application waits dutifully for the reply. This is most familiar and easiest to understand, even if it is the has poor performance characteristics.

Simple or ad-hoc model support
Model? What model? There is no execution environment for the reputation model, which is broken into little pieces and spread throughout the application. Of course, this makes the model code much harder to maintain because future coders will have to search through the source to find all the places the model is implemented. If the programmers think ahead, they might break the common functions out into a library for reuse, but only if time allows.

Implementation details

A typical invisible reputation framework is implemented as in-line code. Taking a typical LAMP (Linux, Apache, MySQL, PHP/Perl/Python) installation as an example, this means that the data schema in the reputable entities tables are extended to include reputation claim values, such as *average rating* or *karma points*, and a new table is set up to contain any stored/reversible user created reputation statements. The database calls are made directly by the application through a standard PHP MySQL library, such as the MySQLi class.

With this approach, simple ratings and review systems can be created and deployed in a few days, if not hours. It doesn't get any quicker than that.

Lessons learned

Assuming your application succeeds and grows, taking the absolutely quickest and cheapest route to reputation will always come back to bite you in the end.

Most likely, the first thing to cause trouble will be the database; as the transaction rate increases, there will be lock contention on writes and general traffic jams on reads. For a while the commercial solutions will help, but ultimately decoupling the application code from the reputation framework functionality will be required, both for reading and for writing statements.

Another set of challenges—tuning the model, adding more reputation uses, and attendant debugging—become cost-prohibitive as your application grows, causing time to market to suffer significantly. Not planning ahead will make you slower than your competition. Again, a little investment in compartmentalizing the reputation framework, such isolating the execution of the model into a library, ends up being a great cost-benefit trade-off in the medium- to long-term.

Whatever you do, compartmentalize!

If the development time budget allows only one best-practice recommendation to be applied to the implementation of a reputation framework, we recommend this above all others: compartmentalize the framework! By that we mean the reputation model, the database code, and the data tables. Yes, you can count that as three things if you must. They are listed in priority order.

The Yahoo! Reputation Platform: Shared, Reliable Reputation at Scale

Yahoo! is a collection of diverse web applications that make it collectively the website with the largest audience in the world. Over a half-billion different people use a Yahoo! application each month. In a single day, Yahoo! gathers millions of user evaluations, explicit and implicit, of reputable entities spread over dozens of topic areas and hundreds of applications. And almost none of it is shared across similar topics or applications. We've already mentioned that it was only a few years ago that Yahoo! Travel and Yahoo! Local started to share hotel and restaurant reviews, and that one-off integration provided no technical or operational assistance to Yahoo! Music and Yahoo! Shopping when they similarly wanted to share information about user DVD ratings.

Yahoo! requirements

Outrageously large scaling requirements and sharing were the driving requirements for the Yahoo! Reputation Platform. The following are Yahoo! Reputation Platform requirements in force-ranked order:

Huge scale: 10,000,000,000 transactions/year

When Yahoo! started its efforts at building a common reputation infrastructure in the form of a standard platform, the current rate of user ratings entering the Yahoo! Music Experience, their real-time music streaming service, had reached one billion ratings per year. This was more than half of the total explicit user ratings it was gathering at the time across all of its sites. The executives were excited by the possibility of this project and how it might be used in the future, when cellphones would become the predominant device for accessing social data, and therefore suggested that the minimum input rate should exceed that seen by Yahoo ! Music by at least a factor of 10×—or ten billion transactions per year. That's an average of about 350 transactions per second, but traffic is never that smooth...common peaks would exceed 1,000 per second.

That may seem huge, but consider how the database transaction rate might become inflated by another factor of 2× to 10×, depending on the nature of the reputation model's complexity. Each stored roll-up could add a (lock)-read-modify-write-(unlock) cycle. Also, using and/or displaying reputation (aka capturing the value) multiplies the number of reads by a significant amount, say 5× in lieu of a concrete example. So by the time things get down to the database, for a typical model, we could see 100 billion reads and 20 or 30 billion writes!

Clearly scale is the requirement that will impose the most challenges on the framework implementation team.

Reputation events sharable across applications and contexts

Why bother building a gigantic reputation platform? One of the driving requirements was that reputation information be shared across applications and Yahoo! sites. Travel, Local, Maps, and other sites should be able to access and contribute user evaluations to the reputable entities—businesses and services—they all have in common. Shopping, Tech, Coupons, and others all have users interacting with products and merchants.

It was clear that the segmentation of Yahoo! applications and sites were not the best contexts for reputation. The properties of the entities themselves—what kind of thing they were, where they were located, and who was interacting with them—these are the real reputation contexts. A common platform was a great way to create a neutral, shared environment for collecting and distributing the users' contributions.

Transaction-level reliability used by most models

Reputation is a critical component of Yahoo!'s overall value and is used throughout the service: from web search to finding a good hotel to identifying the songs you never want to hear on your personal web-radio station.

This value is so important that it creates the incentive for significant reputation abuse. For example, there is a billion-dollar industry, complete with an acronym, for capitalizing on design flaws in search algorithms: SEO, or *search engine optimization*. Likewise, the reputation models that execute in this framework are subject to similar abuse. In fact, for many applications, there are so many targets that the number of user evaluations for each is very small, making the abusive manipulation of roll-ups accessible to small groups or even dedicated individuals (see "Commercial incentives" on page 115).

Generally, it is not technically possible for software to detect small-scale reputation abuse. Instead, social mechanisms are used, typically in the form of a Report Abuse button. The community polices reputation in these cases. Unfortunately, this method can be very expensive, as each report requires a formal review by customer care staff to decide whether the reputation has been manipulated. And each abuser typically generates dozens if not hundreds of abusive reputation contributions. The math is pretty straightforward: even if abuse is reported for 1 in a 100 product reviews, at Yahoo! scale it is not cost-efficient to have humans screen everything.

After identifying a user account or browser cookie or IP address that is abusing the reputation system, there is a requirement that customer care can remove *all* of the related reputation created by the user. Nothing they created can be trusted and everything is presumed to be damaging, perhaps event multiple entities.

This adds a transactional requirement to the framework: every *explicit user input* and its roll-ups that were also affected must be reversible. It is not enough to just delete the user and the specific event; the reputation model must be executed to undo the damage.

Note that this requirement is very expensive and is used only on reputation models that require it. For example, in tracking the user's personal ratings for songs, Yahoo! Music Engine may not require reversibility, because charging a subscription fee is considered sufficient deterrent to reputation abuse.

Also, large-volume models that do not surface roll-up reputation to the users may not be transactional. A good example is the Yahoo! Mail IP Spammer reputation model, as described in the patent application, which does not keep a transactional history of individual IP address but does keep the This Is (Not) Spam votes on a per-user basis for abuse management as described earlier.

Complex and interconnected model support

Between Yahoo!'s existing understanding of reputation abuse in its current systems as well as the strong requirement to share data between applications, it was clear that the reputation models that would execute on this platform would be more complex than simply counting and averaging a bunch of numeric scores.

There was also an original requirement for modular reuse of hypothetical reputation model components in order to speed up the development and deployment of new applications integrating reputation.

Static calculations

As a result of the performance constraints imposed by the scaling requirements, it was immediately clear that models running in the framework should execute with linear, O(n), performance characteristics, which precluded considering dynamic computation. There is no time to grab multiple items from the database to recalculate a custom value for every model execution. All calculations would be limited to roll-forward computation: a roll-up must be updatable using a *fixed* number of repository reads, usually exactly one. This means that the platform will not support per-user reputation contexts, such as *Your Friends Rated This Entity 4.5*. Time-limited contexts, such as Last Year, Last Month, etc., could still be implemented as specific static reputation calculations. (See the discussion of windowing decay systems in "Freshness and decay" on page 63.)

Optimistic messaging system

Given that we can anticipate that the database is going to be the choke point for this platform, a request-reply protocol to the reputation system would be unable to deliver on a reliable service level. There are just too many inputs coming into too many complex model instances to be sure how long it will take for the model to run.

Performance demands an asynchronous, optimistic messaging backbone, where messages are delivered by a load-balancing queue manager to multiple reputation framework instances to be processed on a first-come, first-served basis.

Applications that read reputation claim values directly from the database, not via the framework, will always get the best result possible at that moment.

The application developer that is collecting explicit user reputation events, such as ratings, is offered several choices to deal with the immediate-reply nature of the optimistic messaging system:

- If possible (not displaying a roll-up) assume success and echo the user's input directly back to him as though it had been returned by the platform.

- Implement a callback in the reputation model, and wrap the asynchronous call with one that waits. Don't forget a timeout in best-effort message delivery environments.

- Get whatever the current result is from the database and explain to the user, if needed, that it might take a bit longer for his result to be reflected in the roll-up.

Yahoo! implementation details

The architecture of the Yahoo! Reputation Platform is detailed in two recently published patent applications:

- U.S. Patent Application 11/774,460:"Detecting Spam Messages Using Rapid Sender Reputation Feedback Analysis," Libbey, Miles; Farmer, F. Randall; Mohsenzadeh, Mohammad; Morningstar, Chip; Sample, Neal
- U.S. Patent Application 11/945,911:"Real-Time Asynchronous Event Aggregation Systems," Farmer, F. Randall; Mohsenzadeh, Mohammad; Morningstar, Chip; Sample, Neal

The implementation details we describe here for the platform are derived primarily from these documents, interviews with the development teams, and our personal experience setting the platform's design requirements.

High-level architecture. Figure A-1 renders the Yahoo! reputation framework architectural stack using a traditional layer cake model. Though the onerous scaling requirements make the specifics of this implementation very specialized, at this level of abstraction, most reputation framework models are the same: they each need *message dispatching* services; a reputation model execution engine with an interface reputation statement relational database service; a method to activate or signal external processes; and a separate high-performance, query-only interface to the data for application display and other uses, such as search result ranking.

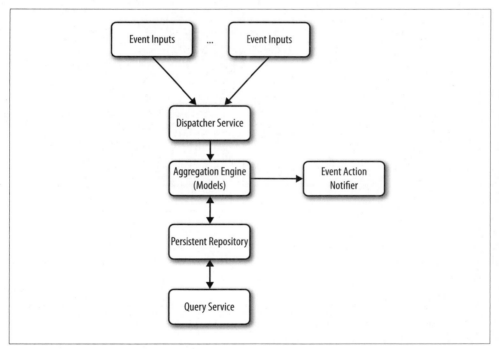

Figure A-1. Yahoo! Reputation Platform layers.

The following sections describe in detail the specific choices that the Yahoo! Reputation Platform team made for implementing each layer.

Messaging dispatcher. Figure A-2 shows the top architectural layer of the framework, a message dispatcher whose job it is to accept inputs, usually in the form of reputation statements (source, claim, and target), transform them to standard-format messages and sending them on to one of many model execution engines to be processed.

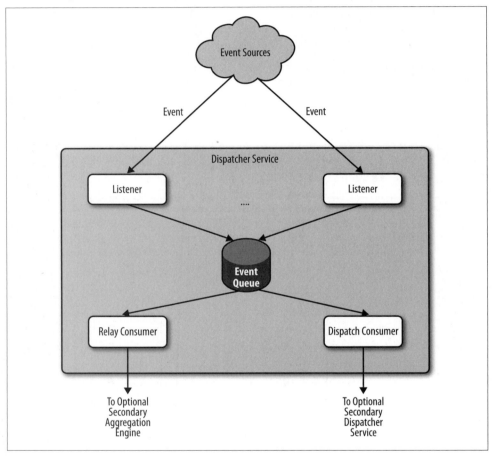

Figure A-2. Yahoo! Reputation Platform message dispatcher.

There are three main components of this subsystem: a set of *input listeners*, a single *message event queue*, and *message consumers*, of which there are two subtypes—*dispatch consumers* and *relay consumers*.

Input listeners

This is the compatibility layer for messaging. Different listeners can have different semantics. For example, some listeners can be implemented to understand asynchronous messages of different data formats, such as XML or JSON. They may be hand-coded function calls to do last-moment data transformations, such as turning a source or target identifier from one context into an identifier from another context. Another common listener enhancement is to add a timestamp to, and/or to write a log of, each message to aide in abuse mitigation or model testing and tuning.

 It is important to note that when reputation models interact with one another across contexts, as is often the case with karma systems, the first model will send a message via this message dispatching service instead of making a direct call to a hardcoded entry point in the second model.

Once normalized into a common format, the messages are then handed off to the message event queue for first-in, first-in processing.

Message event queue

The message event queue holds all of the input messages waiting for processing. This process is tightly optimized and can do load-balancing and other throughput optimizations, not detailed here. There are many books and papers on these methods.

Message consumers

Each message will be fetched by a consumer process, typically to be forwarded somewhere else. There can be several types, each with its own semantics, but the main two kinds are:

Dispatch consumer

The dispatch consumer delivers messages to the model execution engines. Typically there is one dispatch consumer for every known model execution engine. In self-scaling systems, where more resources are brought online automatically, when a new model execution engine starts up, it might register with a dispatcher, which would start a dispatch consumer to start forwarding messages.

Relay consumer

When more than one message dispatcher is running, it is often desirable to separate message traffic, and by extension the ability to modify reputation, by context. This provides data modification isolation, limiting possible damage from context-external applications. But, there are specific cases where cross-context modification is desirable, with karma being the typical example: multiple contexts contribute reputation to the user-profile context.

In order to allow this cross-context, cross-model, and cross-dispatcher messaging, certain predetermined messages are consumed by the relay consumer and passed onto other dispatchers, in effect stacking dispatchers as needed. This way the Yahoo! Movies ratings and review system can send a message to the Yahoo! Profiles karma model without knowing the address for the dispatcher; it can just send a message to the one for its own framework and know that the message will get relayed to the appropriate servers.

Note that a registration service, such as the one described for the dispatch consumer, is required to support this functionality.

There can be many message dispatchers deployed, and this layer is a natural location to provide any context-based security that may be required. Since changes to the reputation database come only by sending messages to the reputation framework, limiting application access to the dispatcher that knows the names and addresses of the context-specific models makes sense. As a concrete example, only Yahoo! Travel and Local had the keys needed to contact, and therefore make changes to, the reputation framework that ran their shared model, but any other company property could read their ratings and reviews using the separate reputation query layer (see "Reputation query interface" on page 298).

The Yahoo! Reputation Platform's dispatcher implementation was optimistic: all application API calls return immediately without waiting for model execution. The messages were stored with the dispatcher until they could be forwarded to a model execution engine.

The transport services used to move messages to the dispatcher varied by application, but most were proprietary high-performance services. A few models, such as Yahoo! Mail's Spam IP reputation, accepted inputs on a best-effort basis, which uses the fastest available transport service.

The Yahoo! Reputation Platform high-level architectural layer cake shown in Figure A-1 contains all the required elements of a typical reputation framework. New framework designers would do well to start with that design and design/select implementations for each component to meet their requirements.

Model execution engine. Figure A-3 shows the heart of the reputation framework, the *model execution engine*, which manages the reputation model processes and their state. Messages from the dispatcher layer are passed into the appropriate model code for immediate execution. The model execution engine reads and writes its state, usually in the form of reputation statements via the reputation database layer. (See "Reputation repository" on page 298.) Model processes run to completion, and if cross-model execution or optimism is desired, may send messages to the dispatcher for future processing.

The diagram also shows that models may use the external event signaling system to notify applications of changes in state. See the section "External signaling interface" on page 297.

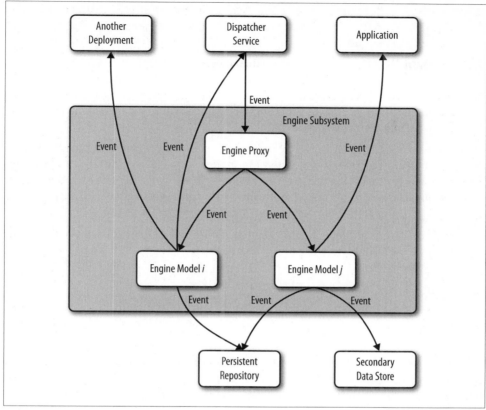

Figure A-3. Yahoo! Reputation Platform model engine.

This platform gets much of its performance from parallel processing, and the Yahoo! Reputation Platform uses this approach by implementing an *Engine Proxy* that routes all incoming message traffic to the engine that is currently running the appropriate model in a concurrent process. This proxy is also in charge of loading and initializing any model that is not currently loaded or executing.

The Yahoo! Reputation Platform implemented models in PHP with many of the messaging lines within the model diagram implemented as function calls instead of higher-overhead messages. See "Your Mileage May Vary" on page 300 for a discussion of the rationale. The team chose PHP mostly due to its members' personal expertise and tastes (there was no particular technical requirement that drove this choice).

External signaling interface. In optimistic systems, such as the Yahoo! reputation platform, output happens passively: the application has no idea *when* a change happened or what the results *were* of any input event. Some unknown time after the input, a query to the database *may* or *may not* reflect a change. In high-volume applications, this is a very good thing because it is just impractical to wait for every side effect of every input to propagate across dozens of servers. But when something *important* (read valuable) happens, such as an IP address switching from good-actor to spammer, the application needs to be informed ASAP.

This is accomplished by using an *external signaling interface*. For smaller systems, this can just be hardcoded calls in the reputation model implementation. But larger environments normally have signalling services in place that typically log signal details and have mechanisms for executing processes that take actions, such as changing user access or contacting supervisory personnel.

Another kind of signaling interface can be used to provide a layer of request-reply semantics to an optimistic system: when the model is about to complete, a signal gets sent to a waiting thread that was created when the input was sent. The thread identifier is sent along as a parameter throughout the model as it executes.

Reputation repository. On the surface, the reputation repository layer looks like any other high-performance, partitioned, and redundant database. The specific features for the repository in the Yahoo! reputation platform are:

- Like the other layers, the repositories may themselves be managed by a proxy manager for performance.
- The reputation claim values may be normalized by the repository layer so that those reading the values via the query interface don't have to know the input scale.

To improve performance, many read-modify-write operations, such as *increment* and *addToSum*, are implemented as stored procedures at the database level, instead of being code-level mathematic operations at the model execution layer. This significantly reduces interprocess message time as well as the duration of any lock contention on highly modified reputation statements.

The Yahoo! Reputation Platform also contains features to dynamically scale up by adding new repository partitions (nodes) and cope gracefully with data migrations. Though those solutions are proprietary, we mention them here for completeness and so that anyone contemplating such a framework can consider them.

Reputation query interface. The main purpose for all of this infrastructure is to provide speedy access to the best possible reputation statements for diverse display and other corporate use patterns. The *reputation query interface* provides this service. It is separated from the repository service because it provides read-only access, and the data access model is presumed to be less restrictive. For example, every Yahoo! application could read user karma scores, even if they could only modify it via their own context-restricted reputation model. Large-scale database query service architectures are well understood and well documented on the Web and in many books. Framework designers are reminded that the number of reputation queries in most applications is one or two orders of magnitude larger than the number of changes. Our short treatment of the subject here does not reflect the relative scale of the service.

Yahoo! used context-specific entity identifiers (often in the form of database *foreign keys*) as source and target IDs. So, even though Yahoo! Movies might have permission to ask the reputation query service for a user's restaurant reviews, it might do them no good without a separate service from Yahoo! Local to map the reviews' local-specific target ID back to a data record describing the eatery. The format used is `context.foreignKeyValue`; the reason for the `context.` is to allow for context-specific wildcard search (described later). There is always at least one special context: `user.`, which holds karma. In practice, there is also a source-only context, `roll-up.`, used for claims that aggregate the input of many sources.

Claim type identifiers are of a specific format—`context.application.claim`. An example is `YMovies.MovieReviews.OverallRating` to hold the claim value for a user's overall rating for a movie.

Queries are of the form: `Source: [SourceIDs], Claim: [ClaimIDs], Target: [TargetIDs]`. Besides the obvious use of retrieving a specific reputation statement, the identifier design used in this platform supports wildcard queries (*) to support various multiple return results:

`Source:*, Claim: [ClaimID], Target: [TargetID]`
> Returns all of a specific type of claim for a particular target. e.g., all of the reviews for the movie *Aliens*.

`Source: [SourceID], Claim: context.application.*, Target: *`
> Returns all of the application-specific reputation statements for any targets by a source, e.g., all of Randy's ratings, reviews, and helpful votes on other user reviews.

`Source: *, Claim: [ClaimID], Target: [TargetID, TargetID, ...]`
> Returns all reputation statements with a certain claim type of multiple targets. The application is the source of the list of targets, such as a list of otherwise qualified search results, e.g., What have users given as overall ratings for the movies that are currently in theaters near my house?

There are many more query patterns possible, and framework designers will need to predetermine exactly which wildcard searches will be supported, as appropriate indexes may need to be created and/or other optimizations might be required.

Yahoo! supports both RESTful interfaces and JSON protocol requests, but any reliable protocol would do. It also supports returning a paged window of results, reducing interprocess messaging to just the number of statements required.

Yahoo! lessons learned

During the development of the Yahoo! Reputation Platform, the team wandered down many dark alleys and false paths. Presented next are some of warning signs and insights gained. They aren't intended as hard-and-fast rules, just friendly advice:

- It is *not* practical to use prebuilt code blocks to build reputation models, because every context is different, so every model is also significantly different. Don't try to create a reputation scripting language. Certainly there are common abstractions, as represented in the graphical grammar, but those should not be confused with actual executing code. To get the desired customization, scale, and performance, the reputation processes should be expressed directly in native code. The Yahoo! Reputation Platform expressed the reputation models directly in PHP. After the first few models were complete, common patterns were packaged and released as code libraries, which decreased the implementation time for each model.

- Focus on building only on the core reputation framework itself, and use existing toolkits for messaging, resource management, and databases. No need to reinvent the wheel.

- Go for the performance over slavishly copying the diagrams' inferred modularity. For example, even the Simple Accumulator process is probably best implemented primarily in the database process as a stored procedure. Many of the patterns work out to be read-modify-write, so the main alternatives are stored procedures or deferring the database modifications as long as possible given your reliability requirements.

- Creating a common platform is necessary, but not sufficient, to get applications to share data. In practice, it turned out that the problem of reconciling the entity identifiers between sites was a time-intensive task that often was deprioritized. Often merging two previously existing entity databases was not 100% automatic and required manual supervision. Even when the data was merged, it typically required each sharing application to modify existing user-facing application code, another expense. This latter problem can be somewhat mitigated in the short-term by writing backward-compatible interfaces for legacy application code.

Your Mileage May Vary

Given the number of variations on reputation framework requirements and your application's technical environment, the two examples just presented represent extremes that don't exactly apply to your situation. Our advice is to design in favor of adaptability, a constraint we intentionally left off the choice list.

It took three separate tries to implement the Yahoo! Reputation Platform.

Yahoo! first tried to do it on the cheap, with a database vendor creating a request-reply, all database-procedure-based implementation. That attempt surfaced an unacceptable performance/reliability trade-off and was abandoned.

The second attempt taught us about premature reputation model compilation and optimization and that we could loosen the strongly typed and compiled language requirement in order to make reputation model implementation more flexible and accessible to more programmers.

The third platform finally made it to deployment, and the lessons are reflected in the previous section. It is worth noting that though the platform delivers on the original

---

requirements, the sharing requirement—listed as a primary driver for the project—is not yet in extensive use. Despite the repeated assertions by senior product management, the applications designers end up requiring orientation in the benefits of sharing their data as well as leveraging the shared reputations of other applications. Presently, only customer care looks at cross-property karma scores to help determine whether an account that might otherwise be automatically suspended should get additional, high-touch support instead.

Recommendations for All Reputation Frameworks

Reputation is a database. Reputation statements should be stored and indexed separately so that applications can continue to evolve new uses for the claims.

Though it is tempting to mix the reputation process code in with your application, *don't do it!* You will be changing the model over time to either fix bugs, achieve the results you were originally looking for, or to mitigate abuse, and this will be all but impossible unless reputation remains a distinct module.

Sources and targets are foreign keys, and generally the reputation framework has little to no specific knowledge of the data objects indexed by those keys. Everything the reputation model needs to compute the claims should be passed in messages or remain directly accessible to each reputation process.

Discipline! The reputation framework manages nothing less than the code that sets the valuation of all user-generated and user-evaluated content in your application. As such, it deserves the effort of regular critical design and code reviews and full testing suites. Log and audit every input that is interesting, especially any claim overrides that are logged during operations. There have been many examples of employees manipulating reputation scores in return for status or favors.

Related Resources

There are many readings on the broad topic of reputation systems. We list a few here and encourage readers who have additional resources to contribute or want to read the most up-to-date list to visit this book's website at *http://buildingreputation.com*.

Further Reading

The Web contains thousands of white papers and blog postings related to specific reputation issues, such as ratings bias and abusing karma. The list here is a representative sample. We maintain an updated, comprehensive list on their Delicious bookmarks: *http://delicious.com/frandallfarmer/reputation* and *http://delicious.com/soldier ant/reputation*.

A Framework for Building Reputation Systems (http://www.windley.com/essays/2006/ dim2006/framework_for_building_reputation_systems), by Phillip J. Windley, Ph.D., Kevin Tew, Devlin Daley, dept. of computer science Brigham Young University. One of the few papers that proposes a platform approach to reputation systems.

Designing Social Interfaces (http://oreilly.com/catalog/9780596154936/), by Christian Crumlish and Erin Malone from O'Reilly and Yahoo! Press. It covers not only the reputation patterns, but social patterns of all types—a definite companion for our book.

"Designing Your Reputation System," (*http://www.slideshare.net/soldierant/designing -your-reputation-system*) a slideshow presentation by Bryce Glass, initially presented before we started on this: book.

"Reputation As Property in Virtual Economies," (*http://yalelawjournal.org/2009/01/19/ blocher.html*) by Joseph Blocher, discusses the idea that online reputation may become real-world property.

The Reputation Pattern Library (*http://developer.yahoo.com/ypatterns/social/people/rep utation/*) at the Yahoo! Developer Network, where some of our thoughts were first refined into clear patterns.

The Reputation Research Network (*http://web.si.umich.edu/reputations/*), a clearing-house for some older reputation systems research papers.

"Who Is Grady Harp? Amazon's Top Reviewers and the fate of the literary amateur," (*http://www.slate.com/id/2182002/pagenum/all/*) by Garth Risk Hallberg. One of many articles talking about the side effects of having karma associated with commercial gain. See our Delicious bookmarks for similar articles about YouTube, Yelp, SlashDot, and more.

Recommender Systems

Though only briefly mentioned in this book, recommender systems are an important form of web reputations, especially for entities. There are extensive libraries of research papers available on the Web. In particular, you should check out the following resources:

Visit *http://presnick.people.si.umich.edu/*. The site is maintained by Paul Resnick, professor at the University of Michigan School of Information. He is one of the lead researchers in reputation and recommender systems and is a prolific author of relevant works.

GroupLens (*http://www.grouplens.org*) is a research lab at the University of Minnesota with a focus in recommender systems.

Robert E. Kraut is another important researcher who focuses on recommender and collaboration systems. Visit his site at *http://www.cs.cmu.edu/~kraut/RKraut.site.files/research/research.html*.

The ACM Recommender Systems conference site (*http://recsys.acm.org/*) contains some great links to support materials, including slide decks.

Social Incentives

The "Broken Windows" effect is cited in this book in several chapters. There is some popular debate about its effect on human behavior, highlighted in two popular books:

Gladwell, Malcolm. *The Tipping Point: How Little Things Can Make a Big Difference*. MA: Back Bay Books, 2002.

Levitt, Steven D., and Stephen J. Dubner. *Freakonomics: A Rogue Economist Explores the Explores the Hidden Side of Everything*. NY: Harper Perennial, 2009.

They focus on the question of the effects (or lack thereof) on crime based on the New York Police Department's strict enforcement. Though we don't take a position on that specific example, we want to point out a few additional references that support the broken windows effect in other contexts:

Johnson, Carolyn Y. "Breakthrough on Broken Windows." (*http://www.boston.com/news/local/massachusetts/articles/2009/02/08/breakthrough_on_broken_windows/*) The *Boston Globe*, February 8, 2009.

"The Broken Windows Theory of Crime is Correct." The *Economist*, November 20, 2008.

The emerging field of *behavioral economics* is deeply relevant to using reputation as user incentive. Papers and books are starting to emerge, but we recommend this primer for all readers:

Ariely, Dan. *Predictably Irrational*. NY: Harper Perennial, 2010.

Howe, Jeff. *Crowdsourcing: Why the Power of the Crowd Is Driving the Future of Business*. NY: Three Rivers Press, 2009. This book provides some useful insight into group motivation.

Patents

Several patent applications were cited in this book, and we've gathered their references here for convenience. Contributors to this section are encouraged to include other relevant intellectual property for consideration by their peers.

U.S. Patent Application 11/774,460:*Detecting Spam Messages Using Rapid Sender Reputation Feedback Analysis*, Miles Libbey, F. Randall Farmer, Mohammad Mohsenzadeh, Chip Morningstar, Neal Sample

U.S. Patent Application 11/945,911:*Real-Time Asynchronous Event Aggregation Systems*, F. Randall Farmer, Mohammad Mohsenzadeh, Chip Morningstar, Neal J. Sample

U.S. Patent Application 11/350,981:*Interestingness ranking of media objects*, Daniel S. Butterfield, Caterina Fake, Callum James Henderson-Begg, Serguei Mourachov

U.S. Patent Application 11/941,009:*Trust Based Moderation*, Ori Zaltzman and Quy Dinh Le

Index

A

abuse
  of karma models, 77
  unacceptable user submissions, 14
abuse reporting, 207
  on Flickr, 85
  report abuse model, 69
  simple system, 33
  watching the watchers, 209
  Yahoo! Answers, 235, 251
accumulators
  display of, 182
  reversible, 49
  simple, 48
achievements of users, 218
adding to collections, 144
advertisers, attracting, 101
affiliations and reputation, 216
agents content control pattern, 108
aggregate source, 23
aggregated community ratings, 153
alpha testing reputation models, 229
altruistic motivation, 113
altruistic or sharing incentives, 113–115
  friendship, 114
  know-it-all, crusader, and opinionated, 114
  tit-for-tat and pay-it-forward, 113
Amazon
  karma example, top reviewer rankings, 191
  top reviewers, 219
  user reviews, 142
application integration, 223–227
  avoiding feedback loops, 226

implementing reputation model, 224
inputs, 225
planning for change, 227
Yahoo! Answers system, 270
application optimization, 231
application tuning, 234, 235
  (see also tuning reputation systems)
Ariely, Dan, 111, 116, 198
asynchronous activations, 134
attention and massive scale of web content, 13
audits of reputation system applications, 127
averages
  problems with simple averages, 59
  reversible, 50
  simple, 50

B

basic social media (content control pattern), 109
best-effort reliability, 282
  invisible reputation framework, 288
beta testing reputation models, 230
bias, 60–63
  first-mover effects, 63
  ratings bias effects, 61
branding, 117
broken windows theory
  online behavior and, 205
  Yahoo! Answers and, 274
browser cookies, input from, 134
bug reports (content control pattern), 105
building blocks, 39–57
  claim types, 39
  computing reputation, 46–54
  routers, 54–57

We'd like to hear your suggestions for improving our indexes. Send email to *index@oreilly.com*.

simple counter, 47

simple ratio, 52

Sims Online, 162

Slashdot
    karma display, 177
    quality thresholds, 206

social and market norms, incentives and, 111

social games, 156

social incentives, resources for information, 304

social media
    attempt to integrate into Yahoo! Sports, 146
    basic social media content control pattern, 109
    harmful effects of leaderboards, 192–195
    news sites, vote-to-promote model, 141
    Orkut, 194
    reputation within social networks, 281

social network filters, 20

social networking relationships, input from, 134

sources, 23

spammers
    excluding, 16
    trolls versus, 245

star ratings
    differing interpretations of, 139
    problems with, 138

stars-and-bars display pattern, 186

static reputation calculations, 280
    Yahoo! Reputation Platform, 292

statistical evidence in reputation display, 183

stored reputation value, 28

submit-publish content control pattern, 107

summary count, 179

surveys content control pattern, 107

synthesizers, 15

T

tagging (on Flickr), 85, 86

targets, 25
    containers and reputation statements, 30

termination (routers), 54

testing reputation systems, 227–232
    bench testing reputation models, 228
    environmental (alpha) testing reputation models, 229

predeployment (beta) testing reputation models, 230
    Yahoo! Answers model, 271

text comments, 40

this-or-that voting, 69

thumbs ratings, 140, 207

time-activated inputs, 134

tit-for-tat incentives, 113

top-X ranking, 191

transaction-level reliability in reputation frameworks, 282
    Yahoo! Reputation Platform, 291

transformation, normalized values, 58

transformers, 53

transitional values for normalized data, 179

trolls
    attack on Yahoo! Answers, 245
    excluding, 16
    spammers versus, 246

tuning reputation systems, 232–241
    excessive tuning and Hawthorne effect, 233
    for behavior, 236–241
        defending against emergent defects, 238
        emergent effects and defects, 236
        keeping great reputations scarce, 239
    for ROI, 232–236
    for the future, 241
    Yahoo! Answers, 271

Twitter, 114
    display of community member stats, 194

two-state votes (thumbs ratings), 140

U

use patterns, measuring, 231

user engagement, goals for, 99

user profiles, 216
    achievements, 218
    affiliations, 216
    historical information, 218

user reputation (see karma)

user-generated content, 15

users
    as source, 23
    full control over content, 110
    matching expectations with appropriate rating scale, 136
    as targets of reputation claims, 25
    understanding and managing, 15

using reputation, 197–221
    abuse reporting, 207
    educating users to become better
        contributors, 209
        course-correcting feedback, 213
        inferred reputation for submissions, 210
        personal reputations, 212
    minimizing or downplaying poor content,
        204–207
    promoting and surfacing good content,
        198–204
    reputation as identity, 214–221

V

viewer activities (Flickr), 83
Vimeo, 200
virtuous circle created by quality contributions,
    17
vote-to-promote reputation model, 28, 68,
    141
    Digg.com, fuller representation of, 29

W

Was this helpful? feedback mechanism, 75
Web 1.0 content control pattern, 104
websites using reputation systems, 18
weighted transform, 54
weighted voting model, 35
weighting, 30
wiki for this book, 21
WikiAnswers.com, 160
    karma display example, 188
World of Warcraft
    egocentric incentives, 118
    identities, 215

Y

Yahoo!
    360° social network, 114
    Autos Custom ratings, 62
    EuroSport message board reputation, 149
    Local, reviews of establishments, 41
    reputation platform, 289–300
        external signaling interface, 298
        high-level architecture, 293
        implementation details, 292
        lessons from, 299
        model execution engine, 296

        reputation query interface, 298
        reputation repository, 298
        requirements, 290
    Reputation Platform
        messaging dispatcher, 294
    Sports, attempt to integrate social media,
        146
    UK Sports Community Stars module, 203
Yahoo! Answers, 243–277
    application integration, testing, and tuning,
        270–272
    attack by trolls, 245
    content control, 250
    deployment and results for new system,
        273
    description of, 243
    displaying source of statistical evidence,
        184
    inferred karma, 160
    leaderboard rankings, 190
    marketplace for questions and answers,
        244
    objects, inputs, scope, and mechanism in
        reputation system, 252–268
    operational and community adjustments for
        new system, 274
    participation points, 182
    project planning for community content
        moderation, 249–252
    reputation system, 248
    Star mechanism and abuse reporting, 234
    teams handling abuse problem, 248
Yelp
    community and public reputations, 171
    egocentric incentives for user engagement,
        106
YouTube
    leaderboard ranking for most viewed videos,
        190
    massive amounts of content on, 13
    statistical data on video popularity, 183
    Symphony Orchestra contest, 108
    video responses, 42, 145

Z

zero price effect, 116
Zynga, Mafia Wars social game, 156